Principles of Quantitative
Development

For other titles in the Wiley Finance series
please see www.wiley.com/finance

Principles of Quantitative
Development

Manoj Thulasidas

A John Wiley and Sons, Ltd., Publication

This edition first published 2010
© 2010 Manoj Thulasidas

Registered office
John Wiley & Sons, Ltd, The Atrium, Southern Gate, Chichester, West Sussex PO19 8SQ, England

For details of our global editorial offices, for customer services and for information about how to
apply for permission to reuse the copyright material in this book please see our website at
www.wiley.com.

Library of Congress Cataloging-in-Publication Data

Thulasidas, Manoj.
    Principles of quantitative development / Manoj Thulasidas.
      p. cm.
    ISBN 978-0-470-74570-0 (hardback),   ISBN 978-0-470-66737-8 (ebk),
    ISBN 978-0-470-97151-2 (ebk),   ISBN 978-0-470-97152-9 (ebk)
1. Speculation.   2. Risk management.   I. Title.
    HG6015.T48   2010
    332.1068′1–dc22

                                                                              2010005779

A catalogue record for this book is available from the British Library.

ISBN 978-0-470-74570-0

Set in 10/12pt Times by Aptara Inc., New Delhi, India
Printed in Great Britain by TJ International Ltd, Padstow, Cornwall, UK

Contents

List of Figures, Tables and Big Pictures

Figures

Tables

Big Pictures

Preface

Times have changed. Not long ago, all that you needed for a successful career in the financial industry were good people skills, and modest arithmetic and accounting abilities. The derivatives market requiring advanced quantitative (or computing) skills used to be miniscule. Now, with the explosive growth of derivatives, those simple times are gone for good. Derivatives and structures have taken the centre stage in recent years.

The world of trading and structuring today relies heavily on mathematical models and sophisticated computational techniques. In order to stay competitive, financial institutions need quantitative talent now. They cannot expect their bankers, specialized professionals themselves, to be adept in other professional domains like computer science and applied mathematics as well. Banks, therefore, import talent from other unorthodox domains. They find a helping hand among physicists and mathematicians who can model and price complex derivatives. They also employ a small army of computer scientists and programmers to deploy the pricing models in systems and platforms that help their traders make money.

This development has created a knowledge gap between the conventional banking staff and the newcomers. Bankers and regulators do not fully understand what the quantitative professionals are up to. The professionals themselves have very little appreciation for how the business side of the financial institution works. Bridging this gap is one of my objectives in embarking on this work.

Coming from a quantitative professional's perspective, I may have tilted this book a bit in our favour. That bias notwithstanding, I feel that it is important for 'quants' (the mathematicians who develop pricing models) and 'quantitative developers' (computer scientists who deploy the models) to understand and appreciate the business aspects of trading so that our efforts may be as fruitful as possible. Once, one of our top traders pointed out that even the most intelligent pricing model is useless unless it can be deployed effectively and in a timely manner. Effective deployment crucially depends on our appreciation of the 'Big Picture'.

Most quantitative professionals, especially at junior levels, are indifferent to the Big Picture. They think of it as a distraction from their real work of taming stochastic differential equations and writing programs. Through this book, I hope to change their mindset to some degree.

However, the scope of the book is bigger than the world of quantitative professionals. There is a flip side to our reluctance fully to appreciate the rest of the value chain. It is the inability of other business groups to realize what is possible and desirable in the quant world or in a trading system. Every business group in a bank is so specialized and requires skills and focus so specific to their duties that they all end up being distinct silos of knowledge. The professionals in other business units, especially in the middle office, will benefit from this book, in being able to formulate their requirements within the realms of feasibility. More than that, they will also gain an insight into how the quantitative work is done and how a mathematical model finally becomes profit-generating systems.

Another group of professionals who are supposed to know everything this book has to say are business analysts whose job it is to interface business needs to systems development. They usually work for technology consultancy firms and talk to their banking clients in order to come up with solutions specifically targeted to the needs of trading, financial computing and risk management. However, their existence is not confined to the technology side of the value chain. Some business associates and analysts work in financial institutions, translating internal business requirements to quantitative development objectives and rolling out new products and processes. These professionals will find this book invaluable as well.

When we change our narrow, albeit efficient, focus on the work at hand to an understanding of our role and value in the organization, we will be able to leverage off each other's work and enhance the overall productivity by leaps and bounds. This big picture view is especially relevant in the current climate (2008–2009) of financial turmoil and in our efforts to avoid or mitigate similar crises in the future. Of the many causes behind the turmoil that we see clearly with the benefit of hindsight, one that this book addresses is the general lack of a high-level understanding of the whole trading process. For instance, most quants, who are often blamed for the hole in which we find ourselves, do not fully appreciate the processes and methodology in managing the credit and market risks, or the interplay between them. Most professionals who manage credit and market risks do not quite understand the risk profiles straddling these two classes of risks that they manage independently of each other. Yet, this deficiency in understanding is neither deliberate nor premeditated. It is a natural consequence of the silo-like concentration and focus, which this book aims to change. In setting its sight at this holistic picture, this book indeed starts with an ambitious goal, but a timely one.

Manoj Thulasidas
Singapore

1

Introduction

Purpose-built trading platforms have become indispensable tools for exotic trading in most modern banks. One reason for their success and prevalence is that exotics and structured products business is highly lucrative to a financial institution. One prerequisite for success in exotic business is the ability to price the products. For pricing model development and hedging or risk analysis, the financial institution can resort to its mathematicians and the quantitative models they develop.

Another vitally important prerequisite is the capability to assess and manage the associated risks. The risks arising from market movements are related to pricing and are managed through sensitivity analyses. However, in order to manage credit and operational risks, especially when the business volume grows, banks need robust trading platforms supporting and augmenting the mathematical effort.

A carefully designed and deployed trading platform can easily recuperate its development costs within a few short months of going live, and turn into an important profit centre for banks. Once they started appreciating the necessity and profitability of an in-house trading system, banks and other financial institutions began to invest resources into developing in-house trading systems.

Resource allocation attracts professionals with highly specialized skills to move into the field. However, their skills, at times, work against them. They think of quantitative development as a purely technical endeavour. Although, at its heart, trading platform development is a technical challenge, it is the myriad of business processes around it that will eventually make or break its viability. The proverbial devil is really in the details.

1.1 WHAT IS A TRADING PLATFORM?

The goal of this book is to help design a robust, durable and reliable trading platform. The first question then is: What exactly is a trading platform (or system)? For our purpose in this book, I define it as a program or a collection of programs that meets the following broad requirements.

1.1.1 Model archival

One of the problems that the quantitative analysis effort in any modern bank faces is the archival and reuse of their pricing models. A trading platform acts as a repository for the quantitative intelligence generated within the bank. A model developed for a particular product is all too often so specialized that it is difficult to deploy it to tackle another product. This lack of reusability results in duplicated effort. A well-designed trading platform can help by imposing the right quantum of structure and standards to encourage generic programming and to enforce reusability. Furthermore, it will hold all the pricing models with standardized interfaces in one place where they can be found, examined and reused.

1.1.2 Incremental deployability

A trading platform should provide means by which the new quantitative models developed or implemented in the bank can be easily integrated and deployed into the revenue generating work streams of the bank. In other words, even after the trading platform is commissioned, as new and innovative products are developed by the mathematicians and structurers, we should be in a position to augment our system to make use of the innovation. This requirement of incremental deployability drives the whole architecture and design of the trading platform, as you will see in later chapters. It also imposes the necessary rigidity in the form in which quantitative analysts deliver their pricing models, facilitating the first requirement.

1.1.3 Live data feeds

A trading platform should talk to the external world to obtain market data (either as live feeds or as snapshots at regular intervals) and archive snapshots of market conditions for bulk processing. Market data feeds reach the trading platform from several data providers who use dissimilar, and often incompatible, technologies and interfaces. For this reason, the market data handling may become another auxiliary project in its own right, providing a uniform interface to the trading platform regardless of the origin of the data provided. This market data project often has its own database back-end for data persistence.

1.1.4 Trade persistence

A trading platform should be able to save trade data into a database and manage all the associated inception and life-cycle events. The database layer of a trading platform has many stringent requirements on security, performance and record-keeping integrity. It should be capable of handling the inception events such as cancellation, cancel and amend, reissue, novation (changing the ownership) etc., consistent with the policies of the financial institution. A cancellation, for instance, is never a database operation of deleting a record, for a complete deletion would erase the necessary audit trails. In addition, the database layer may reside in geographically dispersed locations, and the trading platform may be called upon to provide data replication services that can be challenging when the trade volumes grow.

1.1.5   Regular processing

A trading platform should facilitate and mediate all aspects of regular downstream processing, such as risk management, trade transformation, settlements, etc. This requirement, although summarized in one bullet point, is very vast in its scope, as you will appreciate by the time you finish this book.

It is instructive to benchmark a vended system (such as the trading system currently in use in your bank) against these requirements. All vended systems do an admirable job in meeting the last two requirements. However, they fail miserably in the first two. In fact, the pricing models implemented in vended solutions are the principal intellectual properties that the vendors jealously guard. They have no incentive in facilitating easy deployment of in-house custom models using their trading systems.

The pricing tool that comes with this book is near the other extreme: it implements the first two requirements wonderfully. Using the pricing tool, you can define and deploy new models without even recompiling the core program. However, it has no market data feeds, not even a clear notion of a market, and it does not provide a database layer. The only data persistence it offers comes in the form of XML files that store pricing scenarios.

Most in-house trading platforms find their place in between these two extremes. They do not try to handle every aspect of trade life-cycle management, but they are far more than the prototyping or proof-of-concept pricing programs that the mathematical brains of the bank generate. Depending on the implementation strategy of a particular bank, the in-house trading platform may end up focusing on different aspects of the requirements listed above. In all cases, however, an in-house trading platform attempts to bridge the gap between quantitative pricing models and a deployed and supported system out of which the bank can generate profit. Its emergence has engendered the relatively new domain of quantitative development. Trading platforms are the domain of the quantitative developers (computer scientists who deploy the models) in the bank, who are distinct from the so-called 'quants' (mathematicians who develop pricing models).

1.2   QUANTS AND QUANTITATIVE DEVELOPERS

The term 'quant' is short for quantitative analyst. They are mathematicians who develop pricing models and keep abreast with the cutting edge research on stochastic calculus and quantitative finance. They transform the academic knowledge they assimilate into programs that can generate revenue and profit. Quants usually have an advanced degree in mathematics, physics or other quantitative fields. Ideally, quants have a sound knowledge of markets, business and products, as well as computer science.

The input to quants' work is research and the academia. Their outputs are pricing models, often delivered as programs or functions in a library, aptly called the quant library. They may also deliver standalone pricing programs, usually as spreadsheets and add-ins.

Quantitative developers are computing professionals who make the output from the quants widely usable, often through the in-house trading platform. Their functional duties fall in between the quant output and the programs used at trading desks. Ideally, quantitative developers would have the same skill set as the quants (mathematical aptitude, product/business knowledge and computer science), but with less emphasis on mathematics and much more focus on computing and software engineering. How separated quants and quantitative developers are in terms of job functions and organizational hierarchies depends on the human resourcing strategies of the bank.

In our discussions in this book, we will assume a clean separation between the duties of quants and quantitative developers. The developers start their work from the quant library, the fruits of the quant's labour. The end point of their work is an in-house trading platform and other maintainable quantitative tools.

1.3 NEED FOR SPEED

In today's financial markets, opportunities are transient. The skyrocketing commodity prices of early 2008, for instance, generated a strong demand for cost-effective hedging. Banks that could roll out structured products to meet customized hedging requirements reaped handsome benefits from this demand. Hedging essentially caps the customer's upside exposure while subjecting them to unlimited downside risks. Because of the dizzying fall in commodity prices (especially in energy) that soon followed during the second half of 2008, the banks that could provide the hedging structures again made even more profit. Rolling out such hedging solutions on short notice to benefit from the market fluctuations of this kind necessarily calls for the agility and flexibility that only an in-house trading system can provide.

Due to such enticing profit potential, an increasing amount of assets under management gets earmarked for exotics trading. In fact, this influx of institutional investments was at least partly to blame for the wild fluctuations in commodity prices. However, the influx also underscores the importance of exotic and structured products. Coupled with this emphasis on exotics trading is the increasing sophistication of the clients who demand customized structures reflecting their risk appetite and market views.

The net result of the changing financial market attitude is the need for more mathematical modelling and speedier deployment than ever before. The need for speed, in fact, goes beyond exotics business. In spot FX trading, the time scale of profit making opportunities is measured in seconds or milliseconds. The so-called high-frequency trading tries to capture such small, but prolific, market opportunities. High-frequency trading modes are too fast for human intervention and rely heavily on machine intelligence and algorithmic approaches. The management of high-volume tick data and the real-time decision making requirements hold a challenging fascination for quantitative developers in this field as well.

1.4   IMPLEMENTATION OPTIONS

Once we appreciate the need for a trading platform through which new products can be launched rapidly, we have a few options to choose from.

1.4.1   Outsource to vendor

We can request our vendor to custom-design and integrate the new products into our existing systems, which we are already familiar with. This approach has the attraction that the new product will be native to the existing system, assuring perfect integration, especially in the back-end. In the front-end also, the familiar look and feel of the interface will enhance usability and productivity.

Vendor development, however, tends to be heavy and slow. When we come up with an innovative product, we do not want to wait for months before we can launch it. An innovative product stays innovative only for a brief span of time.

Another disadvantage of this implementation option is that the cost of custom design can be prohibitive, especially if we demand exclusivity on the product developed. The perceived profit attraction of the innovative product can soon evaporate because of the development cost involved. The nonexclusive mode is clearly not attractive because we will see our innovation in the hands of our competitors.

Vendors may be reluctant to accept our quantitative intelligence because of intellectual property considerations. This resistance makes our in-house mathematical talent superfluous. Due to these reasons, vendor development is not the preferred route for deploying new models and products.

1.4.2   Use vendor API

One way to overcome some of the disadvantages of asking the vendor to write code for us is to use their application programming interface (API) ourselves. In principle, this approach should work well. After all, we will have full control over the intellectual property associated with our new product ideas and pricing models. Furthermore, vendor API provides the same level of integration to the downstream processing systems as the vended trading system.

In practice, this approach also suffers from many disadvantages. The vendor provided APIs tend to be incomprehensible and inflexible, which has to be expected because vendors of trading systems have no incentive in encouraging in-house development.

In addition to the shortcomings of the API, we end up battling the process issues related to the release cycles of the systems as well. The vended systems are deployed by the IT team, not by quantitative developers, and the deployment involves the vendors heavily. Thus, deploying new products through the API may still be delayed by the scheduling priorities of other teams over which the product innovators of the front office have no control.

Since the vendor API is usually complicated, it is only one or two key developers in the quantitative development team who turn out to be familiar with it. This concentration of a crucial skill results in significant key person risk to the financial institution.

Finally, vendor APIs are not cheap – after all, it is not in the vendors' interest to help us be totally self-reliant. (However, they do tout the existence of the API as a key selling point.)

Despite these disadvantages, in-house development using vendor APIs is the chosen route for a large number of mid-tier players in the financial industry. If the level of innovation in the bank is low, this implementation option may prove to be the most cost-effective one.

1.4.3   Develop in-house

For larger players in the financial markets with their armies of quants churning out new pricing models and structures, in-house development may be the only viable option. If we choose to go with the in-house approach, we (quantitative developers) can control the release schedule, resulting in a near-ideal response to the front-office demands. A well-designed in-house system can be flexible and extensible.

In-house development is rapid and responsive, although it might prove to be more error-prone than using the inflexible vendor APIs. In addition, supporting such a trading platform may turn out to be costly because of the nature of in-house development, which puts the quantitative development teams and the front-office stakeholders together. The impact of support duties on high-quality (and therefore expensive) quantitative developers can be mitigated either through sound design or through a planned support strategy. For instance, if planned in advance, the less expensive IT teams can take over a large part of daily and routine support load.

Another potential issue with the in-house trading system is a less than ideal integration with the existing settlement and risk management systems. Again, a sound understanding of the downstream systems and processes (of the kind this book is sure to inculcate) and a good design and implementation plan can help avoid nasty surprises during the integration phase.

In-house development also results in obvious key person risk on the chief software architect and the lead developers. This risk has to be managed through sound documentation requirements.

Most of the investment banks (of the pre-2008 financial meltdown era) had well-developed in-house trading platforms. This fact alone is a testimonial to the profit potential of an in-house trading platform. In fact, part of the blame for the financial meltdown can be placed on such systems, which enabled the giants to roll out a slew of new products with such rapidity that the regulatory bodies could not keep up with them.

1.4.4 Replace vended systems

One of the main drawbacks of an in-house trading platform is the ponderous and weak integration with the existing risk management and settlement systems. This drawback plagues both the input side (access to live market data, trade approval signalling, etc.) and the downstream output part (sensitivity report transmission, accounting entries, settlement triggers, etc.) In order to address this weakness, some financial institutions decide to expand the scope of their in-house platform essentially to act as the backbone of their entire trading activity, not merely for their exotics business. In this mode, the in-house platform becomes the master and other trading systems (including the vended ones) become subordinate to it.

Although risky because of its scope and ambition, such a system can enjoy all the benefits of the previous choices listed above, while subjecting the financial institution to an even higher level of key person (or key team) risk. An all-encompassing in-house system soon becomes a viable trading platform in its own right, independent of the financial institution that originally embarks on it. Once the development team recognizes this potentially lucrative independence, the risks become more significant.

1.5 CURRENT TRENDS

Any of the preceding options can be outsourced to IT consultancy firms if the bank wants to minimize the cost of maintaining a dedicated quantitative development team. Most of the advantages and disadvantages of the options apply in the out-sourced approach as well. However, outsourcing brings in a few drawbacks of its own. One is the viability of the IT firm, which becomes a critical consideration. Another is the implications in the intellectual property of the bank's products, practices and processes. There may be additional regulatory issues related to the security of the information accessible to the information technology (IT) firm.

Some traditional banks do take the first approach and entrust an established vendor to deploy their product ideas. However, due to time-to-market and prof-itability considerations, this solution is rapidly falling out of favour. The second approach of exploiting vended APIs is still prevalent, but the lack of flexibility implicit in it will soon make it less than ideal. This approach ties the bank to a particular vendor, with all the disadvantages of the dependency involved.

The last two options are essentially variations on the same theme. The only difference is the scope of the in-house trading platform. Of all the different options listed above, the most popular seems to be the third one – tasking a team of quantitative developers to design and implement an in-house trading platform, plugging the gaps in vended systems, while not attempting to replace them. They also integrate any new products and pricing models coming out of the quant team.

1.6   TECHNICAL AND BUSINESS ASPECTS OF PLATFORM DESIGN

The technical demands of a trading platform are shared by most large-scale software projects. Among them, those important to quantitative development include maintainability, scalability, modularity, robustness, reliability, security and, of course, performance. While these features may look like the standard principles of software engineering, our own special requirements add a twist to their flavours.

The requirement of maintainability has a special significance in a financial institution, where those who design successful trading systems are in demand because in-house trading systems are a relatively recent phenomenon. They tend to move on to greener pastures, rolling out new trading platforms for other financial institutions. Faced with constant disruption, the maintenance of a trading system is always a challenge. The only way to achieve it is through rigorous documentation. Formal documentation requirements are sure to follow as regulators (both internal and external) start reviewing and auditing custom-built trading platforms, which are becoming more and more commonplace. In the absence of policy-driven guidelines, we have to rely on our own discipline to spend time on self-documenting coding practices and conscientious efforts on documentation and mentoring to ensure continuity and maintainability of our in-house trading system.

Modularity is a fundamental design principle that will aid in achieving scalability as well as maintainability. When modular components are used, the purpose of each one of them is usually singular and easily understood, which helps future developers maintain the whole system efficiently. A modular design is essential for a trading platform for an organizational reason as well. In a bank, quantitative analysts are usually organized under asset class banners. Since the trading platform is the conduit of their output, it has to optimally deploy dissimilar pricing tools, emanating from diverse groups. It therefore has to sport a uniform delivery framework and a predefined structure in which the quants can provide their pricing models and tools. Modularity thus becomes an automatic prerequisite. Furthermore, modular components can be replaced with improved versions with more functionality, thereby implementing some amount of scalability.

Scalability, while a desirable trait in any program, is an absolutely vital feature in an in-house trading platform. At the prototyping stage, a trading platform may prove its worth by booking and managing a handful of trades. However, once deployed, the number of trades soon explodes into hundreds of thousands. Unless designed with this exponential scaling in mind, a trading platform will stay as an expensive proof-of-concept exercise. The lack of scalability is a show-stopper.

The real scalability we require of a trading platform, however, is of a more stringent and demanding kind – in addition to scaling performance and capacity, we also demand extensibility. Indeed, the primary reason for embarking on a trading platform project is to deploy and monetize from our in-house quantitative pricing capabilities. Without the ability to plug in new pricing models and products, a trading platform has no *raison d'être*. The functionality of the program needs to be extended with no change (nor rebuilding) of the platform. The software accompanying this book implements such a paradigm, where new products or new models for existing products can be defined and implemented dynamically while keeping the core program untouched.

Security requirements of a trading system also are much more stringent than a standard piece of software. Quantitative developers will need to worry about end users with different levels of credentials and access control. They also have to implement secure and indelible audit trails on all crucial operations. Most of these requirements come as a surprise to quants and quantitative developers, and are often implemented as an afterthought. Understanding, at the design stage, the whole slew of features and operations that a trading platform will need to support will avert much pain and suffering down the road.

Reliability and robustness, again common enough notions in software design, take on special dimensions in our quantitative finance context. In our world, we have to worry not only about the system robustness and reliability but also about transactional integrity. For instance, booking a trade may involve a series of actions:

1. Trade is priced.
2. Confirmation is sought for booking.
3. Trade is written to the database.
4. Trade is placed in the appropriate processing queue.
5. Booking confirmation is given.

Given that these transactions involve multiple computers, usually in a client–server configuration, each of these steps and the associated communication links is a potential point of failure. How we recover from a failure and how far we need to roll back depends crucially on the robustness choices made at the outset, while designing the architecture of the trading platform.

When we dump the performance requirement into the mix, we often end up with conflicting demands on our trading platform. A system that gives us a high level of robustness or flexibility in terms of pricing model deployment may have to sacrifice a bit of its performance.

In assessing the computational efficiency of a pricing model, every iota of performance improvement is significant. For instance, one millisecond saved in pricing a trade may sound like a ridiculously insignificant improvement to a front-office quant. However, the same model will be used to evaluate, say, the Vega scenario of a portfolio over a matrix of eight spot values and eight ATM volatilities. With a volatility pillar count of ten and a portfolio containing 500 trades, the one millisecond time saved soon balloons to over ten minutes. Imagine that, if you waste ten milliseconds on a trade using a suboptimal pricing routine, you may be holding up a downstream report by two hours every day!

The scope and impact of our trading platform may be bigger than we think when we design it. We can fully appreciate the ramifications of our design decisions only if we can see all the associated processes and scenarios in which the final program will be used. We have no alternative but to understand the whole host of business processes that are involved in trading.

1.7 IMPORTANCE OF PROCESSES

A financial institution operates through a system of checks and balances. The rationale behind the system and its processes is not immediately obvious to all involved. To the front-office professionals, for instance, many of these formal processes, implementing the so-called maker–checker paradigm, may look inane and pointlessly bureaucratic.

As a result of this plethora of processes that weigh it down, a financial institution moves like a giant juggernaut, slow and full of deliberate inertia, but purposeful and with a stunningly low error rate.

The front-office quants and quantitative developers need to understand that if the objectives of various business units seem to be in conflict with one another, it is no accident. They are, in fact, designed that way. It is through these incessant conflicts, which may have evolved into a proposer–objector scenario, that a large number of policy decisions are implemented.

The basic job descriptions of risk controllers (namely to minimize risk) and traders (to make profit) are already in conflict. All the processes that we put around these functions will have to reflect and percolate this basic conflict.

Big Picture 1.1:   Conflicts by Design

The conflict-driven implementation of various policies goes well beyond the workflow of a trade or the interactions between the traders and the risk managers. Even in employee compensation schemes, we can see traces of this philosophy.

For a trader, for instance, performance is quantified in terms of the profit (and, to a lesser degree, its volatility) generated by him. This scheme seems to align the trader's interests with those of the bank, thus generating a positive feedback loop. As any electrical engineer will tell you, positive feedback leads to instability, while negative feedback (conflict-driven modes) leads to stable configurations. Thus, we have rogue traders engaging in huge unauthorized trades resulting in enormous damages or actual collapses like the Barings Bank in 1995.

We can find other instances of reinforcing feedback generating explosive situations in upper management of large corporates. The high-level managers, being board members in multiple companies, end up supporting each other's insane salary expectations. If the shareholders, on the other hand, decided the salary packages, their own self-interest of minimizing expenses and increasing the dividend (and the implicit conflict) would have generated a more moderate equilibrium.

Conflict is, in reality, a good tool for policy implementation. It is in the absence of conflict that we see spectacular failures. However, engineering a self-regulating conflict by itself does not guarantee a perfect outcome. Looking at the performance-based incentive schemes again, the incentives may be drawn from a set amount (a bonus pool, for instance). While this mode of compensation can encourage healthy compensation, the inherent conflict in it can also create unhealthy politics – you can benefit not only from your own stellar performance but also from others' poor shows.

The front-office traders taking risk and the middle-office teams managing it form a negative feedback system that is supposed to bring about a predefined equilibrium. Once we understand the philosophy behind risk taking and control processes, we can see the conflict between them, often resulting in ugly office politics, as a good thing.

Once we understand that the conflict between risk taking and control processes is designed to implement the risk appetite of the bank, we can incorporate them in the design of our trading platform in a balanced fashion, rather than satisfying only one side of the risk–reward equation. With the understanding of what needs to go into the thinking process behind the system design, we can start looking at possible strategies of rolling out a trading platform.

It is in the context of a purpose-built system that this book finds its relevance. A robust trading platform design calls for more than computer science knowledge on the part of the quantitative developers and the ability to specify requirements on the part of the rest of the bank. It demands a thorough and reciprocal understanding of the functions, roles and working paradigms of all the stakeholders in the life cycle and risk management of trades.

1.8   OBJECTIVES AND ORGANIZATION

The objective of this book is to lay down the requirements and the ideal design principles of a trading platform, especially one that is built in-house for rapid deployment of quant pricing models. Given the interdisciplinary nature of the beast that is an in-house trading platform, we will organize this book in a top-down fashion, emphasizing the big picture whenever possible. In order to encourage an appreciation for the interconnections among trade life-cycle events and the rationale behind them from this Big Picture perspective, we will pepper the discourse of the book with a series of columns, aptly called 'Big Pictures.'

A short summary of what to expect in each of the following chapters may be of interest. After this introductory chapter, we will delve into the subject matter, starting from an overview of banking in Chapter 2. Here, we will look at the organizational structure of a bank from the perspective of a quantitative developer. While there are aspects of the bank that call for in-depth treatment, they are not of direct relevance to us. We will look at only those departments and business units that affect the flow of a trade (particularly of an exotic or structured product). This chapter is meant to provide a backdrop to those of us who venture into the exciting world of quantitative finance from engineering or scientific fields. For such professionals, the main difficulty is in the finance jargon built around the organizational structure of the bank.

In Chapter 3, we make use of this overview of the banking organization and look at the life cycle of a trade. From its inception to its eventual settlement, a trade goes through a complex web of interrelated operations and processes. Each of these operations will have to be modelled and executed on the trading platform. A thorough understanding of the business processes, therefore, is the key to deploying a trading platform successfully.

In Chapter 4, we bring the two preceding chapters together and examine the trade perspectives held dear in various business units. In order to understand, anticipate and fulfil the requirements coming out of these business units, we have to understand their work paradigms and trade perspectives.

Chapter 5 represents our switch to the technical side of quantitative development. While the previous chapters deal with the business aspects in an attempt to bring a typical quantitative professional up to speed in business knowledge, this chapter does the opposite – it gives an overview of computing to business users. After the initial introductory sections, however, it goes deeper into the language and database choices open to us while designing a trading platform, and their merits and demerits.

Chapter 6 is where we put all these things together and come up with the architecture of a typical trading platform. In this pivotal chapter, we will discuss the considerations and components that need to go into the architecture. We will then complete the picture with an example trading platform design. After describing this fully functional trading platform design, we will present another architecture that has a more ambitious scope.

Once we have looked at sample architectures, we go over some of the recurring programming patterns in Chapter 7. Patterns are a useful and effective means of implementing our design in an object-oriented framework. Since patterns and related topics are discussed in detail in specialized books on programming, we will look at only a few patterns that are commonly used in trading platforms.

Chapter 8 is a description of the design philosophy and the functionality of the program accompanying this book. Although the program, the pricing tool, is no trading platform, it does have certain traits that are desirable in a full-fledged system; in particular, its extensibility and dynamic GUI generations are strong candidates for inclusion in any trading platform. These aspects will be highlighted in this chapter, along with a full description of its other features.

Chapter 9 discusses the technical aspects of the pricing tool. Much more documentation is available to the interested reader on the CD. The discussion in this chapter also includes the gaps between the pricing tool and a real trading platform. Once these gaps are addressed (which is a considerable effort), the pricing tool can indeed become a mini trading platform.

We will sum up our discussion in the final chapter, where we will suggest further reading material and provide some food for thought on the real Big Picture, which the reader may find both interesting and inspiring.

At the end of each chapter, after summarizing the points, we will pose some questions that reiterate the main points of the chapter. Most of these questions are descriptive, rather than mathematical or technical problems. This quiz will serve to benchmark your takeaways from reading the chapter. I would encourage you to attempt the quiz, if not on paper, at least by mentally checking the points you have retained. If you find it hard to answer the questions, it may be a good idea to refer back to the text of the chapter.

QUIZ

1. Why do modern banks prefer an in-house trading system to vended solutions?
2. What are the four high-level requirements of a trading platform?
3. Describe the main development options in deploying a trading platform.
4. How do seemingly conflicting mandates of various business units (like 'increase profit' for the front office and 'minimize risks' for the risk controllers) bring about stability?

2
Overview of Banking

The life of a trade is a complex one. From origination to settlement, a trade goes through numerous operations performed by various business units of the financial institution. All these operations together prescribe the requirements of a trading platform. These requirements are indeed daunting, from a software design perspective. Most vended trading platforms aim to meet the whole trade life-cycle management requirements. An in-house trading platform, however, targets a small subset of the requirements. It typically offers pricing, trade transformation services (fixing, triggering, etc.), risk management reports and database connectivity.

In addition to performing life-cycle transformations on a per-trade basis, a trading platform also needs to service the various views of information demanded of the trade as it evolves, depending on the business unit handling the trade. For instance, product control may need to review profit and loss (P/L) at a per-trade level while market risk management may need the sensitivities of the trades to market conditions at aggregate levels (such as books or portfolios). If you are a quant, all these details may sound mind-numbingly boring. However, if you are a quantitative developer and your job is to design and deploy pricing models on a robust platform, you need to be aware of these stages of the trade life cycle as well as the perspectives held dear in various business units. Failure to meet any one of the requirements or to provide a projection or an aggregation in response to a trade perspective will render the whole platform virtually unusable, resulting in a large amount of wasted effort. A good grasp of the workflow of a trade is essential when designing a trading platform.

In order to follow the trade workflow, we first need to understand the structure of a bank or a financial institution engaged in trading. In general, the structure of a bank is far too complex and calls for a full-length book in its own right. However, luckily for us, we need to concentrate only on those business units that have an influence in the life cycle of a trade. What we are interested in is what these business units do and how they interact with each other.

The following overview of banking structure and functions includes the requirements and expectations of various business units in their interactions with the quantitative world mediated through the trading platform. We will confine ourselves to a functional outline of banking as seen through the eyes of a quantitative development team. This overview will help us in the next two chapters. In the next chapter, we will discuss the trade life cycle as it flows through various business units. In the chapter that follows, we will work on developing an appreciation of

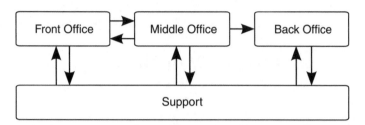

Figure 2.1   High-level overview of the banking structure from a trading perspective. The arrows indicate information flow. Trade information flows back and forth between the front office and the middle office during the lifespan of a trade. It finally ends up in the back office for settlement, general ledger accounting, incentive calculation, etc. All these three 'offices' interact with the support units (IT, HR, finance, etc.)

the perspectives and requirements that various business units place on the trade in greater detail, and their focus and perspectives.

2.1   THE OFFICES

From a trading perspective, a bank is roughly divided into four abstract classes of business units. They are the front office (FO), the middle office (MO), the back office (BO) and the support. In any one bank or financial institution, this division may not be as clear-cut as we present it here. The division is based on a rough depiction of the trade workflow, which tends to be standardized across the industry.

The front office is where a trade originates. It then flows back and forth between the FO and MO validation, and the various monitoring and regular processing purposes. It finally gets settled in the BO. All three 'offices' get help from the support staff, who may also be stakeholders in the performance of the trade. This high-level structure of the bank is illustrated in Figure 2.1.

Note again that the organization in any one financial institution may only be an approximate match to the structure described here. Moreover, even in a faithful implementation of our structure, multiple business functions cut across these 'office' boundaries. Market risk management, for instance, may find its place both in the FO and MO, with different emphasis.

2.2   FRONT OFFICE

The front office is the market-facing side of a financial institution. It consists of economists, structurers, sales staff, trading desks, desk quants, desk risk managers, hedging activities and desk system/platform development and support.

Focusing on the structured or exotic products trading, we can describe concisely the various business units of the front office and their functions as follows. Figure 2.2 shows a detailed look at the structure of a typical front office, and the following

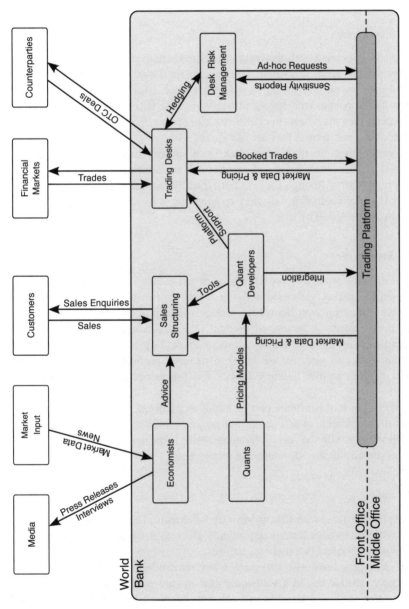

Figure 2.2 The structure and process flows in the front office of a typical financial institution. Arrows indicate activities and workflows. While economists, sales/structuring teams and trading desks interact with the external world, quants and quantitative developers provide the internal muscle. The trading platform mediates most of the FO interactions with the rest of the bank

discussion is based on it. Note that the organizational structure of the front office can vary significantly among institutions.

2.2.1 Economists

Economists associated with the front office are there to predict the future. They study the market trends and summarize the data for traders, highlighting potential opportunities and pitfalls. Acting as the bank's voice to the media, the economists are usually the people who appear most often in the news. Through their media appearances, they may even affect the market to some extent, presumably in favour of the financial institutions they are associated with.

The economists get their input data from sources such as Bloomberg and Reuters, and their predictions and suggestions are announced to the interested trading floor staff. Although they do not typically interact with the trading platform, it is conceivable that they may require access to some of the quantitative tools that are mediated by it.

2.2.2 Structurers

Structuring is the process where a financial expert matches a sophisticated client's risk appetite, market view and hedging needs to a custom-designed product. Structurers come up with innovative products that hold risk–reward appeals to potential customers. A structured product or a structure is a complex derivative product with esoteric names (Inverse Pivot Target Redemption Forward or a Snowball structure, for instance). Structured products are clever combinations of plain vanilla building blocks and are priced and often booked as such.

A structuring tool is often a part of a trading platform, either as an integrated facet of the application or as a standalone program. In either mode, the structuring tool will interact with the rest of the quantitative infrastructure and is an integral aspect of the quantitative development requirement.

2.2.3 Sales

Working hand in hand with structuring is the sales team. They seek and find market needs for the innovative structured products. Once sold, the product becomes one or more trades booked in a trading platform.

The sales personnel will also access any structuring tools deployed by the quantitative developers. In a well-integrated mature trading platform, structurers and sales staff will be able to book temporary trades via these tools and have them transferred to the traders and trading assistants who can book them for real.

2.2.4   Trading desks

The actual trading takes place at trading desks. They are often organized by asset classes as fixed income (FI), equity (EQ or EQD), foreign exchange (FX, FXO or FXD), credit derivatives (CR or CRD), interest rates derivatives (IRD), etc. They may be further subdivided and grouped under the nature of their activity, such as spot, vanilla, exotics and nonexotics trading.

Trading desks are indeed the primary audience of the trading platform, and their requirements are taken very seriously. After all, they take on the profit-generating roles, while everybody else (including quantitative developers) is a cost centre. Tough demanding customers that they are, traders require far more than the basic trade booking, hedging and monitoring capabilities of a trading platform. They may demand particular GUI arrangements or even colour schemes to match their tastes and ease of use.

2.2.5   Desk quants

Exotic desks are supported by mathematicians called desk quants. They generate the mathematical intelligence behind the tools that the structurers, sales teams and traders use. They deliver their output normally in the form of C++ (or other high level language) programs. Deploying these program modules is the primary reason for the existence of a trading platform. While the trading platform puts constraints on the format and modality of the quant work delivery by providing a rigid framework for deployment, it is the quantitative intelligence that drives the trading platform. In fact, the trading platform can be thought of as a conduit between the quants on the input side and the traders on the output side. Although there are many other users and developers involved in making a trading platform a reality, it is these two groups that form its axis.

Often considered the smartest people in the bank, quants go by flattering epithets like rocket scientists, the brain, etc. However, they are also the farthest from the rest of the business units in the bank, both in terms of job functions and process understanding – a deficiency that this book attempts to rectify.

2.2.6   Platform or quantitative developers

Platform developers act as the interface between quants and the rest of the bank, primarily traders. Ideally, quantitative developers are computer science professionals. Front-office platform developers implement the pricing models created by the quants and deploy them in the form of tools that the end users can interact with. The pricing models, as delivered by the quants, encapsulate the most complex intelligence of the trading activity. However, they are not directly usable by any other team. In order to be usable, the models have to access trade and market data form databases, and provide midlife pricing as well as trade life-cycle management and transformations. This is the minimum set of deployability requirements.

2.2.7   Desk risk management

In some banks, trading desks may have associated risk management teams that keep track of their positions and make hedging decisions. Their requirements on the trading platform revolve around daily reports generation. They need sensitivity and trade status reports to understand the profit and loss (P/L) movements. They also need access to limit monitoring resources.

Along with these essential functions, we have other front-office units that take care of contract and term sheet management, actual deal capture and validation, etc. During the inception of a trade, many processes flow back and forth between the FO and MO. These processes include the MO validation and the counterparty credit approval. While most of these process flows are mediated by the trading platform, some (notably credit approvals and live data feeds) may take alternate pathways.

2.3   MIDDLE OFFICE

The middle office typically handles the inception control checks as well as the daily processing, reporting and monitoring of the trades. They also manage the risk aspects of the trading activities at a portfolio or bank book level.

Looking again from the narrow perspective relevant to us, the MO consists of product control, trade control (also known as business or treasury control), risk management (market, credit and operational risks), limits monitoring, rates management, compliance and reporting, analytics, asset and liability management, etc. Figure 2.3 depicts the structure of a typical middle office and the process and information flows in and out of it.

2.3.1   Product control

Product control deals with daily profit and loss (P/L) computations and explanation. Product control houses the middle-office product experts with a thorough understanding of financial accounting. They filter the trading positions and P/L before the numbers reach the finance department in the back office and get reported and disseminated for public consumption.

They also endeavour to understand and explain the P/L. Profit and loss explanation is the process by which product control verifies that the P/L movement is consistent with the market parameter sensitivities of the underlying trades. In

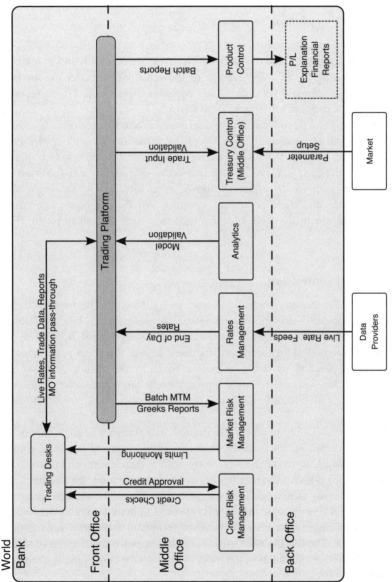

Figure 2.3 The structure and process flows in the middle office of a typical financial institution. The trading platform sits in between the front office and the middle office and mediates most of the interactions. Almost all of the middle business units, such as MRM, rates management, analytics, product control, etc., talk to the trading platform. Some of the information flows may bypass the platform

other words, they use the Taylor series expansion for the P/L (often implemented by quantitative developers) similar to the following:

$$\Delta p|_{\text{today}} = p|_{\text{yesterday}} + \sum_i \frac{\partial p}{\partial m_i} \Delta m_i$$

where p stands for the P/L and the partial derivatives are its sensitivities to market variables. By taking the two-day average of the sensitivities (under the market conditions as of today and yesterday), this equation explains the P/L to second order, although it uses only first-order derivatives.[1]

In explaining the P/L movement, product control actually performs a cross-validation of both the sensitivity (the Greeks) calculations as well as the P/L movements. The input to the P/L explainer (which can be a standalone, post-processing application) consists of the first-order derivatives and the market movements, as seen in the equation above. Also included in the input are market operations and trade population changes. All these inputs come from the trading platform in the form of daily reports, which are fed in to the P/L explainer.

2.3.2   Treasury control unit

In some banks, the treasury control unit may go by the names business or trade control unit, or simply the middle office. Logistically, this team may be a standalone business unit or embedded within or parallel to the product control. Regardless of their name and logistical arrangements, the main task of this team is to validate trade inputs. Depending on how careless the trader or the trading assistant is, up to 60 % of the trade entries may have errors in input parameters, making them fail validation. Without validation, no trade confirmation is given to the customer.

A well-designed trading platform can improve the accuracy of trade inputs in a variety of ways. It can, for instance, maintain an inventory of products, counterparties, portfolios, instruments, etc., along with authentication and restriction information. Since it knows the user by the access authentication, the trading platform can present only those choices to the traders or other end users that are open to them. Thus, an energy trade may not be allowed to book a trade in an equity portfolio. In fact, he may not even see the equity portfolio in his drop-down list of portfolio choices. The trading platform can further improve the fraction of valid trade inputs by active validation of the input fields with the help of the underlying quant library.

---

[1] See Quiz question 4.

2.3.3   Market risk management

Market risk refers to the fluctuations in the value of an investment due to movements in the market parameters such as equity or commodity prices, or foreign exchange or interest rates. Market risk management (MRM) is the business unit that is tasked with managing this risk. It is important to note that MRM does not attempt to eliminate all possible risks of loss due to market movements. Instead, its task is to ensure that the risk-taking arm of the business (namely the FO traders) is exposing the bank to exactly as much risk as the top management has decided to take on. In order to accomplish this task, MRM monitors the trading positions on a daily basis, computes risk measures such as value at risk (VaR) and prepares reports for senior management and regulatory bodies.

When compared to product control, MRM is more interested in aggregate levels. They monitor the P/L at different levels of grouping. They also perform scenario, stress test and historical value at risk (VaR) computations. In stress tests, they apply a drastic market movement of the kind that took place in the past (like the Asian currency crisis or 9/11) to the current market data and estimate the movement in the bank's book. In historical VaR, they apply the market movements in the immediate past (usually one year) and estimate the 99th percentile (or some such predetermined number) worst loss scenario.

Limits monitoring, which may fall under the purview of market risk management, sets and monitors desk and bank-wide limits on the positions traders can take. The limits are specified in terms of the notional, P/L, sensitivities or risk measures. Thus a particular desk may have a limit on its Delta equivalent or on VaR.

From the trading platform, MRM would expect regular reports facilitating their work. These reports include a sensitivities report (such as Delta, Gamma, Vega, PV01, etc., at multiple levels of aggregation) as well as other risk measures (such as VaR, stress test analysis reports, etc.). They may also demand a framework where they can design their own reports on the fly as and when they need. All these are reports for the inputs to further process and reporting by MRM.

2.3.4   Credit risk management

Credit risk management (CRM) concerns themselves with the possibility of entities that owe us money defaulting on their obligation. Credit risks arise, most obviously, from loans, but they also arise from trading activities in the form of counterparty credit risk and settlement risk. The settlement risk is a measure of the small (but nonzero) probability that the counterparty may go bankrupt during the normal two-day settlement period between the time an obligation falls due and the time when it is actually settled or delivered.

The credit exposure at the inception of a trade is close to zero. This is to be expected because most deals between financial institutions are entered into with a PV close to zero – otherwise, why would they strike a deal? However, as the markets move during the lifetime of the trade, they may move in favour of one of the counterparties, which ends up with large credit risk. In order to manage the risk, therefore, the credit controllers will have to understand the exposure profile during the lifetime of the trade. Only with this information can they approve the trade, and only with their approval can the FO book it. The potential future exposure (PFE) computation tends to be complex and computationally intensive. In order to minimize the resource requirement, the credit controllers may ask the FO to provide them with the so-called credit replicates, which are simplified equivalents of the trades with roughly the same payoff profile.

In recent times, credit and market risks have started merging thanks to the advent of credit derivatives. For instance, a popular credit derivative, CDS (credit default swap), offers protection against the possibility that a specified company may default on their obligation. If we have credit exposure to this company, we can use a CDS to reduce or offset our credit risk. However, we can buy the CDS even if we do not have any exposure, expecting the company to get into trouble, at which point, the CDS would be worth more in the market. Used for this speculative purpose, the CDS makes the credit rating of the underlying company a driver in the market risk involved. When we consider that we can buy a CDS based on credit indices, we can see further mixing of market and credit risks in a manner not easily modelled.

2.3.5 Operational risk management

Operational risk is the risk of loss resulting from inadequate or failed internal processes, people and systems, or from external events – this is the formal definition according to Basel II. In practice, operational risk management (ORM) handles systemic risks that are not market or credit related. They worry about integrity of systems and processes, business continuity plans during disasters and so on. While not specifically linked to trading, a trading platform will have to respond to requests coming from ORM, for a good reason. It is in an in-house trading platform that the biggest chunk of the front-office operational risk is likely to reside.

Operational risk management and their detailed Business Continuity Plans are thankfully acknowledged only during catastrophic terrorist attacks and other disasters. However, the operational risks that do affect trading are of a more mundane kind. Seemingly innocuous practices such as sharing of system passwords among trusted colleagues may lead to crippling consequences, like the seven billion dollar loss in Société Générale. Insufficient or inappropriate access control or wrong process flow implementation in a trading platform can and does introduce operational risk.

Big Picture 2.1:   Operational Risk in In-House Platforms

Most of the difficulties related to in-house trading systems stem from the lack of communication between various business units and the consequent emergence of what we can call the silos of knowledge. For instance, quants, whose work drives the need for the in-house system to begin with, are way too mathematical for anybody else in the bank. The developers, who bring the pricing models to the trading systems, are computer science professionals – again far removed from the rest of the banking world. Traders, who end up using the models on the in-house systems, tend to be more nimble, market-oriented people, quite unlike the quants and the developers.

The knowledge gap is even bigger when we move to other aspects of trade life-cycle management. Although risk management professionals use methodologies similar to the front-office staff, their philosophical focus (on risk reduction rather than risk taking) puts them at variance, and often in conflict, with them.

One efficient way to fight operational risk issues arising from the development of an in-house system is to spread the specialized knowledge residing in the various business units – break the silos, as it were. This need is what prompted me to embark on writing this book. Here, I endeavour to develop in each professional team a healthy respect for all other business units, by pointing out the various functions, their needs and the associated trade perspectives.

While designing an in-house trading platform, the architects have to spend a long time understanding the trade perspectives and the work paradigms in various business units, and fully appreciate the requirements arising from them. It may be wise to reuse as much of the existing infrastructure (for trade settlement, accounting rules etc.) without trying to reinvent the wheel. Because of the compelling reasons for their existence, in-house trading platforms are here to stay, and we need to bring them under operational risk management.

Operational risk is different from market risk in many ways. First, assuming a risky position (from a market risk perspective) opens the possibility of higher returns, albeit with higher volatility. Assuming operational risk, however, only leads to pain and loss (not counting the minor cost savings and conveniences of practices like password sharing). Second, market risk is well understood and modelled mathematically. Operational risk is not amenable to mathematical modelling, despite the efforts on the part of the operational risk practitioners to quantify their efforts. Third, market risk can be mitigated by hedging – by taking opposing position in the market; operational risk can be mitigated only through policies and practices in an essentially nonquantitative way.

We can draw a similar comparison with credit risk as well. We take on credit risk only when we see a profit making potential. Modern credit derivatives make it relatively easy to manage credit risk, although the credit crisis and the subsequent financial meltdown serve to highlight the pitfalls involved.

In a trading platform, operational risk requirements manifest themselves as policy-driven implementations such as a prescribed access control framework, a source code control system and/or an approved software development process.

2.3.6 Rates management

The rates management team usually finds itself embedded in product control or market risk management. This critical team, working in conjunction with the information technology (IT) team, ensures the integrity and availability of live market data like spot values, volatilities, interest rates, etc. Live data reach the trading desks through feeds from data providers such as Reuters and Bloomberg, or from brokers. The rates management team, through periodic and regular monitoring, validates the market data.

While traders use any data that may give them a price, information or time advantage, the official pricing (marking-to-market) process uses specific end-of-day (EOD) rates that are snapshots of predefined live sources at predefined points in time. The EOD data may have to flow into the trading platform depending on its scope. If the trading platform is also required to run the end-of-day batch processing, we had better ensure that we have the data structures and conduits ready to accept the EOD rates and process the trades using them.

In a modern trading platform setup, the rates feeds may need to be abstracted away in order to provide a uniform interface to multiple data providers, as well as for archiving or performance reasons. Such a market data system may form a part of the trading platform, or evolve into a major software project in its own right. In any case, it is best not to underestimate the scope of the function that comes under the purview of rates management.

2.3.7 Static data management

While the rates management team deals with dynamic market data, there is usually another team that concerns itself with static data. Examples of static data include definitions of instruments such as equities, bonds, etc., maintenance of holiday calendars, currency pair names, rates pillar definitions, portfolio and counterparty setup, maintenance and so on. In fact, every single piece of static information that goes into the trade details needs to be created, verified and stored for future reference. Thus static data management is also as daunting a task as rates management. For this reason, the software framework to manage it may very well end up being a standalone application or service.

Documentation management is another business group that may be lumped along with static data management. They take care of trade-related documentation such as term sheets and contracts. While quite removed from the trading platform, they also place requirements (such as a unique trade reference that survives trade amendments and reissues, for instance) that may impact the design decisions of the trading platform.

2.3.8   Compliance and reporting

Compliance refers to complying with the local regulatory bodies. A compliance and reporting group, which may also come under market risk management, takes care of the mandatory and extensive regulatory compliance reporting. Depending on the country of operation, compliance may vary from reporting daily marked-to-market values to detailed risk analysis. In addition, in response to market events (the Lehman collapse, for instance), regulatory entities may request other ad hoc analyses. The senior management also needs to have a high-level view of the trading positions and activity on a daily basis.

The starting point of the compliance reporting is also the trade population and, in the case of the exotic trade residing in the trading platform, the compliance and reporting group will demand regular and ad hoc reports on their statistics as well as risk characteristics.

2.3.9   Market risk management analytics

Analytics group, comprising quantitative analysts working for risk management, mainly handles model validation. The objective of model validation is to ensure that the pricing (and other) quantitative models deployed in the bank are appropriate and implemented correctly. An analytics group may also handle other mathematical tasks of risk management such as counterparty credit exposure, liquidity modelling, etc. Because of the nature of their work and their facility with the mathematical lingo of quantitative finance, they serve as the primary point of contact for the front-office quantitative professionals with the middle-office operations.

Although of direct relevance to the deployment of new models in the trading platform, the MRM analytics group does not place too many requirements on it. Their work is largely independent of the trading platform, and revolves around approving or rejecting the quant models that can be deployed.

2.3.10   Asset and liability management

Asset and liability management (ALM) is the precursor to risk management and has a scope much bigger than trading. While ALM assesses the position of the bank by the book value through accrual account (acquisition cost minus depreciation), risk management looks at the transient replacement cost or through market value accounting.

The interactions between the risk management and the trading room at times seem conflicting or adversarial, prompting the front office to see them as hindrances to revenue generation and engage in a war of attrition with them. The perceived conflict between the functions of these business units is real. The role of the risk manager is to ensure that the positions assumed during revenue generation are as close to risk-free as possible. The role of the revenue-generating front office is to ensure that enough risk is taken to make huge returns a possibility. It is in the conflict between these roles that the risk appetite of a financial institution is expressed.

Big Picture 2.2:   Risk–Reward Seesaw

Modern organizations reward their employees based on performance. In a financial institution, it is easy to quantify performance, it would seem. After all, in an organization that deals with money, performance is easily equated with profit. This practice, although it sounds natural, results in treacherous skews in incentive schemes and associated moral hazards.

In any financial institution, we will find profit-generating units, which take risks, as well as risk-controlling units, which seem to curtail profits. It is the dynamic equilibrium between these units that expresses the risk appetite of the organization.

If performance is measured solely on the basis of the direct contribution to the bottom line of the bank, the risk takers tend to get better rewarded than the risk controllers. Such an incentive scheme is good during boom times. It will encourage more productive employees to move from the middle-office risk-controlling functions to the front-office trading and modelling roles. The lack of adequate risk management talent will become painfully obvious only during economic and financial downturns such as the aftermath of the subprime crisis.

Another undesired side effect of the skewed incentive scheme is the moral hazard it generates, resulting in the much touted 'greed' of Wall Street. Risk takers enjoy something similar to a one-way bet: they get rewarded when they make profit, but if their bets do not pay off, all they have to lose is their job. In this sense, they seem to be long a free call option. On average, it is best for the risk-taking arm of the bank to take as much risk as they are allowed to hold. After all, if they are giving out options for free, why not grab as many as you can? They always have some nonnegative value.

Risk controllers, on the other hand, seem to be short an option. When the risk controls they put in place work perfectly, they reduce the returns to the risk-free rate. When the markets move the wrong way and the controls do not work, the risk controllers have an unlimited downside.

Risk controllers also have to weather unreasonable expectations from business units that fail to understand and appreciate the real nature of risk management. They are expected to eliminate or mitigate the downside risks, while keeping all the upside rewards intact. In reality, the best any risk manager can do, and indeed should try to do, is to minimize the volatility in returns, which means flooring downside losses as well as capping upside gains.

At the start of the 2008 financial turmoil, faced with the skyrocketing oil prices, the risk controllers of many airlines tried to hedge their energy exposure against even higher oil prices. However, after hitting an all-time high of $147, oil prices plummeted, shedding over 70 % of their price in the next five months. Consequently, the well-hedged industries ended up owing large sums of money to the financial institutions that sold them the hedging structures. Instead of reaping the benefits of the falling oil price, they ended up suffering huge losses because of it. We can only imagine the severe grilling these careful risk controllers had to face.

2.4 BACK OFFICE

Farthest from our sphere of influence, the back office is involved in accounting operations and settlement. Their responsibilities also include regulatory compliance such as capital allocation, cash management, collateral management and so on. Most of our interaction with them takes place through what are known as accounting entries. They are numbers generated using specific accounting rules in a downstream system from the trade details captured during the booking process. The accounting entries make it possible for the back office to settle the trade.

In a typical in-house trading system, we do not try explicitly to implement the accounting rules generating the accounting entries. The accounting rules are intelligible to only those with a background in accountancy. It is not efficient for quantitative analysts and developers to study and implement them. A far better idea would be to leverage on the existing implementations in vended solutions.

2.5 SUPPORTING UNITS

Among the support functions most critical to a quantitative developer is information technology. They handle all the access rights, network and hardware procurement, performance and disposal, licence management for software and similar functions. In most organizations, IT teams have software projects handling eCommerce, transaction banking, etc. Information technology has projects cutting across the whole operation of the banks, rather than just trading. In fact, it is possible to organize quantitative developers also under the purview of IT, although such an organization de-emphasizes the special niche they fill as cross-domain specialists. IT projects tend to run as replicas of large-scale software efforts in standardized development mode, churning through the phases of requirements, design, implementation, version control, unit and user acceptance tests, release cycles, etc. This mode of operation, while robust and reliable, may not be nimble enough to respond quickly to changing market conditions.

The finance department handles all aspects of cash management in the bank. They are also responsible for accurate assessment and presentation of the net position of the bank, for instance in annual reports and regulatory disclosures. The numbers that they generate, though distant from our arena of the bank, depend on the trades the front office engages in and the systems we deploy to support them.

Other groups that may look equally distant include human resources, legal, corporate communication, etc. Although relevant only in special circumstances, we do interact with these teams during our work as quantitative developers, albeit not necessarily via the trading platform. Writing this book, for instance, called for the approval from the corporate affairs group, and to some extent, a green light from the legal and the intellectual property managing groups. Similar approvals are mandatory if we are called upon to present anything to the wider world, be it through TV or media appearances, conference presentations or journal articles.

2.6   SUMMARY

Before we can understand the trade workflow, it is necessary to keep a working picture of a bank in our mind. Note that what I described above may not be implemented exactly in any bank, but most banks will have equivalent business units with functions segregated roughly along these lines. I must highlight again that we are looking only at a small subset of banking operations that are relevant to our field of quantitative finance and platform development.

A bank or a financial institution is a complex and vast organization. Citibank, for example, had about 380 000 employees at the height of its staff strength. It is only a small fraction of them that are engaged in operations that directly affect an exotic financial instrument such as a structured product. The rest of the staff and business units of most major banks are engaged in other activities, like Consumer/Retail Banking, Wholesale Banking, Private Banking, Investment Banking, Corporate Banking, etc. Some banks may be more specialized in one activity rather than the others. Although important and interesting in their own right, these activities do not all come under a quantitative developer's portfolio of tasks. What is most important to us are the operations of the global treasury, where exotics trading activities take place, and the associated business units that handle different aspects of the trade workflow.

QUIZ

1. What are the main categories of risk that banks strive to manage?
2. Classify the following events into the three types of risk:
   (a) Because of the 9/11 attack, the stock market takes a dip. The value of your portfolio goes down.
   (b) Because of an earthquake in Taiwan, your counterparty suffers a catastrophic collapse from which they cannot recover. You lose money.
   (c) Because of the same earthquake, your Taiwan operations suffer prolonged closure. You cannot access your counterparty information and you lose money.
3. What are the strategies to mitigate the risks involved in each of the scenarios in question 2?
4. Prove mathematically that taking a two-day average of the first-order market sensitivities in P/L explanation is equivalent to considering the second-order sensitivities.
5. What is the difference between the product control and the market risk management given that both of them worry about trade PVs?
6. Check your understanding of the following business units and their functions:
   (a) Rates management
   (b) Credit risk management
   (c) Static data management
   (d) Market risk – analytics
   (e) Documentation.
7. What is the difference between credit risk and settlement risk?

3
Trade Life Cycle

Trades are dynamic entities. During the course of their life, they evolve and transform. Their evolution can be thought of as the flow of the trade object (in software parlance) in and out of the various business units that work on them. These business units may go by differing names depending on the financial institution we work in, but the trade workflow shows remarkable similarity across the financial industry.

Thanks to the increasing sophistication of our customers and the complex, interconnected nature of today's markets, the modern financial marketplace demands customized structures and solutions. Such solutions call for a high level of quantitative input, both in innovative models as well as the imperative of robust platforms to launch them in a timely fashion to capture transient market opportunities.

Most modern banks build such platforms in-house. This trend towards self-reliance is easy to understand, for the generic trading platforms that vendors provide are mainly set up to handle the established vanilla products well. They also do a good job in taking care of the established processes such as compliance, reporting, settlements, audit trails, etc. However, they are inefficient or downright incapable when it comes to pricing a hitherto unknown structure, and we face a dilemma. If we ask the vendors to develop and deploy a new pricing model for the innovative structure, they typically take a long time to respond. Furthermore, they either hold the associated intellectual property, nullifying the competitive advantage of the innovation, or sell it back to us with enormous markups, thereby eradicating any associated profit potential.

Because of these considerations, we often deem vended solutions inappropriate for rapid deployment of complex structures. We turn to in-house development of a trading platform. It is when we design an in-house system that the 'Big Picture' becomes crucial. The quantitative developers will need to understand the whole trade workflow through the various business units and processes in order to design a system that can respond to all the requirements. Furthermore, they will have to develop an appreciation for the trade perspectives and paradigms associated with these business units.

Trade perspectives stay invisible because they are entrenched in our business activities and our thinking process. Yet, in order to be efficient in their jobs, quantitative professionals and business associates need to appreciate the nuances of the paradigms and perspectives behind the business processes. For instance, depending on our perspective, we can think of the starting point of a trade as a structuring effort or a sales event. If we think of structuring as the starting point, it is because we are mentally classifying all the trades of the same structure as one entity. In other words, we are thinking from a quantitative professional's perspective. If we think of the sales event as the starting point, each instance of the structure is a trade, which is a more commonly held perspective.

In the previous chapter, we looked at the static structure of a bank. The structure is important because it provides the backdrop for understanding the dynamics of trade evolution. In this chapter, we will go through the life cycle of a trade, from its inception to its eventual termination. We will highlight the processes, life-cycle events and their implications in the system design. The objective is to understand why trades transform the way they do, and why the transformations are important for the bottom line of the financial institution (and yours). Wherever possible, we will also highlight the conflicting perspectives and the 'gotchas' in the implementation process.

For most of the players in the life of a trade, it is best to regard each instance of a structure as a trade – as a software object that flows back and forth among the various business units described in the previous chapter. We should keep in mind that this trade-centric perspective of ours is only one of the many possible views, even from the limited vantage point of quantitative development. For flow products that trade in high volume with fixed configuration, for instance, a product-centric view may be more appropriate. For the purpose of this chapter, we will stick to a trade-centric view. From this perspective, we can describe the life of a trade from start to finish in different stages, as described below.

3.1   PRE-TRADE ACTIVITIES

After commissioning a trading platform and before the first trade is booked in it, we have to complete a series of validation and approval steps at the product level (see Figure 3.1). These general steps include evaluating the structured product and modelling it. First, the mathematical quants develop the model and deliver it in the form of a standalone program or source code. The developers then integrate the model into the trading system. After the integration, the model validation team in the middle-office analytics team (usually under market risk management) verifies the model characteristics and implementation. The model is then presented for user acceptance tests. Once these steps are completed successfully, a trader is ready to book the first instance of the product.

In addition to these general pre-trade activities, we have other specific trade-level steps to complete before each trade. First of all, the sales team has to make a sale, which involves term sheet generation, negotiations and contract evaluation in the light of ISDA or netting agreements.

A novel product is approved and added to the product repository in a trading platform as the end point of a pricing model from a quant. For a quant, the most interesting point of a trade is the mathematical model behind it. Once he figures

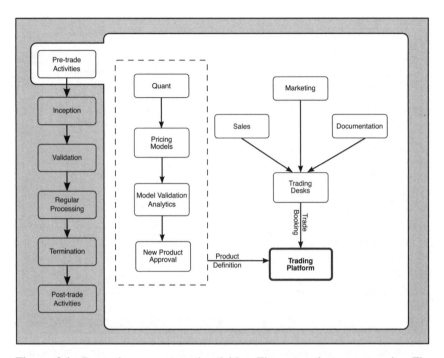

Figure 3.1 Pre-trade processes and activities. They come in two categories. The first one is the approval processes before a model goes into the trading system and the products are rolled out. These processes are shown in the dashed rectangle. The second category of processes takes place before each trade is booked, and includes marketing, sales, documentation, etc.

out how to write down a closed-form solution for the price and sensitivities of the derivative under consideration (or puts it in a numerical form or a Monte Carlo simulation framework), his work is done. Typically, a model quant is much more interested in the price at the inception of the trade rather than its life-cycle management.

3.2 INCEPTION

The inception of a trade takes place in front-office units such as sales, structuring and trading desk (see Figure 3.2). They study their customers' needs and risk appetite, and assess the market potential and the viability of the trades. Once they see and grab a market opportunity, the trade is born.

After these inception steps are completed, the trade goes through the pre-booking approval processes. It needs a green light from the credit controllers, who worry about the extent of the counterparty credit exposure arising from it. They

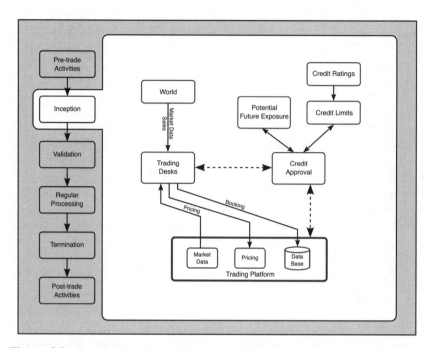

Figure 3.2 Trade origination and inception processes and activities. The main activities at the inception stage are pricing and credit approval. The trade is booked into the database during inception

also monitor the credit limits allocated to the counterparties and their usage. The counterparty credit control team uses historical data, internal and external credit rating systems and their own quantitative modelling prowess to come up with counterparty credit limits and maximum per trade and netted exposures.

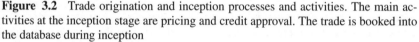

Big Picture 3.1:   Collateral versus Credit Lines

Consumer banks manage credit risk using two distinct paradigms – through collateral management or through credit line allocation. In the consumer credit market, these paradigms correspond to secure lending (such as automobile financing or home mortgages) and unsecured loans (e.g. personal credit lines and overdrafts). The unsecured loans are clearly more prone to credit defaults and, consequently, attract high interest rates.

In dealing with financial counterparties, banks use the same two paradigms. Collateral credit management is generally safe because the collateral pledged against one obligation cannot be used for other credit exposures. However, when a counterparty enjoys a credit limit based on their credit ratings, banks face a problem. While the credit rating of a bank or a financial institution may be accurate, it is almost impossible to know how much credit is loaded against the rating of that particular entity. The difficulty in estimating the credit 'loading' is in the fact that complex financial products like derivatives are all 'off-balance-sheet' instruments. The off-balance-sheet nature means that the existence and, consequently, the credit exposures of these instruments do not figure in the balance sheets of the companies holding them, making credit research difficult, if not impossible.

This situation is akin to a bank's inability to check how much a consumer owes against his other credit lines when it offers him an overdraft facility.

This blind spot in credit limit management leads to dangerous levels of leverage against the credit rating without counterparties realizing it. The painful deleveraging soon takes place when a credit event (such as lowering of the credit rating) occurs, which was one of the tough lessons learned during the credit crisis of 2008.

Since the credit exposure changes during the life cycle of the trade, the peak exposure (called the potential future exposure, or PFE) is the quantity that the credit controllers need to consider. They estimate PFE using simple quantitative models. Only with their approval can the front office do the deal.

Once all the origination, pre-trade work is done, the trade gets priced and booked. It is in these two steps that an in-house trading platform plays its crucial role.

On a commissioned trading platform, the inception pricing usually can take place without a hitch. After all, it is on inception pricing that quants and quantitative developers focus their mathematical and computing prowess. Pricing typically takes place on an Excel spreadsheet, although more and more banks are spending considerable energy in developing customized and flexible user interfaces.

After pricing, the trade needs to be booked. Trade booking is the process of putting the trade in a database and initiating its workflow through the software platform. It is at this stage of the life of a trade that a quantitative developer's role is most obvious. Once in the database, the trade is open to simultaneous access by multiple business units.

This relatively simple process of inserting a trade record in a database is, in practice, a battle of perspectives. While the quants really do not care about the trade identification number, the quantitative developer would like it to be something unique per trade. A structurer would like to have one identifying reference for the trade with possible sub-IDs for the individual subtrades that make up a structure. While this requirement is easy enough to implement, the software architecture also has to cater to trade cancellation and amendment requirements from the FO and MO. What happens when a structure is modified or cancelled? How do we find and deal with all the related trades? This problem will almost invariably end up requiring a link ID in the database. Trade number amendments on a live deal create problems for documentation and operations staff as well, who might demand another immutable external reference number attached to each trade. Audit will require integrity and indelibility on everything, demanding database record duplication. As we can see, the perspectives and work paradigms of each business unit translate to often conflicting requirements on the program design at a fundamental level. It is for this reason that we will take a close look at the trade perspectives in the following chapter.

Although functionally identical, the model quant's idea of pricing is different from the pricing in a trading platform in one crucial aspect – in the notion of market data. The quant may think of market data as a static set of numbers necessary for running the pricing model. In a trading platform, however, it is the dynamic and critical representation of the market comprising a large volume of numbers such as prices, volatilities, rates and correlations, and so on. The difference comes about precisely because of the difference between the inception pricing that the quant focuses on and the 'aged' pricing that the trade life-cycle management calls for.

3.3   VALIDATION

After it is booked, the trade moves to the treasury control team of the middle office to get validated (see Figure 3.3). Their job is to ensure that the trade accurately

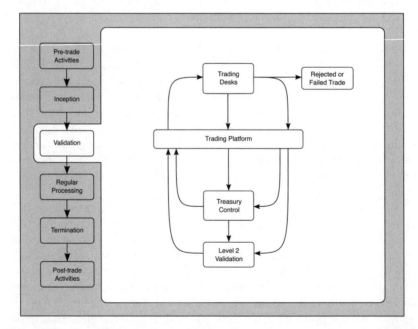

Figure 3.3   Trade validation in the middle-office treasury control team is a complicated process with multilevel approval processes and full audit trails

reflects the specifications in its term sheet and contract. They verify the trade details, validate the initial pricing, apply some reasonable reserves against the potentially inflated profit claims of the front office and come up with a simple 'yes' or 'no' response to the trade as it is booked. The reply from the MO, in fact, is something like an 'ACK' (trade is valid and acknowledged) or a 'NACK' (not valid). Depending on how careful the traders (or their assistants) are, a large proportion of the trades may get NACKed and bounced back to the trading desk. The desk then will correct the errors and re-book.

Once the trade passes the validation, a trade confirmation is sent to the counterparty. Note that even in the absence of validation, the trade is still 'live' and has to be risk-managed.

Big Picture 3.2:   Workflow Engine

The processes around inception, approval and event management are sufficiently complex and interrelated that a specialized workflow engine may be called for. Such workflow engine solutions (also know as Business Process Management – BPM – tools) make it easy to define complex process flows that are initiated in response to specific triggering events. In our case, a trade booking event can trigger the MO validation process. A fixing request from a trade can trigger another process. Depending on the outcome of the validation or the fixing process, other processes (second-level confirmation, or bouncing back to the FO, for instance) can be triggered.

The BPM system isolates the trade workflow logic from its implementation, thereby making the overall system more robust and flexible. It usually has an interface that allows its business users to define and modify process flows. These interfaces are designed to be user friendly and require little or no programming knowledge – at least, that is the objective. The actual orchestration of what the process does will involve quantitative developers.

The workflow engine often offers additional benefits. It has built-in audit trails, data persistence and performance measurement tools. It can, for instance, answer questions such as what fraction of fixings get done within a specified span of time. It can also have role-based authentication or talk to an authentication and entitlement service to ensure that only the right employees are permitted to carry out specific tasks.

The business process management programs are complex pieces of software, almost as complex as the trading platform itself. They are, therefore, expensive as well, and all their advantages come at the cost of increased expenditure, as well as the complexities of maintaining another large vended system. There really is no such thing as a free lunch in banking and finance.

3.4   REGULAR PROCESSING

The next destination in the trade workflow is again the middle office, specifically the market risk management and product control professionals (see Figure 3.4). They handle a large number of processes on a regular basis after the trade is booked in the system. They monitor the trades at a per-trade level basis as well as at the portfolio level.

Product control worries about the trade valuations every day. They worry about the daily profit and loss movements both at the trade and portfolio levels. They also modulate the profit claims by the front office through a reserving mechanism and come up with the so-called unrealized P/L. The unrealized P/L has a direct impact on the compensation and incentive structure of the front

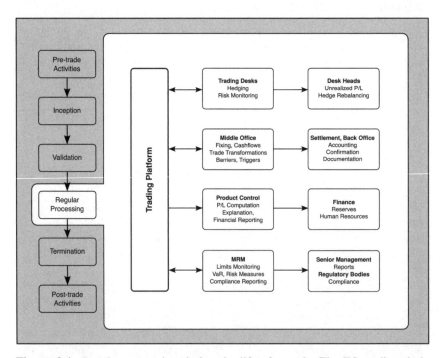

Figure 3.4 Regular processing during the life of a trade. The FO trading desks monitor their trades for performance and hedging. The MO life-cycle management team keeps track of rate fixings and cash flows, and monitors triggers, barrier breaches and termination events. The product control unit studies the P/L in conjunction with finance. They pass on reserve and unrealized profit to finance and human resources for compensation incentives. The market risk management deals with VaR and limit monitoring on a daily basis, and may handle regulatory and compliance reporting as well at predefined, regular intervals

office in the short run, which may explain the perennial tussle over the reserve levels.

Market risk management monitors the P/L at different levels of aggregation. They also study and report various market risk measures. In computing the commonly used risk measure of historical value at risk (VaR), MRM assumes that the daily returns from the trades follow a Gaussian distribution, which corresponds to the so-called lognormal assumption. They collect a large number of historical daily movements (typically one year or 252 days) in the market conditions and apply each one of them to the current market, generating a market scenario. They price each trade with each of the market scenarios and aggregate the prices. They then sort the resulting 'P/L vector' and take the 99 % worst movements (or some such predefined percentile) as the VaR.

Many questions have been raised about the efficacy of VaR as a risk measure by practitioners who believe that catastrophic market movements are more drastic than predicted by Gaussian distribution – the 1987 Black Monday and the Asian Currency Crisis were 5σ events. They further point out that such unlikely events do take place more often than expected – the so-called Black Swan effect. There are many sound practical arguments why VaR may be inadequate. Because of the human psychology (the herd mentality, for instance) that plays a crucial role in precipitating market swings, it may be impossible to model catastrophic scenarios accurately, even with the help of historical data. Therefore, historical VaR may always be suspect, at best.

In order to allay these suspicions, MRM does stress tests and tail risk analysis. In stress tests, they apply a drastic market movement of the kind that took place in the past (like the Asian currency crisis or 9/11) to the current market data and estimate the movement in the bank's book.

Tail risk analysis asks a rather unmathematical question: If the VaR condition of the 99th percentile move actually occurs, what is the expected loss? Given the lognormal assumption, the expected loss is predetermined. However, by using the available historical data, we may get a different expectation value, albeit with dubious mathematical validity and usefulness.

Such analysis is of enormous importance to the senior management and in regulatory and compliance reporting. MRM also takes care of compliance reporting to regulatory bodies, as well as risk reporting to the upper management.

Risk analysis is carried out, by and large, by studying the sensitivities of portfolio values in response to market movements. In calculus, the sensitivity of a function (f) to a variable (x) is the derivative $\partial f / \partial x$. However, when it comes to measuring financial sensitivities, banks operate with a set of conventions. In other words, the Greeks are not quite the same as pure mathematical derivatives. This apparent lack of rigour is not hard to understand. As with any physical quantity, financial functions (price of a derivative, for example) have units and dimensions (dollars and money in our example). So do observables on which they depend. As we learned in freshman physics, once we have units and dimensions, we have to agree on conventions and adopt standards so that we can compare numbers.

In finance, these conventions can get complicated and arbitrary. For instance, Vega (the sensitivity of price with respect to the volatility of the underlying) is defined as the change in the price for 1 % absolute change in the volatility. Theta (time sensitivity) is the change in the value when we roll the date by one day.

Once we appreciate that the market observables can be vectors and surfaces (interest rates and volatilities, for instance), the complexities in defining sensitivity standards multiply. Add to that the possibility that the market observable may not be observable at all (zero rates, for instance), and the proliferation of conventions reaches an alarming level of complexity. Market risk professionals and the front-office quants alike are expected to be well-versed in such conventions so that they can work effectively with sensitivity reports to manage their risks.

In addition to these passive risk methodologies, MRM also actively manages the risk at different levels of granularity, such as the risk assumed by a trader, a desk or the institution as a whole. They use the process of limit monitoring to accomplish this task. At each level of aggregation, MRM allocates a certain limit on risk-sensitive quantities, such as notional, Delta or Gamma, VaR and so on. Market risk management then monitors the usage of such quantities against their limits. Any breach of the limit is a serious issue, potentially resulting in disciplinary action. Traders also actively monitor their trades for risks and for hedge rebalancing.

Big Picture 3.3:   To Hedge or Not to Hedge

In July 2008, just before the financial crisis, the oil price (WTI) hit $147 a barrel, with a general expectation of sustained $200 levels. The possibility of such high levels rang alarm bells in the hearts of the senior management of most airlines. These levels were beyond their critical survival thresholds, they rightly felt. With such high oil prices, they ran a real risk of going bankrupt.

Faced with such a possibility, the CFOs and the risk managers of the airline industry rushed to put in place hedges against the potentially devastating oil prices and spent a small fortune on structured products implementing the hedges. Hedging essentially fixes the fuel price for the airline at around the same level as it is with the WTI price of $150 a barrel, no matter how the market moves.

This well-intentioned safeguard soon backfired when the WTI prices (and consequently fuel prices) started plummeting, contrary to all expectations. Because of the hedges, the airlines were basically pegging the cost of fuel for them at its highest level in history.

Thanks to the hedgers' honest work, airlines (and even countries) ended up handing over huge sums of money to energy traders in the second half of 2008 and early 2009. In fact, the amount of money owed by some government-linked investment bodies was so huge that there were reports of countries defaulting, or planning to default.

One can only imagine the plight of the risk managers involved in such hedging exercises. Risk managers always have a thankless job. When the market is bullish, and things are going well, risk managers try to curtail the risk appetite, thereby reducing the profit potential. When things go south, hedges based on positional views come back to haunt the organization, with the risk managers taking the blame.

3.5   LIFE-CYCLE EVENTS

Monitoring processes include more than risk management. Each trade has to be monitored for events such as option exercises, triggering or barrier conditions. In addition to these unpredictable events, there are regular fixings and cash flows to be processed as well. Managing and monitoring such events is a complex process because of its impact on the P/L. Besides, it calls for persistence in a database, audit trails and integration with specialized user interface elements facilitating the related MO operations. Take an interest rate swap (IRS) as an example. Its floating leg may call for fixings on its interest rate index every three months. The rate fixings happen in the middle office. One rate fixing may affect multiple IRS (and potentially other) trades because the interest rate index (and the associated fixing source) may be shared among them. Once the rate is fixed, a part of the value of the associated trades becomes the 'realized' P/L in the form of past cash, and the stochastic part gets restricted to the future. In order for the pricing models to handle this change in pricing, they need to access the fixings in a consistent way, which implies a database back-end specific to their storage.

Although we design a trading platform primarily for exotics trading, there are instances when we may consider using it for flow business as well. The reason for this inclusion of flow trades involving exchange-traded derivatives (ETD) is not hard to understand. One of the requirements of risk managers and traders is the ability to have an aggregate view of the portfolios under their management. As the aggregate view often involves both over-the-counter (OTC) trades as well as exchange-traded instruments, they may find it necessary to import their positions from multiple vended systems as well as in-house trading platforms into their risk management tools or spreadsheets. They would then have to combine and reconcile these positions on ad hoc spreadsheets. Such repetitive and unproductive tasks soon prompt the FO and MO professionals to demand that all positions be processed through one system – typically our in-house trading platform.

Big Picture 3.4:   Exchange-Traded versus Over-the-Counter

Stocks and futures are normally traded on centralized and established exchanges. You can buy or sell stocks via the New York Stock Exchange, for instance, or commodity futures via the Chicago Mercantile Exchange. Some plain vanilla options are also traded on exchanges. Instruments that trade on exchanges are called, naturally, exchange-traded derivatives, or ETD.

When you trade on an exchange, your counterparty is always the exchange. Thus, if you buy 1000 IBM shares through NYSE, you are not buying it from some other trader who wants to sell IBM shares, but from the exchange itself. All transactions go through the exchange that acts as an intermediary.

Since the exchange is the counterparty in all your transactions, you can be sure that your contracts will be honoured and all the monies due will be paid. In other words, the counterparty credit risk is all but eliminated in exchange-traded derivatives. Exchanges accomplish this risk minimization by demanding initial margins from the traders they deal with. As the market moves and the value of the traded derivatives changes, margin calls may become necessary for maintaining this credit guarantee.

Over-the-counter or OTC contracts are, in principle, negotiated privately between two counterparties. In practice, banks act as market makers for OTC instruments such as bonds, interest rate swaps, forward rate agreements, etc. In other words, they are willing to sell and buy the instruments at published rates. If you want to buy a particular bond, you will only have to look for a bank selling it. When you wish to sell the bond, you can sell it back to the bank at the prevailing price. Of course, there is a spread between the bid and offer prices.

When it comes to exotic options and customized structured products, you will find individual price quotes rather than published market making. Since OTC trading is expected to happen between sophisticated participants, its market is largely unregulated. Furthermore, the volume of OTC traded instruments is not readily available, leading to unknown leverages in the market. The counterparty credit risk involved in OTC trading is something that the participants take on and price into the traded instruments.

From a life-cycle management perspective, this requirement poses an interesting challenge. Life-cycle events include fixings, cash flow generation, exercises, barrier and trigger monitoring, and so on. These events form the ageing process and clearly affect the mark-to-market value and the P/L of trades. Such life-cycle events, in the case of customized OTC trades, vary from trade to trade. Each trade has to be monitored and aged individually.

For ETD trading, however, the situation is completely different. Their mark-to-market comes directly from their market values. Thus, a plain vanilla option traded on an exchange will be marked-to-market using its market spot price rather than a Black–Scholes or Binary Tree model. Furthermore, the trade volume on such exchange-traded derivatives may be large in terms of the number of trades, and the life-cycle events tend to be corporate actions and automated option exercises. These actions are common to all trades on a particular ETD. For this reason, it would seem natural to track their ageing process using the bank's net positions on them so that a large number of trades on one ETD can be handled at once, with potential savings on computational resources.

What this discussion shows is that in a trading platform design with an overarching scope, the nature of the instruments traded can and does impose conflicting requirements. A quantitative developer therefore needs to be resourceful and cognizant of the underlying business dynamics for such requirements.

3.6 TERMINATION AND SETTLEMENT

Settlements (cash and/or asset exchanges between counterparties) can take place during the life of a trade or at its termination (see Figure 3.5). In swap kinds of trades (interest rate swaps, for instance), there are net cash flows at regular intervals as specified in the contract. These cash flows are computed in the trading

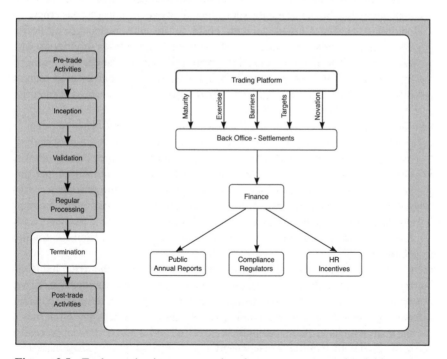

Figure 3.5 Trade termination events and settlement processes and activities

platform and settled by the relevant back-office team. The settlement takes place after a delay, as specified in the contract or term sheet. The settlement delay is usually two business days for most asset classes, but it can be longer for some commodity trades, for instance.

A trade may terminate in a variety of ways:

1. Normal termination at maturity. In the case of noncancellable, noncallable swaps, the trade lasts till its maturity. In addition to any periodic cash flows, the trade may have a final settlement as well. For an option, the termination at maturity does not involve settlement if it matures out of the money.
2. Exercises. When an option is exercised, it generates a settlement trigger. Depending on the nature of the option, the exercise may or may not coincide with the maturity of the trade. A European option, if in the money, is exercised only at maturity. If it is out of the money, it matures worthless. American options, on the other hand, may be exercised any time during their lifetime generating a cash flow, although they are rarely exercised before maturity because they always have a positive time value. In other words, they are always worth more as an option than their intrinsic value, and you can make more money by selling them in the market rather than exercising them.
3. Barrier breaches. Barrier options are options that come alive or get knocked out depending on whether or not the spot value of an underlying asset has crossed a predefined barrier. A knock out with rebate, for instance, is one type of barrier option that becomes null and void if the underlying crosses the barrier. The associated rebate is a compensation given to the option holder for getting it knocked out. The rebate settlement is triggered when the barrier breach takes place. Note that the rebate may be settled at the barrier breach or at maturity after the usual settlement delay.
4. Target conditions. Another termination event of a trade is when a target is reached. For example, in a target redemption note, coupons are paid periodically until the cumulated payoffs reach a predefined target cap. When the target is reached, the trade is terminated with one final payment. Other target redemption options include forwards, where the profit or loss of a forward contract accumulates towards a predefined target. All target redemption trades are monitored for trigger conditions and the associated cash flows generate accounting entries and settlement directives from the trading platform.
5. Callability exercises. A callable instrument is one in which the writer holds the right to terminate the trade. Because of the implicit option that the buyer of the option has given to the writer, the instrument is cheaper than the corresponding noncallable version. Since callability is essentially an American option, when the instrument is 'called', the option is exercised and all the settlement processes associated with exercises are triggered.

6. There are a couple of market operations that cut across the boundaries of the front-, middle- or back-office divisions. One such operation is novation, where one participant of the trade replaces the other with a third party, after mutual negotiations and agreement. Depending on the marked-to-market value of the trade, the third party may pay or receive cash, generating a settlement trigger.

3.7   POST-TRADE ACTIVITIES

Once the trade is terminated, either early (through trigger, target or exercise conditions) or at maturity, it flows into the hands of the massive accounting apparatus of the bank. All the accounting after the termination of the trade is handled by the finance department. They keep track of the general ledger (GL), the statements and reports, which will end up in annual reports and other public disclosures.

The post-trade accounting calculations, although done independently of the trading platform, do impact the staff involved in the trade life-cycle management from inception to termination. The impact is through performance-based compensation and incentive schemes. Such schemes are managed by the human resources (HR) department, who think up many clever means of aligning the employee's financial interests with the bank's performance in the stock market. For instance, HR may offer incentives in the form of employee share options with long vesting periods or may come up with employee share purchase plans with attractive terms.

3.8   SUMMARY

During the course of its complex life, a trade undergoes several transformations and operations performed on it by various business units. As a software object, the trade services the information requests from these business units. For instance, product control may request daily P/L, market risk management may require the Greeks aggregated at different levels, the middle-office control units may need to set flags and put trades in operation queues based on status, and so on. All these requirements put together define and determine the architecture of the trading platform. As quantitative professionals, we need to understand the rationale behind these requirements and be able to prioritize them.

From our perspective, a trade is conventionally a software entity persisting in a database and loaded into a computer memory as an object. In a more modern architecture, a trade may be a distributed entity whose projections are served, on demand, by a trade data provider or service. Regardless of how we model it, the trade entity will have to satisfy the business requirements coming from the numerous corners of the organization. The only way to design a lasting, robust and maintainable trading platform is to anticipate and understand as many of these requirements as possible before we start implementing them.

Although we view the trade as a software object, ours is not the only perspective in the bank. The trade perspectives are paradigms that help various business units carry out their tasks. These paradigms are derived out of the static structure of the bank (as described in the previous chapter) as well as the nature of their tasks (this chapter) and, perhaps most importantly, convention. As quant developers, we need to appreciate these varying perspectives as well, which we will take a stab at in the next chapter.

QUIZ

1. What is the difference between inception pricing and aged pricing of a trade?
2. What is historical VaR and why do people mistrust it as a risk measure?
3. Can you recall six trade termination events that trigger settlement?
4. What is the difference between the model validation (performed by the market risk management) and the trade validation (performed in the middle office)?
5. How do human resources align the employees' and the bank's financial interests?
6. Why is it important for quantitative developers to appreciate the various trade perspectives and work paradigms of other business units?

4

Trade Perspectives

All business units that manage some aspects of the life cycle of a trade view it through their own preferred paradigms. Paradigms are metaphors or representations employed to handle data and information efficiently. Due to long usage and the consequent familiarity, paradigms become synonymous with what they represent. The process paradigms, in a financial institution, are not all compatible with one another across various business units.

As quantitative developers, we come across a variety of paradigms because our trading platform services many different business and support units while handling the trade workflow. In order to excel in our job and enhance communication with these business users, we have to be aware of these paradigms, which are filters through which they view trades and trade-related operations.

The last two chapters outlined the static organization of a bank and the dynamics of how trades flow through the static apparatus. In this chapter, we will examine the views and paradigms held dear by various teams at different stages of a trade life cycle. The trade paradigms or perspectives help the bank employees carry out their tasks efficiently.

Once we understand the trade perspective of a particular team, we will be able to formulate their requirements and implement them successfully. In this chapter, we will also look at some of the information and presentation required of the trading platform that the trading and processing teams demand, based on their views, and some sample reports generated to meet their demands.

4.1 TRADE-CENTRIC VIEW

The trade perspective that is most common these days is trade-centric. In this view, trades are the primary objects of interest. A trade-centric view is the reason that most trading systems index trades as the primary objects. By putting together a group of the primary objects (trades), we get a portfolio or folder. Put a few portfolios together and we get a book. The whole trading activity of the financial institution is merely a collection of books. This paradigm, which has served us well for a long time, represents the best compromise between different possible views.

Still, the trade-centric perspective is only a compromise. As we will see, the activities of the trading floor can be viewed from different angles. Each view corresponds to a paradigm and has its role in the bigger picture when it comes to designing the trading platform.

Regardless of the trade perspectives of the various business units, the trade-centric view is going to be implemented in any trading platform because trades are the primary units of work. However, this view does run into trouble when applied to structured products, which can be thought of as a composition of several simpler trades. The simpler trades, though necessary for booking and pricing the structures, are not the primary units, and consequently they have to carry along some identifying tag or attribute to link them together as one structure. Such considerations become vitally important during certain trade operations. For example, if the structure is cancelled (in response to some trigger or termination event), we have to be careful to remove all the linked trades.

In addition to the structures made up of simpler trades that have to be considered as a group, there may be other trades booked, at times automatically in the trading platform. For instance, the trading platform may autogenerate an array of trades to replicate the counterparty credit risk associated with a trade and propagate them

Big Picture 4.1:   Back-to-Back Trades

Back-to-back trades are special deals where the bank buys a derivative product from another financial institution on behalf of a customer. The bank does this when it does not have the mathematical or technical capability to assess and manage risks associated with the product (which, in trading floor jargon, is known as 'warehousing' or 'in-housing' the risk or the product). When the bank cannot warehouse it, it passes on the associated market risk to a counterparty through the process of back-to-back trade booking.

Although it perfectly transfers the market risk, the back-to-back technique exposes the bank to greater credit risk than a customer-facing trade. The increase in credit risk comes about because the bank has two positions, and indeed two trades – one with the counterparty and the other with the customer. However, the potential future exposure (PFE) computation will overestimate the associated credit risk because it sees the two trades.

Traditionally, the credit risk is estimated by simulating the trade a large number of times, calculating the amount the counterparty is expected to owe the bank and taking a certain percentile value of this future exposure. The derivative product being traded on the back-to-back basis can be in the money for the bank from both ends, but not at the same time. When one side of the trade is in the money, the other side has to be out of the money. Since the potential future exposure calculation for estimating the credit risk does not take this fact into account, it is usually an overestimation. The credit risk on back-to-back trades needs to be netted using this fact.

to other credit management systems. If the trading platform does not provide the necessary tools to link the credit replicates as part of the same structure, we will find it impossible to ensure that they are removed in tandem when we terminate the trade or structure.

4.2   MODEL-CENTRIC VIEW

A model-centric view is what quants hold on to. Quants are the mathematical brains of the bank. Their deliverables are mainly pricing models. A pricing model is the end result of a set of assumptions on how the market evolves and how the evolution reflects on the value of the trade. Once the pricing model is developed and delivered, the quant can consider his task accomplished for the particular product under consideration. Therefore, their natural view of trades is from this angle.

A simple example may help elucidate the model-centric view. In order to come up with a model to price an equity option, we can make a reasonable assumption about equity prices that the daily returns of a particular stock is a random variable with a Gaussian distribution. The resulting probability distribution of the spot price of the underlying equity is the well-known lognormal distribution. The standard deviation of the daily returns is related to the volatility of the stock, which we can determine from historical price data. Once we annualize it (to consider the standard deviation of the annual returns), we get the stock volatility.

If we make a further assumption that the volatility is constant over time, we have all the ingredients for the famous Black–Scholes partial differential equation, which equates the returns of a portfolio consisting of the option and a fraction of its underlying to the risk-free rate of return. The Nobel Prize winning solution to this equation is the Black–Scholes pricing formula. The pricing model corresponding to the Black–Scholes pricing formula, as the quant delivers it, would be a collection of functions in a library.

Given that the Black–Scholes formula applies only to European options, the quants may decide to develop a binomial tree pricing model, which can also handle American type exercises. Again, the quants will deliver the binomial tree model as another set of functions in the quant library. Although binomial trees can be applied to European options as well, the two distinct models are two units of deliverables from the quants in this simplified example. This view, in essence, is the model-centric perspective (see Figure 4.1).

Looking at trades or products from a model-centric perspective optimizes the productivity for quants. For instance, if they can use the same model to price different products, even across asset classes, they save on their mathematical and programming work. Note, however, that in most financial institutions, quants tend to specialize in a chosen asset class.

Quants deliver their work in the form of libraries (the quant library), which contain the models and their associated helper functions. In addition to this primary

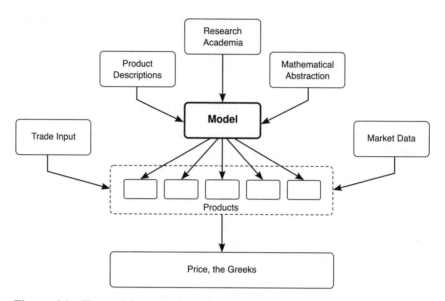

Figure 4.1 The model-centric view of trading activities, as seen by the quants. The quants may deploy the same model to multiple products with minimal modifications. The products, once given market data and the input parameters, produce prices and sensitivities using the quant models

deliverable, they may also create pricing tools (programs built using the quant library) either for themselves for testing purposes or for trading support.

A mathematician or a physicist just switching to a quant career has a focus quite different from a professional quant. The newcomer may think of the mathematical aspect or the quick implementation as the most important aspect of the job. A professional quant knows that the mathematical part is only the tip of the iceberg. He has to worry about all the devilish details like day-count conventions, holiday calendars, market data and other parameter definitions (such as rate curves, interpolation methods and so on).

However, even the more experienced quants tend to stop at inception pricing and leave the rest of the implementation to quantitative developers. If the quants implement anything other than inception pricing (like aged-trade pricing, past-cash management or even the Greeks computations), they usually do it as an afterthought. For this reason, such implementations are not as robust or scalable as they should be.

The model-centric view of the quant has implications when it comes to deploying products. Quants may develop macro languages or other configuration description tactics to modify the model easily to suit new product variants.

Because of the ad hoc manner in which downstream processes are implemented, the products may, however, be hard to deploy, validate and monetize.

4.3   PRODUCT-CENTRIC VIEW

Quantitative developers are product-centric in their trade view. Their work starts with the quant library. Each product or product variant put together using the models in the quant library needs to go into the trading platform, which forms the basis of the quant developer's bread and butter (see Figure 4.2).

The trading platform makes the models and programs from the quants usable to the rest of the bank. To the quantitative professionals who develop the trading platform, each product or product variant is a complete and independent unit of work. By and large, it does not matter to them whether the new product uses the same model as an existing one. They have to implement the necessary plumbing for all the downstream processes, regardless of what model is being used. Therefore, the work paradigm that makes most sense to quantitative developers is product-centric.

In our example of Black–Scholes and binomial tree models, the quantitative developers would probably find the largest superset of products that can use the two models. The pricing tool that comes with this book, for instance,

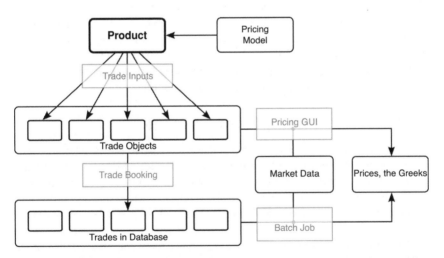

Figure 4.2 The product-centric view of trading activities, appropriate in the trading platform. This view, entertained by the quantitative developers, is more detailed than the model-centric view. Here, each product is a unit of work. When the product gets input parameters and the market data, it instantiates a trade, which is stored in a database. The trade knows how to price itself using market data and its own pricing models

defines vanilla options as the product, with call/put, European/American and Black–Scholes/binomial tree variants. This product-centric organization (starting from plain vanilla) minimizes the effort needed to deploy and maintain the trading platform and the products available on it.

By looking at the implementation task from this product-centric perspective, the quantitative developers can leverage on common user interfaces, utility extensions (such as visualization tools, finite difference sensitivity computations, etc.). In fact, even in implementing products with a vastly different topology, it is in the interest of the development team to find as much commonality as possible.

There are modern approaches that may change this product-centric view. For instance, it may be possible to design a trading platform so flexible and intelligent that new product development and deployment are virtually indistinguishable from each other. In other words, the trading platform provides tools that help you design a new product, potentially using a new model that your quant team has developed. While you are designing the product, the trading platform automatically configures the process chains and generates downstream hooks such as approval templates, accounting rules, a settlement trigger setup and so on. The automatic configuration takes place behind the scene, without you (the end user) realizing it. By the time you have completed the product design phase, it is already integrated in the system.

This mode of operation cuts down the time delay between product conceptualization and deployment to mere minutes. It also changes the work paradigm of quantitative developers from the current product-centric view to a much higher level of abstraction. While this route may be the right choice for reasons of efficiency and pure elegance of design, I personally believe that the process specificity and rule exceptions present in our current financial and regulatory environment make it an extremely difficult, if not impossible, undertaking.

4.4   ASSET-CLASS VIEW

Trading desks are primarily organized under asset classes. We have trading desks dealing with fixed income (FI – bonds trading), equities (EQ – stocks), foreign exchange (FX or forex – currencies), commodities (COM – precious and base metals, energy, etc.), interest rate derivatives (IRD – swaps) and so on. Because of this organization, traders use an asset-class-based paradigm to view trades and trading systems.

The hierarchy of trading desks, however, is much more complicated than simple asset class categorization. We have derivatives trading desks, structured products, exotics, day trading, etc. These desks may be organized by asset classes or by the nature of their activity. Thus, a commodities structured products trader may have a reporting line that does not go through the rest of the commodities or energy trading. However, looking at their skillset and knowledge requirements, it is best to view trading desks under their asset class banner.

The trading platform interacts with the trading desks at the input (booking) as well as the output (reporting) levels. Although many of the input and output requests are asset-class-specific, some of them cut across all asset classes. The generic requests are, for example, sensitivity and scenario analysis reports. An example of a scenario analysis is given in Table 4.1 and Figure 4.3. (This analysis is performed using the pricing program that comes with this book.) In a deployed environment, such reports would be generated as a part of a daily batch job.

Although traders may be asset-class-centric in their organization, their work metaphor is not very different from that of quantitative professionals. They think of trades from a model-centric or product-centric perspective as needed, and demand processed data and booking services on a per-trade or per-portfolio level. Since this view is close to the view of the quants and quantitative developers, we need not do anything special in the trading platform. In other words, the whole trading platform is already designed and implemented with traders' requirements in mind.

4.5 QUEUES AND STATUS FLAGS

The business unit that checks and validates the trade inputs uses a queue paradigm to visualized trades. This unit is usually named the treasury control or business control unit, or simply the middle office. To facilitate their job, they have to get a list of trades that demand their attention. Furthermore, they would like to collect trades into separate lists depending on the actions to be performed.

It is natural for them to think of trades awaiting actions as a queue. The validation queue, for instance, can become longer as more and more trades are booked at the trading desks. The validating professionals, attacking the queue from the other end, try to make the queue shorter. By the end of the day, prior to the daily batch processing, the queue has to be cleared.

An in-house trading system has to place all trades waiting for market operations to be performed on them on appropriate queues to enable the middle-office people to locate and process them easily. Market operations can be complicated, with multiple stages of approvals and full audit trails. Figure 4.4 shows a typical process flow as seen by the middle office.

How do we implement the queues? If the trading platform works with a trade-centric paradigm, the queues are merely collections of trades. However, we have to add on status flags as properties of the trade objects to handle queues. Since the trade status is something that needs to be historized and timestamped for audit purposes, it may be wise to track it using another dedicated database table. Although it may be possible to start our design process keeping this queue obsession in mind, it is not advisable, given that the queue view of the middle office is just one of the many differing views. However, we need to be aware of this particular

Table 4.1 A sample trade scenario risk analysis. The dependence of the Delta on the volatility and spot price is studied in this simple European call option. Such analyses, especially for complicated structures, are essential for the trading desks to understand and manage their risks

Volatility (%)	Spot										
	50	60	70	80	90	100	110	120	130	140
10 %	0.000	0.000	0.000	0.003	0.010	0.023	0.043	0.067	0.093	0.121
14 %	0.000	0.001	0.007	0.024	0.050	0.083	0.118	0.153	0.188	0.220
18 %	0.001	0.017	0.053	0.100	0.147	0.1925	0.232	0.269	0.302	0.331
22 %	0.046	0.122	0.192	0.249	0.296	0.335	0.367	0.395	0.420	0.442
26 %	0.307	0.372	0.414	0.444	0.467	0.486	0.503	0.518	0.531	0.544
30 %	0.709	0.665	0.644	0.632	0.626	0.624	0.624	0.626	0.629	0.633
34 %	0.934	0.866	0.815	0.780	0.755	0.737	0.725	0.717	0.711	0.707
38 %	0.991	0.958	0.916	0.878	0.847	0.822	0.803	0.789	0.777	0.769
42 %	0.999	0.989	0.966	0.937	0.909	0.833	0.862	0.844	0.830	0.818
46 %	1.000	0.998	0.987	0.969	0.947	0.925	0.904	0.886	0.871	0.858

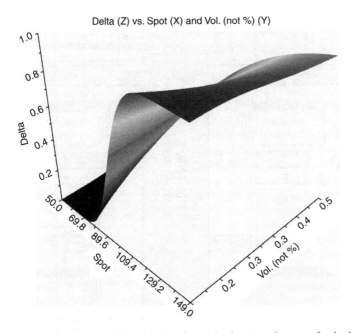

Delta (Z) vs. Spot (X) and Vol. (not %) (Y)

Figure 4.3 A sample scenario analysis of a trade that a trader uses for hedging it. This surface plot is generated by the attached pricing tool. In a real trading platform, such reports and plots will be generated in batch

view of the trading world in order to anticipate and respond to the requirements from the middle office and validation teams.

4.6 AGGREGATE VIEWS

When the trade reaches the market risk management group, there is a subtle change in the perspective from a trade-level view to a portfolio- or book-level view. We can think of portfolio or other groupings as aggregate views. Aggregation is a trivial process mathematically. After all, when you put a bunch of trades together, you get an aggregate view like a portfolio. How robust the portfolio hierarchy needs to be is a design consideration in the trading platform.

A weak portfolio structure can be implemented, for instance, by adding an attribute to the trade object. In this design, any modification to this attribute creates a portfolio implicitly. Such autogeneration of portfolios without any checks and approvals may not be compatible with the workflow and policies of the bank.

A more robust portfolio hierarchy would live in the database where the trades are booked, with specific access controlled user interfaces for creating and managing portfolios. Regardless of where the portfolio is defined, it is still necessary to

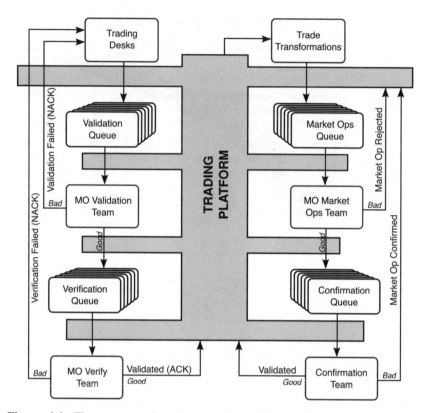

Figure 4.4 The queue paradigm that the middle office uses for managing their daily work. There are validation and various market operations queues and multiple levels of approval processes

decide how to lay it out in the memory when the trading platform is running. Do we make collection or container classes to hold trades in portfolios? Or do we keep it as a trade attribute? Does the hierarchy need to be nested with multiple levels and overlaps? We need to address all these considerations at the design stage in order to avoid incompatibilities and weaknesses after the implementation of the trading platform.

Big Picture 4.2: Pluses and Minuses of VaR

Value at risk (VaR) helps the market risk management team to estimate and anticipate extreme negative movements in P/L. The underlying assumption in historic VaR methodology is that the probability of change in the P/L from today to tomorrow has a (possibly unknown) distribution that is stationary and modelled by the historical market movements in the immediate past. Since this assumption and the whole methodology are a hotly debated subject, let us look at them a bit more closely.

Let us say the value of our book as of yesterday is P_0 and that the market moves as it usually does (which is a statement that hides the stationarity assumption), resulting in a new value today of P_1. Then the change in the value of the book is $P = P_1 - P_0$, and it has a distribution perhaps similar to what is shown in the figure in Exhibit A below. Looking back in time; we can build this distribution over a large number days. The history usually used is a year or 252 business days. Even without knowing the shape of the distribution, we can estimate the 99 % confidence level of the P/L tomorrow, and call it VaR. In other words, we can say with 99 % confidence that the value of our book tomorrow is going to be better than the VaR number.

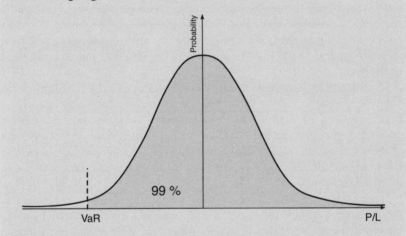

Exhibit A Illustration of the VaR computation methodology on the X axis, the P/L moves based on historical market moves and, on the Y axis, the probability of that move is shown. The distribution is, in fact, a smoothed histogram of the simulated P/L moves, with the negative side indicating the losses. VaR is defined, in the case shown, as the value of the P/L move corresponding to the 99 % confidence level. To put it differently, we expect the P/L shift to be better than the VaR number with 99 % probability.

Clearly, we can change the confidence level percentile to 95 % or any other number and for the time horizon we can look forward from one day to one week or whatever. The resulting estimate is a VaR with the characteristics that we define.

The first question is: How can we assume that the past history of market moves is an indicator of how the future is going to look? The VaR methodology crucially depends on the assumption that the market moves are 'normal'. Therefore, we can start from the historical market scenarios, typically of 252 days, and apply the market moves in those scenarios to the current market to get an ensemble of 'normal' markets tomorrow. Based on these simulated markets, we get 252 P/L changes for our book. The 99 % value is halfway between the lowest second and third P/L movements. In other words, we sort the 252 P/L values in descending order and look for the value corresponding to the 248.48th (252×0.99) position. The fractional position is estimated using interpolation. If a different percentile p is prescribed for VaR with a P/L vector of size n, then the position to seek would be $n \times p$.

Note that the VaR computation does not make an explicit assumption on the probability distribution of the P/L movements of the whole book. It does, however, assume that the market moves causing the P/L shifts have a distribution that is represented by the 250 or so historical scenarios that form the input to the VaR computation. Since P/L shifts depend on a large number of factors with unknown probability distributions, we can assume that the central limit theorem applies. The P/L shifts of the book are likely to follow a Gaussian distribution.

There are many arguments against the use of VaR as a risk measure – some emotional, some technical. VaR methodology is computationally intensive – if we have, say, 10 thousand trades in our book, we make about 2.5 million pricing calculations to get the 250 P/L numbers. After that, we throw away most of them and use only one or two (the second and third lowest, for instance) to compute our VaR. One or two bad market scenarios can affect our VaR for an extended period of time.

If we assume a Gaussian (or at least a symmetric) distribution for the P/L moves, we may be able to improve the accuracy of the VaR measure by using the profit side as well. That is to say, in the case of 99 % VaR, we can also consider not only the second and third loss moves but the profit moves as well, interpolate between them and invert their sign. This will improve the accuracy of the VaR estimate by about 30 %. However, if we permit ourselves to assume a Gaussian shape for the distribution of the P/L moves, we can use curve-fitting techniques vastly to improve the accuracy and stability of the measure.

4.7   BOTTOM-LINE VIEW

Of all the various trade perspectives, the one that all of us should appreciate is that of the senior management, narrowly and steadily focusing on the bottom line. This is the view that is presented to the shareholders of the financial institution in annual reports and other public announcements. Since a financial institution such as a bank is primarily a profit-generating organization, this bottom-line view is appropriate.

Furthermore, it helps the senior management prioritize actions in terms of the profit they bring to the stakeholders – including employees, shareholders and customers. Such prioritization and the consequent resource allocation have a direct impact on all of us.

This view, however, is at a level so high that pricing models and trades are invisible, unless, of course, rogue traders lose a lot of money on a particular product or by using a particular model – or, somewhat less likely, they make huge profits using the same tricks. However, this lack of visibility does not mean that the trading platform designers can ignore this view. We have to design in the capability of generating appropriate reports catering to this view as well.

4.8 OTHER PERSPECTIVES

When a trade comes to the finance department, it is no longer in the booking system. The finance professionals manage trading desks and asset classes as profit and cost centres. This notion of profit and cost centres, which we can implement using a flexible portfolio structure, may impose other constraints on the platform design. In order to come up with a robust design, we need to understand the accounting structure well enough to respond to the specific requirements coming from the finance and accounting departments as well.

Some aspects of the trade data come under the purview of regulatory bodies and secrecy laws. Since financial data contains sensitive information, access to it is understandably highly regulated. Since a trading platform operates over international boundaries in today's globalized financial markets, it has to cater to multiple, disparate regulatory requirements related to banking secrecy and privileged data. The very definition of what 'privileged data' means is different in different countries. In some countries, the fact that the bank has business dealings with a specific counterparty is already privileged information, while in others, it is only the trade details (like the notional or exposure) that are confidential.

Some countries may have geographic constraints on the physical location of the databases – South Korea, for instance, demands that all trade-related data involving entities on their land be housed domestically. Even a lookup of counterparty names from abroad is forbidden. Like all other perspectives described so far, this regulatory view also has an impact on the trading platform design. For instance, if we design a user interface for trade entry with a type-ahead or drop-down feature on the counterparty name, we have to ensure that the static data populating this feature is aware of the geographical location where the end user is.

An information technology (IT) team views the trading world from a completely different perspective. Theirs is a system-centric view, where the same product using the same model appearing in two different systems is basically two different beasts. This view is not particularly appreciated by traders, quants or quant developers. Most of our troubles in communicating with the IT team stem from our lack of understanding of their work paradigm. When we think of a trade, they think of a record in a database. When we talk about a new product roll out, they hear an additional module in an existing piece of software or a version upgrade.

Quantitative developers and IT professionals, while staying close in their syntactical lingo, have completely different semantic contexts in their views of the trading world. These views are not going to change just because of one book. However, this book may bring about an appreciation for the differing views and their semantics so that the deployment of the trading platforms can proceed as smoothly as possible.

4.9 SUMMARY

Big Picture 4.3:   Big Picture and Narrow Perspectives

The trading platform is a system that brings multiple domains of expertise together. It calls for specialized knowledge in computing, finance and business processes, problem solving and so on. As quantitative developers are the professionals closest to the trading world, their need to embrace a Big Picture view is the greatest. Other professionals may entertain narrow perspectives and may still be effective, though with stunted advancement prospects.

Most quants, especially at junior levels, despise the Big Picture. They think of it as a distraction from their real work of marrying stochastic calculus to C++. All traders, however, will agree that the best model in the world is worthless unless it can be deployed. Deployment is the fast track to the Big Picture – There is no point in denying it. Besides, in an increasingly interconnected world where a crazy French man's actions instantly affect our bonus, what is the use of denying the existence of the Big Picture in our neck of the woods? Instead, let us take advantage of the Big Picture to empower ourselves.

When we change our narrow, albeit effective, focus on the work at hand to an understanding of our role and value in the organization, we will see the potential points of failure of the systems and processes. We will be prepared with possible solutions to the nightmarish havoc that computerized processes can wreak.

A trading platform finds its users primarily in the front office and the middle office, where various teams manage and process trades, their life cycle, settlement, reporting, etc. All these teams demand an array of features in the trading platform depending on the established perspectives and subtle paradigms they use to visualize and work with trades. As the architects of the trading platform, quantitative developers need to understand these perspectives.

The trade perspectives differ from each other to such a degree that they may even seem to us incompatible. In this chapter, we went through many views – from the developers' product-centric through the quants' model-centric to the big bosses' view that sees only the bottom line. The challenge of designing a successful trading platform is in shaping the ability of the final application to express any of these views. The successful trading platform is one that exhibits multiple personalities and satisfies all its users. In the next chapter, we will start looking at the technical choices that will eventually lead us to this holy grail.

QUIZ

1. Match the business units in the left column with their favourite trade perspectives on the right. (Note that it is not necessarily a one-to-one map.)

Quantitative modelling	Trade-centric
Quantitative development	Model-centric
Trading desks	Product-centric
Middle office	Asset-class-centric
Market risk management	System-centric
Credit risk management	Processing queues
Information technology	Aggregate views
Senior management	Profit and cost centres
Finance	Bottom-line view

2. What is the difference between trade queues and portfolios?
3. What is a quantitative developer's trade perspective? What is its advantage?
4. Why do we need to understand all the various trade perspectives?

5
Programming Languages – Basics and Choices

In the last three chapters, we went through the structure of financial institutions and the business units that handle the various aspects of the trading activity. The business processes and practices that we explored in these chapters will resurface during the design phase of a trading platform project or, somewhat more painfully, during its implementation phase. These processes and practices form the basis of the user requirements of the trading platform. In order to meet these requirements, we need a sound understanding of the business. Though necessary, business knowledge is by no means sufficient because a trading platform is, first and foremost, a software design challenge. We therefore need to have a firm footing on computer science, software engineering and programming as well if we are to succeed in rolling out a robust trading platform.

Those of us who come with a more quantitative and mathematical, rather than technical and engineering, background may lack the formal knowledge to be good quantitative developers. This chapter, which represents a transition from the business requirements to the technical aspects of platform design, recapitulates the basics of computing and programming, all with a view to bridging the gap in technical knowledge in some of us so that we can come up with a robust design and sound implementation strategies.

The first order of business in designing a trading platform is likely to be technical choices such as the computing and database platform that will meet the requirements and objectives of the program. Only with the help of some formal knowledge in software engineering and our experience can we hope to understand the technical choices open to us, and choose wisely. However, given the importance and the scope of the trading platform for the business, the technical choices are likely to be decided in a collaborative fashion, often with strong voices exerting prescriptive influences on them.

The rationale behind the technical choices is our subject matter in this and the following chapters. We first look at the choice of the computing language itself, starting from its basic features. In the following chapter, we will expand on this knowledge with an example design of a trading platform. We will then look at more advanced and detailed aspects of the design in the subsequent chapter.

5.1   LANGUAGE CHOICE

Since the most commonly used programming language for developing trading platforms is C++ (or, at least, an object-oriented language), we will discuss design considerations assuming the object-oriented programming (OOP) environment. In particular, we will choose to provide examples almost exclusively in C++. This choice of examples does not imply an endorsement of the language for implementing trading platforms. In fact, OOP methodology, while holding considerable advantages as an ideal environment for developing trading platforms, also suffers from some significant weaknesses. These weaknesses are usually addressed using programming idioms and patterns. A more drastic approach to overcoming the weaknesses of OOP involves resorting to other programming methodologies. We will go through both these approaches later on in this chapter.

Writing a book on computer programming is always a difficult undertaking because the author has to guess and assume the level of programming expertise of his potential readers. My style is to assume nothing so that every reader of this book has a fair chance of following the ensuing discussion. However, this approach runs the risk of alienating those who are experienced programmers. Although they can safely skip over the introductory sections of this chapter, it may still be worth their time to go through this chapter in its entirety. This chapter starts with the often forgotten basics that may inspire novel and original approaches in the thinking process of even accomplished programmers.

Big Picture 5.1:   Zeros and Ones

A basic computer processor is deceptively simple. It is a string of gates. A gate is a switch (more or less) made up of a small group of transistors. A 32-bit processor has 32 switches in an array. Each switch can be either in an off position representing a zero or on (representing one). So a processor can hold a 32-bit binary number and it can perform only one function – add the contents of another array of gates (called a register) to itself. In other words, it can only 'accumulate'.

In writing this last sentence, I have already started a process of abstraction. I wrote 'contents', thinking of the register as a container holding numbers. It is the power of multiple levels of abstraction, each of which is simple and obvious, but building on whatever came before it, that makes a computer enormously powerful.

We can see abstractions, followed by the modularization of the abstracted concept, in every aspect of computing, both hardware and software. Groups of transistors become arrays of gates, and then processors, registers, cache or memory. Accumulations (additions) become all arithmetic operations, string manipulations, user interfaces, image and video editing and so on.

Another feature of computing that aids in the seemingly unstoppable march of Moore's law (which states that computers will double in their power every 18 months) is that each advance seems to fuel further advances, generating an explosive growth. The first compiler, for instance, was written in a primitive assembler-level language. The second one was written using the first one and so on. Even in hardware development, one generation of computers become the tools in designing the next generation, stoking an inexorable cycle of development.

While this positive feedback in hardware and software is a good thing, the explosive nature of growth may take us in wrong directions, much like the strong growth in the credit market led to the banking collapse of 2008. Many computing experts now wonder whether the object-oriented technology has been overplayed.

5.2 BASICS OF COMPUTING

5.2.1 Development cycle

It is instructional for a developer to review the basic process of building a program from its source code. Once the developer has created the source code file, he will go through the cycle of compile–link–run–debug until he can call the program relatively bug-free. No nontrivial program can be guaranteed to be bug-free, because the elimination of bugs is rarely an absolute concept; the developer can only minimize the number and probability of bugs.

Modern integrated development environments (IDEs) hide these distinct steps of compilation, linking, etc., from the developer's view. At times, however, we have to tweak the compiler or linker options, which requires us to know what is involved at each step.

A developer writes his code almost always in a high- level language, such as C, C++, etc. These languages are human-readable, however cryptic they may look to the uninitiated. For instance, a simple declaration such as int $n = 0$; (in C or C++) indicates to the human developer that he has access to a memory location that has labelled n, and that it can take integer values. Hidden from his view are the steps necessary to allocate this memory location and keep track of it, and to move a zero integer value into it. These steps are machine-dependent operation codes (opcodes), which are mere series of binary numbers, completely unintelligible to a human being.

Compilation is the process by which the source code written in a high-level language (such as C, C++, etc.) is translated to a low-level machine language and optimized. The compiler, a program by itself, first launches a language preprocessor (to handle macros and other preprocessor directives in C, for instance). Then it does a lexical analysis, followed by more thorough syntax and semantic checks. Then it optimizes the code, finally generating a machine-readable code called the object (not to be confused with the object in the OOP paradigm). This intermediate object file, which needs to be 'linked' before running, has an .o or .obj extension.

On a Unix-like machine, a compiler such as the GNU C compiler (gcc) is invoked with a command like `gcc -c file.c -o file.o`, which instructs the machine to compile `file.c` and put the output (the object file) in `file.o`. The source code (`file.c`) can be edited using any text editor such as emacs, vi, notepad etc. On the VAX computer of yester year, which came with its own C compiler, a similar command `CC FILE.C` would create `FILE.OBJ` out of the source code file. On Windows running the popular Visual Studio development environment, we do not usually see the command line, but if we must, we can examine it in one of the configuration settings.

The complier program, while thorough in checking the syntax of the source code, does not try to resolve any so-called external symbols. To illustrate it by an example, if we say `int n = getTradeNum();` (with an adequately declared `getTradeNum()` function), the compiler would create the object code assuming that `getTradeNum()` is an external reference. It does not yet know what this external function is, but it takes it that all will be revealed in due course. This function may be defined in another object file or in an object library (which is an aggregate of object files). The process of finding this function ('resolving' it) is called linking, which is why we occasionally encounter the 'unresolved external symbol' error from the linker.

The linker is another computer program that we need to run before our program is ready to execute. The linker collects multiple object files and puts them together to make an executable image. It uses libraries, both custom specified and standard, to resolve the function references in the object files at its input. The output of the linker is the executable file (with an .exe extension in Windows), a dynamic load library (.dll) or a shared object (.so in Unix).

In an IDE like Visual Studio, the compilation and linking processes come under one command 'build', invoked by a mouse click or a keyboard shortcut. In command-line based environments (like VAX, Unix, Linux, etc.), the linker is invoked by typing in a command `LINK FILE.OBJ`, which creates an executable image `FILE.EXE` on a VAX machine. In the GNU C compiler, the command gcc invokes the linker as well.

Once successfully linked, we have our program ready to run – we have the seal of approval from the compiler (certifying that our source code is syntactically correct and can be translated to machine instructions) and from the linker (stating that all the function references that we want to use do exist). We still have no guarantee that our program is going to do what we want it to. It seldom does. It is a rare and gifted programmer who consistently gets it right the first time around. In all likelihood, we will encounter 'run-time' errors where the program flow we implement attempts to do something that it should not. The run-time errors usually result in predictive failures and are relatively easy to locate and fix.

The next wave of errors, those in the logic of the program, may be far trickier to handle. They are considered semantic errors, where we have implemented something that we did not mean to. In our earlier example, `int n = getTrade-Num();`, if we actually meant to get the number of trades as n rather than the trade number (or the trade identifier), we have a logical error. The memory location n may end up holding a valid integer (and therefore may not trigger any run-time failure), but it is a wrong integer.

In order to squash the bugs that show up during execution time, whether syntactic or semantic, we often need a debugger. The debugger is a program that lets us go through the sources code, executing one step (in the high-level language) at a time, while letting us examine the context and the variables in scope. Modern debuggers let us do much more. Here is a partial list of things we expect to see in a debugger.

- Set break points, which are lines in the high-level language source code where the execution of the program pauses so that the developer can examine the context, memory locations, etc.
- Watch variables so that the program flow pauses when a watched memory location changes.
- Examine the call stack, which lets the developer see how the program flow gets to a particular point.
- Set variables so that the developer can try out what-if scenarios.
- Skip over part of the program.
- Attach the debugger to a running process.

In IDEs like Visual Studio, the distinction between the editor, compiler, linker and the debugger is not immediately obvious. They carry out the compile–link–run steps behind the scene. They also let us compile and link (and run) with one mouse click, use the code editor as the display for a debugging purpose and hide the options and building process from our view. When we need more control over their options or switch between IDEs, we will need an understanding of their inner workings.

5.2.2 Dependencies and Makefiles

The compile–link–run cycle described above may work fine for simple programs. For complex projects such as a trading platform, this development cycle poses many problems. Such huge projects are made of potentially millions of lines of code organized in thousands of files. Their compile–link process may take hours. What happens if the developer needs to change a few lines in a limited number of files and rebuild the executable? Compiling every single file is clearly less than productive. Keeping track of the files changed and compiling only the affected files also is not optimal. A developer should focus his colossal brain on designing and writing code rather than wasting it on such mundane tasks as looking up file names to compile. Besides, such manual dependency checking is dangerous, for instance, if the developer needs to change an include file.

Luckily, we have an elegant solution that makes use of dependency rules and file timestamps. Since we know that the object files depend on the underlying source files and the final executable files depend on the object files, we can get the computer to look up the timestamps, and compile and link only the required targets. On Unix systems, the command `make` does precisely that. The `Makefile` that forms the input to the make command specifies the dependencies and targets, and can have automatic, built-in rules as well as our amendments.

Integrated development environments such as a Visual Studio also use the same technique to minimize build delays, but the Makefiles (or their equivalents) are often hidden from the developer. The pricing tool that comes with this book has a `Makefile` that can be used on Cygwin (a Linux-like environment that runs as a subsystem under Windows). The interested reader can download this file (and other up-to-date information) from the book website: `http://pqd.thulasidas.com`.

5.2.3   Lexical structure of a programming language

A computer program specifies a series of steps or computations that the processor has to execute in a sequence. While resembling mathematics in their form, computer code is far from algebraic statements. For example, $x = x + 1$ in a computer source code means something very different from the mathematical falsehood it seems to state, as all programmers know. It instructs the computer to take the contents of the memory location labelled x, add 1 to it and store the result back in the same location x. In programming lingo, it 'increments' x.

In this example, x holds a number, perhaps an integer. Integers are one of the many built-in types in a high-level programming language. Other types include float, char and so on. How does the computer program know the type of a variable? After all, the term 'variable' is a euphemism for a location in the computer memory. The program can 'guess' the type from the context of the variable. For instance, the statement $y = x + 1$, where x is an integer, implies that y is likely to be of int type. Such guesswork often leads to nasty surprises. Therefore, most modern languages are 'strongly typed', requiring the programmer to explicitly declare the variables and their types.

A variable declaration assigns a certain type to a memory location you are planning to use. For instance, the declaration statement int x tells the computer that you need enough memory to hold an integer, which you will access using the label x. Variables declared in this way have a scope, which in C and C++ are defined by the enclosing braces, $\{\ldots\}$.

Since an integer is also a rational number (`float` or `double` in computer parlance), we can 'cast' an `int` to a `float` as: `float y = (float) x` (or somewhat more formally in C++ as: `float y = static_cast<float>(x)`), which tells the computer that we want to take the contents of the memory location x, interpret it as an integer and place it in another location y encoded as a floating point number of the same value. This kind of type casting is considered explicit. Casting can also be automatic (by simply stating `y = x`), where you expect the compiler to infer the variable types and cast accordingly.

While some languages force us to declare the type of each variable (or label for a memory location, as I will never tire of pointing out) under use, which is always a good practice, others do not. C and C++ are languages with strong typing, while PHP does not let us declare variable types. Still others (VBA and Fortran, for instance) let us decide whether we want to enable strong typing.

In addition to the basic types like `int`, `double`, `char`, etc., most modern languages have structures like arrays that put variables together. If we want to treat a collection of trade numbers as a unit, it may make sense to use an array of integers, or, if we have a string of characters (like the optimistic string 'Hello World' that managed to convince us all that computers would be self-aware someday), we can again use an array. While a quantum leap from the basic types, arrays are still primitive structures. It forces the developer to guess the size of the memory storage needed (or resort to dynamic memory allocation with its own set of problems) and deal with painful bounds-checking issues. It often results in the dreaded array-overflow and memory-corruption errors. In order to overcome such problems the standard template library (STL) in C++ comes with other, far more powerful container classes such as vectors, maps, strings and so on.

As we design increasingly complex applications, the built-in types (and the richer STL structures) will soon prove inadequate. We will need to design our own data structures and define types based on them. Variables and types give us the components with which we can access the computer memory and manipulate data. They are put together using the lexical elements of the language to define how the instructions flow in a program.

Although a program is a series of instructions for the processor to execute, we are not constrained to follow its sequential flow. We can change the control flow by `if then ... else ...` or `switch` conditional statements. We can also set up loops that operate a certain number of times or until a condition is met, such as `for (...)` or `while {}` statements. These lexical constructs drastically reduce the code required to implement repetitive operations. For instance, if we have a large number of trades and we want to price them, we can set up a loop to do it.

Loops help us minimize repetitions to some extent and introduce the notion of code reusability. However, in order to really reuse code snippets, we need functions. Functions are self-contained units of code that carry out specific tasks.

Using functions and loops, it is possible to organize a series of steps that accomplish most simple (and many complex) programming tasks.

Ideally, functions take arguments and return results based on their values. However, in computing, functions may carry out other operations, and their behaviour may depend on the state of the program, not merely their arguments. Since arguments are, in reality, labels of memory locations in a conventional programming language, the implementation of function calls becomes a matter of choice – not ours, but of the language designer's. How exactly does it pass an argument to a function? Consider a simple function call $y = f(x)$. For a computer, it can mean, 'Take the contents of the memory location x, and pass it to the function $f(x)$'. It can also mean, 'Pass the label x to the function $f(x)$.' The former is called passing argument by value, while the latter is passing it by reference.

The intricacies of a function call do not end there. When an argument is passed to a function by value, in reality it is the label of a temporary memory location, containing a copy of the original argument, that is passed. This implicit copying may be innocuous for simple built-in types, but when functions start passing complex and large data structures (like trade objects), the copy process takes time. Worse, the copy may be imperfect. Passing large data structures happens mostly in object-oriented programming, where we have explicitly to define good copy constructors.

We can always get around the restriction of temporary copies being passed to functions by explicitly sending the memory locations (or pointers) of the arguments. In other words, we can pass the references ourselves. In C, we can define a function: `double sum(double *x, double *y)`. We would invoke this function as:

```
double a, b;
double ab = sum(&a, &b) ;
```

The & operator gets the address location. Beware, though, that passing the pointer to a function can give it unwarranted power. The function sum here can modify the values of its arguments. If sum sets `*x = 0` at the return from the function, the value of a would be zero, which breaks all things sacred about encapsulation.

In C++, the function itself can demand the address of its arguments. We can write `double sum(double& x, double& y)`. You may invoke it as:

```
double a, b;
double ab = sum(a, b) ;
```

Note the absence of & in the function call. However, you are in for a surprise if the function sum actually changes its arguments. You can get around this problem by other lexical constructs (`const`), but the trouble is that such modifications have to take place in the function you are using, and you are at the mercy of the developer of the function (who 'owns' it) for safety implementations.

The example a above illustrates how we pass arguments to a function by reference. Of course, in the case of `double`, passing by reference only makes sense if we want the function to change the values of the arguments. It does not buy us any advantage in terms of performance or efficiency. However, if we are dealing with complex data types and passing them to functions, it is best to pass them by reference. For instance, if we use a function price a set of trades, it may have the prototype: `std::vector<double> price(const std::vector<trade>&);`. The `const` declaration reassures the user of the function that the function will not attempt to modify the vector of trades.

With the help of the lexical elements that modify the control flow of the program execution, and functions and procedures that handle specific computations and tasks, a developer sets up a program that responds and adapts to its inputs. Because of the sequential nature of the underlying flow, the design of a (simple) program is best illustrated in a flowchart. As an example, consider the task of pricing a bunch of trades and generating a price report (in a non-OOP framework).

The flowchart in Figure 5.1 illustrates the program flow for carrying out this task. The 'Start' bubble indicates the initialization phase, including setting up the report parameters, opening a dispatch channel (which may be an in-memory object, a local file, an intermediate database, etc.) After the program initializes, it accesses the trade database and loads the trades of interest in its memory. Although summarized in this short statement, this I/O operation is far from simple. First, the database may be housed in a distant location, perhaps in a different country, and the access is likely to be mediated by a middle layer. This layer is also responsible for ensuring that the user attempting to access the trades has the credentials and clearance to do so, because the trade data are confidential and privileged information in most jurisdictions. It may have to log the access for audit purposes.

Once the trade set is in its memory, the price report program will count the number of trades. If there are not trades read in, there is little point in continuing. The program exits in that case, which is indicated by the 'End' branch of the decision diamond. The 'End' processing will summarize the price report (stating, in this case, that there are no trades), dispatch it and exit the program.

If the program gets at least one trade, it proceeds to price it. This statement is another of those deceptively terse ones, for 'pricing a trade' is what the whole of mathematical finance is all about. Besides, pricing involves multiple database accesses to get the history of the trade and the market data needed, with the associated access control checks and audit trails. Once the program prices the trade, it accumulates the price in the report either in its memory or in a temporary storage, and proceeds to the next trade. When it processes all trades, the number remaining to be priced reaches zero and the program exits via the 'End' branch, after summarizing and dispatching the report.

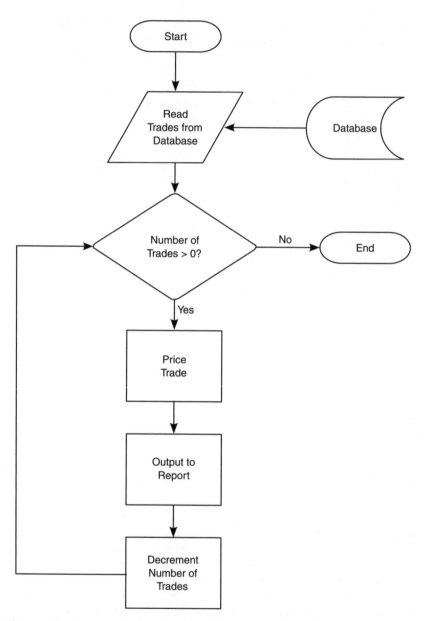

Figure 5.1 The example flowchart illustrates how a portfolio can be priced by loop-
ing over each trade in a portfolio. Trades read in from the database are complex
structures. The number of trades is perhaps declared an int in the program. 'Price the
trade' possibly invokes a function price(). Reading from the database and writing
to the report are I/O operations

This scheme will work quite well for a portfolio of trades that are all of the same kind. What happens if the trades are of different kinds with different pricing functions? That is where the more powerful approach of OOP makes its entrance.

5.3   OBJECT-ORIENTED LANGUAGES

In a traditional, non-object-oriented framework, we have a few options in implementing the price report in Figure 5.1, knowing that the trades in the set we are reporting on are of different types. We can examine the trade type in the loop and call the right pricing function depending on what kind of trade it is that we are handling. Alternatively, we could loop over each kind of trade separately, creating multiple loops, or we could call the same pricing function, which can examine the trade type and take the appropriate action. All of these options are far from elegant.

If we could associate the pricing function with the complex data structure that describes a trade, we will keep the same simple program flow in Figure 5.1, while accomplishing customized pricing for each trade type. This functionality of encapsulating and associating functions with data structures is provided by object-oriented programming (OOP) methodology. In OOP terminology, the functions are methods and structures are classes or objects. A class can be thought of as a data structure with associated functions specific to it and an object is an instantiation of a class. With a trade class defined, the declaration `Trade t` ; creates an object t of the `trade` class. In this sense, a class is like a type and an object is a variable of the class type.

The object-oriented paradigm originated out of the difficulty in maintaining large and complex programs in the conventional sequential languages. The object-oriented technology has many features that make it particularly suited for modular development in a collaborative environment with a large number of developers working together. It is an embodiment of sound software engineering principles. While we can still break the principles even in an OOP language, the lexical structure of the language makes it difficult to do so. Object-oriented languages become even more powerful by incorporating the notions of function overloading, polymorphism, inheritance, encapsulation, etc. In order to understand how the structure of an OOP language and software design principles go hand in hand, let us quickly survey the OOP terminology.

5.3.1   Basics of object-oriented methodology

Class defines an object and specifies its characteristics and capabilities. An object can be anything that needs a representation in the software. This overwhelming generality makes OOP extremely powerful and unwieldy at the same time. We will soon illustrate the concept using an example of a product that can be traded.

Members are elements that define the internal structure and characteristics of an object. Members can be other objects belonging to other classes. For example, in order to define a product object, we may have members such as the notional (a double), a pricing model (an object belonging to the class model) and so on.

Methods (also called member functions) describe the capabilities of the object. They are functions within the class. For our product object, we may have a method to return its notional, which simply returns the value of the notional member. Another less trivial method could be to price the product using a particular model.

Constructor is a special method for building the object.

As an example, let us look at how we define a product.

```
class Product{
public:
  //constructor
  Product(const string& name, const string& desc,
          const Model& m, const vector<Param>& p)
          : model(m), pars(p) ;
  price() ;
private:
  Model model ;
  vector <Param> pars ;
};
```

The constructor `Product` is a special `public` method (which means anybody can access this method) with the same name as the class. The other public method `price()` will use the `private` member `model`, presumably to compute a price of an instance of the product. The array of `Param`, `pars` are also `private` members of the product. Note that `model` and `pars` are in fact other objects, not basic types.

As you can see, class is merely a complex data structure with functions specific to it. By associating data and functions, OOP helps the developer encapsulate them in classes. The notion of encapsulation is a powerful idea that shaped OOP development in its early days. It is an extension of the idea that started with function calls. A function returns a value depending on its inputs. How the function does its work is largely unimportant to the users as long as the function signature (which represents the number and types of its arguments and its return value) remains unchanged. In that sense, the function encapsulates the computational logic that is modular to it (broken only by our ability to pass pointers as arguments, and define global variables).

In OOP, the encapsulation idea applies to the whole object. The object interacts with the rest of the program through a set of published interfaces. The private data and the internal implementation methods are all hidden from the view of its users. The immediate benefits to the programmers, both to the users of the object as well as the developers of the class, is that as long as they honour the interface, they can make modifications both within and outside the class without affecting each other. This benefit translates to perfect modularity at the class level. It also puts enormous demands on the care needed to define the interfaces.

Object-oriented languages also support inheritance, which makes the hierarchical ordering of classes a breeze. In our product example, we have the name and description members. However, these attributes also apply to the objects of other classes such as models and parameters. We can therefore define a base class (say 'thing') to handle these attributes along with the methods to set and display them. Other classes then inherit 'thing' without worrying about how to handle these common attributes.

Inheritance greatly improves modularity. In our example, suppose we want to add another attribute, say a comment, to all objects derived from the base class thing. We can do that by modifying only the base class, without touching any of the derived classes.

Another feature of the OOP paradigm is polymorphism, which lets the programmer treat all derived classes originating from a base class on an equal footing. In Figure 5.1, for instance, in an OOP implementation, the programmer could cast all the trades to its base trade class, put them in an array or a vector, loop over them and call the price method for each. The right price method, as implemented in the derived trade class, will be invoked, providing an elegant solution to our earlier problem, without resorting to ugly run-time checks. In more complex situations, this ability to invoke the right function depending on the object under consideration (the so-called single dispatch) makes the program elegant, simple and easy to maintain.

Closely related to polymorphism is the concept of function overloading. In C++, we can define the same function with different signatures, making them polymorphic. In our example of trade pricing, we could have a function price(), which will be invoked as:

```
product t ;
// construct the product
double p = t.price() ;
```

Presumably price() would use a default model, but we could have a price function that takes a model as an argument. So we can write:

```
product t(name, desc, model, pars) ;
// construct the product
double BlackScholesPrice = t.price() ;
model m ;
// construct a new Binomial Tree Model;
double BinomialPrice = t.price(m) ;
```

Our ability to define functions with the same identifier name, but with different signatures, is the function overloading facility provided in OOP. We can also overload operators such as the plus and minus signs (+, −), etc. Operators are also methods (member functions), but presented differently to the user. The addition operator (+) is a function that takes two arguments. Therefore, we could add an int to an int, a double to an int, a string to a string (concatenation) and so on, all using the same plus (+) operator.

Big Picture 5.2:   Magic of Object-Oriented Languages

To someone with an exclusive background in sequential programming, all these features of object-oriented languages may seem like pure magic. However, most of the features are really extensions or variations on their sequential programming equivalents. A class is merely a structure, and can even be declared as such in C++. When you add a method in a class, you can imagine that the compiler is secretly adding a global function with an extra argument (the reference to the object) and a unique identifier (say, a hash value of the class name). Polymorphic functions can also be implemented by adding a hash value of the function signature to the function names and putting them in the global scope.

The real value of the object-oriented methodology is that it encourages good design. However, good programming discipline goes beyond mere adaptation of an object-oriented language, which is why my first C++ teacher said, 'You can write bad Fortran in C++ if you really want. Just that you have to work a little harder to do it.'

5.3.2   Advantages and disadvantages of the object-oriented approach

The object-oriented methodology has a lot going for it as an ideal environment for implementing an in-house trading platform. In fact, OOP is flexible enough to handle most large-scale software projects. Because of its predominance in the software industry, we can easily find and hire high-quality developers adept in OOP to implement our trading platform.

The discussion above may seem to recommend OOP for trading platform development. However, OOP suffers from some significant handicaps. One of the major disadvantages of the OOP methodology is, in fact, one of its basic design features. Objects are memory locations containing data as laid down by the programmer (and the computer). Memory locations, by definition, remember the state of the object. What state an object is in determines what it does when a method is invoked. Thus the OOP approach is inherently stateful.

In a pricing user interface, where the developer does not have much control over the sequence in which various steps are executed, we might get erroneous numbers if the end user follows a certain sequence of operations. While we can eliminate such errors through careful design and implementation, the possibility of statefulness clearly has an impact on the amount of testing needed.

Such considerations related to statefulness and data dependency are especially important when we work with parallel computers in complex situations. One desirable property in such cases is that every function returns a number solely based on its arguments. This property is the basic design feature of functional languages.

5.4 FUNCTIONAL PROGRAMMING

Functional programming is the programming methodology that puts great emphasis on statelessness and religiously avoids side effects of one function in the evaluation of any other function. This property, termed 'purity', is the basic design goal of most functional languages, although even their architects will concede that most of them are not strictly 'pure'. Functions in this methodology are like mathematical functions. In the conventional programming style, on the other hand, statements are considered 'imperative' and represent instructions to the computer for accomplishing computing tasks.

Adapting this notion of functional programming may sound like regressing back to the pre-object-oriented age and sacrificing all the advantages thereof. However, there are practitioners, both in academia and in the industry, who strongly believe that functional languages are the only approach that ensures stability and robustness in financial and number crunching applications.

Functional languages, by definition, are stateless. They do everything through functions, which return results that are, well, functions of their arguments. This statelessness immediately makes the functions behave like their mathematical counterparts. Similarly, in a functional language, variables behave like mathematical variables rather than labels for memory locations. A statement like x = x + 1 would make no sense. After all, it makes no sense in algebra either.

This strong mathematical underpinning makes functional programming the darling of mathematicians. A piece of code written in a functional programming language is a set of declarations quite unlike anything in a standard computer language such as C or C++, where the code represents a series of instructions for the computer. Because a functional language is declarative, its statements are mathematical declarations of facts and relationships, which is another reason why a statement like x = x + 1 would be illegal.

The declarative nature of the language makes it 'lazy', meaning that it computes a result only when we ask for it. (At least, that is the principle. In real life, full computational laziness may be difficult to achieve.) Computational laziness makes a functional programming language capable of handling many situations that would be impossible or exceedingly difficult for procedural languages. Users of Mathematica, which is a functional language for symbolic manipulation of mathematical equations, would immediately appreciate the advantages of computational laziness and other functional features such as its declarative nature. In Mathematica, we can carry out an operation like solving an equation for instance. Once that is done, we can add a few more constraints at the bottom of our notebook, scroll up to the command to solve the original equation and re-execute it, fully expecting the later constraints to be respected. They will be, because a statement appearing at a later part in the program listing is not some instruction to be carried out at a later point in a sequence. It is merely a mathematical declaration of truism, no matter where it appears.

This affinity of functional languages toward mathematics may appeal to quants as well, who are, after all, mathematicians of the applied kind. To see where the appeal stems from, let us consider a simple example of computing the factorial of an integer. In C or C++, we can write a factorial function either using a loop or making use of recursion. In a functional language, on the other hand, we merely restate the mathematical definition, using the syntax of the language we are working with. In mathematics, we define the factorial as

$$n! = \begin{cases} 1, & n = 1 \\ n \times (n-1)!, & \text{otherwise} \end{cases}$$

In Haskell (a well-known functional programming language), we can write:

```
bang 1 = 1
bang n = n * bang (n-1)
```

and expect to make the call bang 12 to get 12!.

This factorial example may look artificially simple. However, we can put even more complicated problems from mathematics directly to a functional language. For an example closer to home, let us consider a binomial pricing model, illustrating that the elegance with which Haskell handles a factorial does indeed extend to real-life quantitative finance problems as well.

The binomial tree pricing model works by assuming that the price of an underlying asset can only move up or down by constant factors u and d during a small

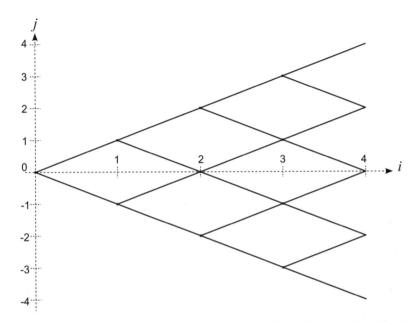

Figure 5.2 Binomial tree pricing model. On the X axis, labelled i, we have the time steps. The Y axis represents the price of the underlying, labelled j. The only difference from the standard binomial tree is that we have let j be both positive and negative, which is mathematically natural, and hence simplifies the notation in a functional language

time interval δt. Stringing together many such time intervals, we make up the expiration time of the derivative instrument we are trying to price. The derivative is defined as a function of the price of the underlying asset at any point in time.

We can visualize the binomial tree as shown in Figure 5.2. At time $t = 0$, we have the asset price $S(0) = S_0$. At $t = \delta t$ (with the maturity $T = N\delta t$), we have two possible asset values $S_0 u$ and $S_0 d = S_0/u$, where we have chosen $d = 1/u$. In general, at time $i\delta t$, at the asset price node level j, we have

$$S_{ij} = S_0 u^j$$

By choosing the sizes of the up and down price movements the same, we have created a recombinant binomial tree, which is why we have only $2i + 1$ price nodes at any time step $i\delta t$. In order to price the derivative, we have to assign risk-neutral probabilities to the up and down price movements. The risk-neutral probability for an upward movement of u is denoted by p. With these notations, we can write down the fair value of an American call option (of expiry T, underlying asset price S_0, strike price K, risk-free interest rate r, asset price volatility σ and number of time steps in the binomial tree N) using the binomial tree pricing model as follows:

$$\text{Option price}(T, S_0, K, r, \sigma, N) = f_{00}$$

where f_{ij} denotes the fair value of the option at any node i in time and j in price (referring to Figure 5.2):

$$f_{ij} = \begin{cases} \max(S_{ij} - K, 0), & \text{if } i = N \\ \max\left\{S_{ij} - K, e^{-\delta tr}\left[pf_{(i+1)(j+1)} + (1-p)f_{(i+1)(j-1)}\right]\right\}, & \text{otherwise} \end{cases}$$

At maturity, $i = N$ and $i\delta t = T$, where we exercise the option if it is in the money, which is what the first max function denotes. The last term in the expression above represents the risk-neutral backward propagation of the option price from the time layer at $(i + 1)\delta t$ to $i\delta t$. At each node, if the option price is less than the intrinsic value, we exercise the option, which is the second max function.

The common choice for the upward price movement depends on the volatility of the underlying asset; $u = e^{\sigma\sqrt{\delta t}}$ and the downward movement is chosen to be the same $d = 1/u$ to ensure that we have a recombinant tree. For risk neutrality, we have the probability defined as

$$p = \frac{e^{r\delta t} - d}{u - d}$$

For the purpose of illustrating how it translates to the functional programming language of Haskell, let us put all these equations together once more:

$$\text{Option price}(T, S_0, K, r, \sigma, N) = f_{00}$$

where
$$f_{ij} = \begin{cases} \max(S_{ij} - K, 0), & \text{if } i = N \\ \max\left\{S_{ij} - K, e^{-\delta tr}\left[pf_{(i+1)(j+1)} + (1-p)f_{(i+1)(j-1)}\right]\right\}, & \text{otherwise} \end{cases}$$
$$S_{ij} = S_0 u^j$$
$$u = e^{\sigma\sqrt{\delta t}}$$
$$d = 1/u$$
$$\delta t = T/N$$
$$p = \frac{e^{r\delta t} - d}{u - d}$$

Now, let us look at the code in Haskell.

```
optionPrice t s0 k r sigma n = f 0 0
    where
      f i j =
          if i == n
          then max ((s i j) - k) 0
          else max ((s i j) - k)
                    (exp(-r*dt) * (p * f(i+1)(j+1) +
                    (1-p) * f(i+1)(j-1)))
      s i j = s0 * u**j
      u = exp(sigma * sqrt dt)
      d = 1 / u
      dt = t / n
      p = (exp(r*dt)-d) / (u-d)
```

As we can see, it is a near-verbatim rendition of the mathematical statements, nothing more. This code snippet actually runs as it is, and produces the following result.

```
*Main> optionPrice 1 100 110 0.05 0.3 20
10.10369526959085
```

Looking at the remarkable similarity between the mathematical equations and the code in Haskell, we can understand why mathematicians love the idea of functional programming. This particular implementation of the binomial pricing model may not be the most computationally efficient, but it certainly is one of great elegance and brevity.

While a functional programming language may not be appropriate for a full-fledged implementation of a trading platform, many of its underlying principles, such as type abstractions and strict purity, may prove invaluable in programs we use in quantitative finance, where heavy mathematics and number crunching are involved. The mathematical rigour enables us to employ complex functional manipulations at the program level. The religious adherence to the notion of statelessness in functional programming has another great benefit. It helps in parallel and grid, enabling the computations with almost no extra work.

Big Picture 5.3:   Back to Basics

Computers are notorious for their infuriatingly literal obedience. I am sure anyone who ever worked with a computer has come across the lack of empathy on its part – it follows our instructions to the dot, yet ends up accomplishing something altogether different from what we intend. We have all been bitten in the rear end by this literal adherence to logic at the expense of common sense. We can attribute at least some of the blame to our lack of understanding (yes, literal and complete understanding) of the paradigms used in computing.

Rich in paradigms, the field of computing has a strong influence in the way we think and view the world. If you do not believe me, just look at the way we learn things these days. Do we learn anything now or do we merely learn how to access information through browsing and searching? Even our arithmetic abilities have eroded along with the advent of calculators and spreadsheets. I remember the legends of great minds like Enrico Fermi (who estimated the power output of the first nuclear blast by floating a few pieces of scrap paper) and Richard Feynman (who beat an abacus expert by mentally doing binomial expansion). I wonder if the Fermis and Feynmans of our age would be able to pull those stunts without pulling out their pocket calculators.

Procedural programming, through its unwarranted reuse of mathematical symbols and patterns, has shaped the way we interact with our computers. The paradigm that has evolved is distinctly unmathematical. Functional programming represents a counterattack, a campaign to win our minds back from the damaging influences of the mathematical monstrosities of procedural languages. The success of this battle may depend more on might and momentum rather than truth and beauty. In our neck of the woods, this statement translates to a simple question: Can we find enough developers who can do functional programming? Or is it cheaper and more efficient to stick to procedural and object-oriented methodologies?

5.5 SUMMARY

Like all large-scale applications, the trading platform also demands that we make sound choices in the beginning and design it wisely. The main difference between the trading platform and any other standard program is that the former is designed to evolve and assimilate new products and pricing models gracefully. This feature of planned growth places additional constraints on the design.

Because of its power and flexibility, an object-oriented language may present itself as the ideal development environment, and an in-house trading platform is likely to be deployed using an object-oriented language. The powerful features of OOP that are attractive include polymorphism (which allows us to handle disparate products on an equal footing), encapsulation (helping us maintain modularity and maintainability), inheritance (hierarchical structuring of the design), function overloading (reuse of intuitive function names and compile-time function lookup), etc.

For all its power, OOP suffers from certain handicaps that are, in fact, the basis of some of its features. Among them are statefulness (the property that the output from a piece of code depends on the state of the program, which is inherent in constructing an object and then using its methods) and the associated lack of functional purity (the inability to guarantee that the operation in one part of the program will not have undesired, global side effects). The ability to avoid statefulness and side effects has implications on data dependency and thread safety, and therefore in parallelization and grid computing – a common trend in modern financial computing.

To address these drawbacks, we may rely on sound development discipline, or design patterns. A drastically different computational paradigm that addresses these drawbacks is functional programming. In addition to statelessness and purity, functional languages also give us computational laziness and a declarative source code, which mathematicians find attractive.

While functional programming may offer some solutions, it has not yet matured as an ideal development environment. However, because of its desired features, functional programming ideas may appear as part of the in-house development effort, either as a hybrid (in conjunction with a standard OOP language like C++) or as guiding principles and policies in the design and architecture.

QUIZ

1. Define the following in the context of OOP.
   (a) Polymorphism
   (b) Overloading
   (c) Encapsulation
   (d) Inheritance.
2. What is the difference between
   (a) A data structure in C and a class in C++
   (b) A class and an object
   (c) A function and a method
   (d) A function and a loop
   (e) The declarative nature of a functional programming language and variable declarations?
3. Why is computational laziness a desired property?
4. Why do we need to pay attention to copy constructors? After all most OOP languages give us default copy constructors.
5. What are the disadvantages of OOP?
6. Why do people believe that functional programming is better suited for grid computing than OOP?
7. What does $x = x + 1$ mean in a conventional procedural language and why is it illegal in a declarative functional language?

6
Trading Platform Design

In the previous chapters, we went through the generalities of banking and computing. We explored the need for a trading platform and the choices open to us in implementing it. Our explorations took us through the structure of a typical bank engaged in exotics trading, the associated processes and the perspectives from which various business units view the trading activities. These processes and perspectives echo the requirements of our trading platform. Finally, we looked at the technical aspects of computing, including choices of languages. We went into some detail the guiding principles behind the design considerations (such as the need for grid computing), some of which may take us away from the traditional object-oriented programming. Now it is time to delve deep into specific implementation strategies. How do we translate the requirements into the features of our trading platform?

Although this chapter will discuss specific design choices, it will stay away from absolute prescriptions. It will, instead, present implementation strategies suitable for various features of the platform as guidelines. To drive the guiding principles home, we will describe the architecture in two steps. The first one will correspond to a full-fledged trading platform, albeit limited in its scope. We can roll out a design of this kind in a matter of months with a handful of developers. The second architecture that we present has a more ambitious scope, and will take several parallel teams working in collaboration and coordinating to realize it.

In the next chapter, we will look at some of the programming idioms and patterns that tend to recur in financial computing. One of the subsequent chapters, describing the accompanying pricing tool, will get even more specific and detailed in describing the design and implementation strategies.

6.1 GENERAL DESIGN CONSIDERATIONS

Like any other large-scale programming project, the trading platform also needs to be designed and implemented with sound software engineering principles in mind. These general principles include maintainability, scalability, performance, etc. However, they mean something more in the context of financial computing.

6.1.1 Maintainability and documentation

Maintainability may sound like a purely technical challenge related to how well the software architecture is designed. In practice, however, it is very nontechnical and almost cultural or sociological in nature. In our fast-paced field of mathematical finance, quantitative developers routinely leave their organizations looking for better career prospects. Because of this rapid turnover, we may find ourselves without the system architect and the lead developers of the trading platform actively in use. Such disruptions in development and support occur more often than we care to admit. Faced with disruptions of this kind, how do we ensure continuity of operation and support, let alone software maintainability?

Documentation may suggest itself as an obvious means. However, requiring documentation has some serious drawbacks. Developers and quants usually consider documentation a boring task and a distraction from their real job. They have good reasons to feel that way. In a job environment where employee turnover is high, it is important for the newcomers to make their mark quickly. They do not have the luxury of time to create good documentation – a thankless task that takes a significant amount of time and effort when done right. The net result of this time pressure is that whatever is deemed the least important aspect of the deliverables gets postponed or ignored, and documentation usually falls in that category.

Another unfortunate consequence of this hurried attack on the deliverables is that we seldom have enough time to study the existing documentation, meagre as it may be, to understand fully the current architecture and design philosophy. We therefore tend to extend and build on the existing trading platform without adequate regard for the underlying architecture. Such efforts will soon lead to an unmaintainable mess where the only real option to maintain continuity is to redesign and rewrite the whole program.

One viable solution to this lack of incentive to document is to move the documentation effort to the code development phase. By writing in-line comments during coding, and extracting them into a comprehensive source code description, we can partially automate documentation and eliminate the painful, post-coding effort. We have powerful tools at our disposal (Doxygen, for instance) to accomplish this task. Good source code documentation is essential if we are to have a shot at maintainability.

A second means of ensuring continuity is at the people management layer. We have to make a conscious effort to embed and mentor junior members of the development teams during the design phase so that the high-level knowledge about the architecture of the trading platform gets disseminated. Lastly, the architectural aspects of the trading platform should be proudly showcased, not merely hidden in self-documenting source code, so that they are widely known. With such deliberate and constant visibility, the design philosophy of the trading platform will be widely known and appreciated, thereby generating some level of continuity.

6.1.2   Scalability and extensibility

The common notion of scalability in software engineering is in terms of the computational power required, or in terms of the bandwidth requirements. For instance, if we have a trading platform designed to deal with 100 trades, and if we book 10 times as many trades in it, we will expect a tenfold increase in the computational requirement, or in computing time.

This simple scaling, and how the trading platform can respond to it, is on the first dimension of the scalability requirement of a trading platform. Even at this basic level, the scalability requirement is more stringent that we first perceive. Imagine that the 100 trades in the system (in our previous example) take five hours to go through the daily end-of-day (EOD) batch job that computes the sensitivities and risk measures. The batch job starts at around 9 pm after the daily live data snapshots are finalized for the EOD processing. The output of the batch is ready by 2:00 am, well before the business and the risk management start looking for it.

Now imagine a tenfold increase in the number of trades requiring a corresponding increase in the duration of the batch job. The hedging and risk monitoring staff will have to wait for two days for their EOD reports, which is unacceptable. Even if we increase the hardware power, this linear time requirement of the trading platform is clearly not scalable in terms of the number of trades.

It is this quasi real-time feature of the trading platform that makes its scalability requirement challenging. The only way to meet this requirement is some sort of parallelization, which involves software decisions taken early during the design process.

Parallelization is not the solution for all our scalability problems. When the number of trades is scaled, in addition to the time scaling of the batch job, it also affects querying, network performance and trade-set loading on the client's computer, impacting the experience of the end users of the trading platform. Similar degradation may happen when the number of users increases as well. Such scalability issues, though somewhat more challenging than those encountered in normal software engineering, can be remedied with standard approaches – increased computational resources, parallelization, grid computing, better design, etc.

The real scalability requirement of the trading platform is a dimension quite unlike that of any other programs. It is the requirement that the trading platform be able to extend itself to deploy new products and pricing models. In fact, the main reason for embarking on an in-house trading platform project is that the financial institution wants to deploy pricing models and new products as rapidly as possible. Without meeting this extensibility requirement efficiently, the trading platform has no *raison d'être*.

Extensibility can also be demanded in terms of the scope of the program. For example, a trading platform originally designed for trade pricing, booking and daily processing may be called upon to provide settlement or credit risk management services. It is always difficult to anticipate such extensions. The best we can do as quantitative developers is to make the software design as modular and flexible as practical.

To add to the difficulty, we have to deal with asset-class specificity as well. When we design and deploy a trading platform as a proof of concept or as an advanced production-ready prototype, we typically do it for one asset class, say FX. The choice of the initial asset class depends more on political considerations (such as which trading desk head is most vocal in supporting the trading platform or in demanding it, and who puts up the funding for it, etc.) rather than a technical evaluation. Once the trading platform proves itself, other asset classes would want to get their business on it and reap the rewards. Therefore, the extensibility required of a trading platform goes beyond new product and pricing models; it also includes new asset classes.

Providing this type of extensibility is particularly challenging because of the plethora of asset-class-specific practices and conventions. In addition, we will find asset-class-specific operations and market data. In the equity world, for instance, we find corporate actions such as stock splits and dividend payouts affecting trade values and characteristics. The rates and spot fixing processes also vary among asset classes, and are usually carried out by different business units. In fact, the asset-class specificity is so great and acknowledged that quantitative analysts end up specializing in one asset class. It is therefore no surprise that the trading platform should reflect the same specialization.

6.1.3 Security and access control

In all programs running in a bank, security is a primary concern. Since the trading platform deals with real money that will be settled between counterparties at some point, operational risk issues like data security, access control, etc., are scrutinized with extreme care.

The access control to the user interface of the trading platform is only the tip of the iceberg. Since the trades and the market data are stored in a database, the access to the database also needs to be secured. Data integrity even during transit is an operational risk issue that the trading platform design has to worry about.

Banks operate on a policy of functionally separating the front, middle and back offices as much as possible. Trade booking, for instance, belongs in the front office. If the middle-office validators find an error in the booking, they are not supposed to correct it and get on with their work. They have to flag it and send it back to the front office that has the access rights to modify trades. Furthermore, each of these operations (rejection, modification, re-booking, etc.) needs to appear in an audit trail with timestamps and user names so that the trade evolution can be reconstructed in the future, if needed.

Another point to keep in mind is the possible regulatory requirements (like the Banking Secrecy Act in Singapore), which prohibit staff from accessing client data unless they can demonstrate a professional need to do so. Since the trading platform and its database will hold all the data associated with the trade, we need to worry about such regulatory constraints as well. The security and access control requirements are so stringent that often we delegate them to commercial technology providers while keeping the rest of the trading platform an in-house effort.

The ever-present access control has created many practical problems and innovative solutions. One consequence of the access control is that employees will have to log on to multiple systems multiple times a day to carry out their daily tasks. In addition to the loss in time and productivity due to this constant self-authentication, we may have problems when an employee decides to write down his passwords or store them in plain text files.

Another problem with this distributed access control shows up when employees leave the organization or are reassigned to other tasks. The subsequent amendment in the employee credentials will have to percolate into all the various access control databases.

A modern solution to this access control problem is to implement a single sign-on system. Given that most employees sit in front of a computer running a Windows-based operating system, the bank can secure the access to these computers with a centrally administered access control coupled with strong password policies. The access to all other systems can then be granted based on these initial sign-on credentials. This scheme is similar to the way we access our email client, for instance. Once we log on to our personal computer, we usually do not need to sign on again to read our email. While the email access information is stored in unsecured local resources, the corporate access to privileged systems would be administered in a secure fashion. However, in both cases, the physical security of our workstation becomes more critical. If we leave our workstation logged on, an intruder can access the trade data just as easily as he can read our emails.

6.2   ARCHITECTURE COMPONENTS

The technical requirements described above all have special significance in the context of an in-house trading platform project. In addition to these special requirements, we have all the standard requirements of any large-scale software project that also apply to a trading platform. We touched upon these generalities in our introductory chapter. Armed with the knowledge of the requirements of a trading platform, both technical and business-driven, we can begin to design a trading system ourselves. Design is the process of aligning the features of the trading platform with the business requirements, while choosing and planning around the best technology solutions to handle the technical requirements.

First, let us look at the high-level components that make up the overall architecture. They are:

1. Trade representation
2. Market representation
3. Static data management
4. Quant library
5. Trade transformations and operations
6. Settlement triggers or pathways
7. Batch processing and grid computing
8. Credit replication
9. Security and audit model
10. Documentation and support model.

While all of these components are important, the first few are more important than the rest from a design point of view because they form the foundation on which the whole trading platform stands. We will therefore look at them, and the choices open to us in implementing them, more closely.

Our eventual implementation choice is always a compromise because each option comes with its own advantages and disadvantages. We will have to evaluate the pluses and minuses in the light of our understanding of the expectations and requirements of the trading platform, its scope in our particular organization and our own business needs and processes. It is this understanding that this book promotes, so that our choices are optimal and decisive. The book will not recommend any specific implementation strategy because the trading platform appropriate for a particular organization will be necessarily specific to that organization. If it were not so, there would be general purpose vended candidates for trading platforms, given the profit potential involved.

6.2.1 Trade representation

To a quant developer, in our product-centric view, a trade is an object belonging to the `product` class, with a few extra identifying and bookkeeping pieces of information. It is a complex object though. It holds information about the model, the market, the curves and conventions from its term sheet, fixing and cash flow schedules, and details of the trade itself, such as its notional amount, maturity date, counterparty, etc. Representing this complex entity calls for careful consideration.

To complicate matters further, we have many different contexts in which we need to represent the trade as data, often with conflicting requirements. Building the trade in the computer memory is not difficult, especially in an object-oriented programming (OOP) environment. The object constructor method takes care of the building process. In this process, the main concerns are memory resources requirements and performance. The trade object has links to models and market objects, either explicitly as pointers in the trade object or implicitly as members of other objects contained within it. A trade pricer contained within the trade object, for instance, may contain these helper objects.

It is when we demand persistence of the trade object that we have to weigh various design options. Trades are saved into databases so that they can 'persist' between computing sessions. Even in a scenario where we have a small number of trades, a flat file database (where the whole trade is saved as a row in a table) will prove inadequate. Because of the complex nature of the trade data structure, it is practically impossible to design a table format to contain the data unless we are dealing with identical types of simple trades.

A relational database, where the trade data are stored in multiple interrelated tables, may fare a little better. The only realistic way of dealing with the complex trade details is to implement some kind of marshalling or serialization of the trade data. Serialization is the process by which an object in memory is converted into a byte stream (or a human-readable text form) that can be stored, transmitted, retrieved and transformed back into the original object. If human readability is a requirement, XML serialization is appropriate. There are standard libraries and language extensions (including unswizzling, which takes care of the pointer references within the objects that need serialization).

Serialization, while unavoidable, eats into the querying power of the relational database. The serialized trade object needs to be deserialized before its semantic structure can be understood or queried against.

Another database choice that we need to evaluate for the trading platform is the object database. Object databases store objects directly in the database, if supported by the programming language. Since this way of storing data mimics the programming structure, it can support queries based on object members by traversing the pointer structure within the stored object. In this sense, the object database can be more powerful than a relational database, which may get bogged down by the necessity of joining multiple tables to retrieve a queried record. While this necessity is a disadvantage, relational databases have a stronger mathematical foundation and, therefore, a richer set of tools than object databases. However, the tools are useless if the relational database stores serialized data.

The difference between object and relational databases is more philosophical than it appears. Object-oriented methodology thrives by implementing how an object behaves under different circumstances, which is reflected in an object database as well. A relational database, on the other hand, uses an attribute-identifier paradigm, which makes the database querying easy to implement. By exposing the attributes to the whole world to query against, the relational database philosophy breaks the fundamental encapsulation idea of an object-oriented paradigm.

Ultimately, the choice of the database may well be taken for reasons other than technical rationality. It may depend on the cost, anticipated support level, availability of trained database administrators and the existing database infrastructure of the bank. In all likelihood, the database that a trading platform will run on will be a relational database.

Other modern approaches to trade representation include a streaming or network model, where the trade can be passed from computer to computer (or from one instance of the trading platform to another) to traverse the trade workflow. This model simulates the scenario where the trade (and market) data reside on the network. The back-end storage, security and synchronization issues are all abstracted away, certainly from the end user, and, to a large extent, from the developers as well. While it is good to know that such ideas exist, it is not clear how secure and robust their deployment can be and how different their implementation is from a quantitative developer's perspective.

In addition to the static design of the database, we also need to worry about its behaviour in the light of audit and bookkeeping requirements. The behaviour is something we implement in the program that services trade-related requests. How do we implement a trade cancellation request? We could simply delete the database record, but that would be unwise. We lose the information about who booked the trade, who deleted it, and when and why. We could attach a flag to the trade record, which we change in response to the cancel request, and create a new one with proper timestamps, which will satisfy most of the requirements. Even this scheme is not flexible enough to handle the cancellation reasons or to respond to more complex requests like cancel and amend, or bulk operations on multiple linked trades, such as structured products.

Linking trades brings about the need to have a hierarchical structure in the database. We may need to include a master trade record and multiple slave trades, possibly in different tables. Since the trade identifying number also has special significance to various business units (the documentation team, for instance, would like to have a unique trade number that lives across trade cancel-amend reincarnations), even the simple trade identification is a tug of war among conflicting requirements. From a technical perspective, we need to implement a unique database key, or a collection of attributes that would uniquely identify the trade. We would then use this key to link trades and their attributes residing in multiple tables in the database.

The detailed database design is beyond the scope of this book because it is specific to the organization, its business needs and technical capabilities. It is best left to experienced database professionals and system architects. What is important, though, is not to underestimate the complexities of this pivotal step. A lot of the trading platform architecture depends on it. It is therefore essential to spend time and resources on it and to deploy talent and experience to get it right.

6.2.2 Market representation

If trade representation is a daunting problem, market data representation is an even harder challenge. Even in the absence of an in-house trading platform, market data setup and update processes demand the coordinated attention of various business units, such as a static parameter setup, rates management, information technology, external data providers, etc. In a trading platform, we have to come up with a robust and scalable design for representing this complex data structure, while leveraging on the processes of these business units, without duplicating their work.

All too often, the importance of market data and its setup is underestimated in the design of a trading platform, resulting in a poor representation and unnecessary duplication of work. This lack of forethought is understandable though. In a prototype implementation of a trading platform, or a pricing program, there is little difference between normal trade parameters and market data. This similarity may give the quant and the quant developer a false sense of security where a simple data structure, possibly based on the trade representation, would suffice.

In addition to this underestimation, there is an insidious programming inertia that can lead to a lot of headaches later on. While testing their models, the quants may come across the need to set up a handful of market parameters. They may use a temporary text file or a local database to accomplish this task and get on with their programming. When it comes to integrating their model and deploying it, the quantitative developer may stay with the temporary data structure, with the noble intention of assimilating it in a better market data representation on a later day. However, this day may never come and the 'temporary' database may become an unmanageable and poorly controlled mess.

The only way to avoid such pitfalls is to develop an appreciation for the enormity of the effort required in market representation. Although less visible, market data representation is at least as important as trade representation. It certainly is more complicated because of its scope and the existence of strange market conventions, constraining how we can massage it into a class or a set of database tables.

In reality, the market representation needs to be robust enough to accommodate multiple types of operations:

1. Market data setup, which includes securities configuration, curve and pillar definition and modification, addition of new security types, etc. As we can see in Table 6.1, the setup and the periodic modifications can be a significant amount of work.
2. Rates and volatility feeds, which will populate the tables and structures set up in the first step above. They can be live, real-time feeds from commercial data providers or, in a more modern bank, a rates server. They can also be an automatic, periodic uploading of a rates dump from other trading or rates management systems.
3. Daily data snapshot, or processing a pre-prepared snapshot for the daily batch job.
4. Potential ad hoc changes by the user, with the option to save it back to the database with audit trails, if the user has the privileges to do so.

Table 6.1 A partial list of the components of the market data. The first column lists the market quantities or parameters that we need to set up once and modify only rarely. Each of these quantities has a corresponding table in the database and a structure in the trading platform. The second column lists the live market data that will populate the table or the structure. Depending on the scope of the trading platform, it will have to take a daily snapshot of the market data for its batch processing

Setup	Live data
Holidays calendars	Rare changes
Equities Bonds Currencies Currency pairs Commodities	Spot prices
Curve definitions Rate pillars	Interest rates
Volatility pillars Volatility/Skew definitions	Volatilities
Correlations	Correlation values
Credit ratings	Ratings

In order to accommodate the asset-class specificity in market data, we have to design its representation with a large quantum of flexibility built in. Table 6.1 describes two aspects of setting up market data. First, we need to set up indices, like equities, bonds, currency pairs, etc. Once the one-time setup is done, the spot prices start coming into the database, either manually copied in at regular intervals or through live feeds. What 'spot' means depends on the asset class.

An equity index has only a spot price that is relevant to pricing. A commodity index, on the other hand, has a whole vector of numbers (futures prices) lumped under the spot column. When it comes to volatility and correlations, the asset-class specificity may become too great for us to massage the market data into any uniform format, regardless of how flexible our design is. We may end up putting the data into different tables or structures, depending on the asset class. In any case, it is best to be aware of these complications at the architecture design phase so that we can maintain appropriate high-level uniformity in our market data abstraction and representation schemes.

In principle, market data can live in a database distinct from the one used for the trade data. However, it is likely to end up in the same relational database, and it may be best to unify the database layer so that we can reuse the existing code. We must pay particular attention to the table layout, indices and relations. It may be wise for us to model our market representation after some established trading systems. Although they tend to keep such implementation details proprietary, we can browse through the market data in an established system to see the intricacies, conventions and interconnections involved.

6.2.3   Static data management

A large amount of data that the trading platform deals with is common to multiple systems across the bank. It includes approved products, counterparty details, access rights of staff, account information, portfolio names and hierarchies, profit and cost centre setup, etc. Since such data rarely change, they can be considered static. Our in-house trading platform may share such data with the other vended systems in the bank where it has already been set up. Duplicating the data to the trading platform database is a waste of time and effort. Furthermore, it may actually risk various systems being out of sync and introduce errors.

One possible solution to this need to access the same static data is to create a database application or service to manage it. We can treat one trading system as the source or master database, read and process the data into our own static data management system and have all other systems in the bank query it to get the information needed. The master system is likely to be the oldest and most used vended trading platform in the bank.

Another efficient, albeit harder to implement, solution is to create this new static data management as the master and treat all trading systems (including the legacy vended ones) as consumers of data, querying it when needed. We can then design robust workflows around the in-house static data management system to handle new counterparty/portfolio/user creation with proper auditing.

In addition to this static data, which are common to all trading systems, we have another class of data that may be system-specific, but not as transient as live market data. We described it as 'setup' market data in Table 6.1. It includes index setup, holiday calendar management, fixing sources, etc. In most banks, it is considered as another class of data called something like reference data, and is administered independently of market and static data. How these reference data are managed depends on the organizational structure of the bank. If static data management is more of a technology-driven effort, it is perhaps appropriate to leave the reference data management to some middle-office team. If, on the other hand, the technology department merely provides a tool to manage static data, it is worthwhile integrating both reference and static data management to the same middle-office team, or to parallel teams.

6.2.4   Quant library

Quant library is the term we use in this book to denote the output from the quantitative analysts (or quants). The library is assumed to contain ready-to-use modules of pricing models. By loading the right module and calling its functions from the trading platform, we can price the corresponding instrument. The quantitative developer can set it up such that a new instrument thus delivered can be priced and risk-managed (or integrated) on the trading platform.

What form the quant library takes depends on the architecture of the trading platform. It can be a set of functions or classes with a well-documented application programming interface (API) or it can be a set of dynamic link libraries (DLL). It can also be in the form of modules specific to the platform, like spreadsheet add-ins. Regardless of the form in which the quant intelligence is delivered to the rest of the bank, it is imperative to agree upon the interface and the quality standards of the delivered code well in advance, preferably during the design phase of the trading platform. A well-defined interface, coupled with high-quality code to be integrated, will result in a clean design and a relatively painless integration effort.

In the pricing tool that comes with this book, the delivery mode uses DLLs. The pricing tool defines an interface and enforces it by providing skeleton implementation templates for pricing models, as we shall see later.

6.2.5 Trade transformations and operations

Trades go through a large number operations during their lifetime, as we have seen earlier. Each operation can be modelled as a state change in the trade representation. In order to ensure that our representation is robust enough to handle all transformations, it is wise to list and go through the processes and compare them against the capabilities and features we need to handle them.

Like most features in a computer program, the ones in a trading platform servicing the processes and operations have a few internal parts:

- The user interface, which exposes the capabilities of the program to the end user and lets him initiate a state change.
- The computational elements, which interact with the user interface and carry out the requests and the state changes needed.
- An internal representation, which facilitates the computation and presentation.
- A persistent representation, for instance, in a database.

The routine trade transformation and the related operations that need to be implemented include trade input validation, fixings, fixing sources setup and selection, confirmations of trade transformations, etc. For each of these operations, we have to come up with an appropriate user interface. For transformations, which change the trade state, we can display a variant of the trade booking dialogue to the end user, where he can modify a status flag and re-save it. Thus, we can reuse the trade pricing and booking interface for all validation and confirmation operations.

Trade transformations are relatively simple to implement in the back-end of the program as well. We can think of the state of the trade as one or two status flags. When the end user attempts to modify the flags through a user interface, we first establish that the user has the right credentials to request the change and then change the flag as requested. If not, we throw an error message.

Since the flags are attributes of the trade, their representation becomes part of the trade data structure, both in the platform program memory as well as in the persistent database storage. A more scalable and flexible design would be to have a separate database table for states management and to join it with trade data when trades are queried. This design avoids the unnecessary duplication of potentially large trade data.

Fixings are a bit more complicated. They may affect multiple trades at once and may have multiple sources. Let us look at fixings a bit more closely. Fixing refers to the process of a middle-office professional deciding on what the spot price or the rate of a particular index is on a given day. The fixed value will be used for generating cash flows to and from the organization, and hence the fixing process is mission-critical and sensitive from an accounting perspective.

The process of fixing involves examining all live trades to see if they call for a fixing operation on a given day. The trading platform will accomplish this part of the task by going through the trades table either in the database or in memory. Once this is done, the trading platform will have to examine a different table to see if all the required indices have been fixed. It then displays the outstanding fixings (after verifying the user's access rights) in an interface where they can be modified, if authorized. The trading platform will have to worry about the concurrency issues associated with multiple users accessing the fixing table.

At times, the trading platform would be called upon to set up a new fixing source, which entails the database operation of creating a new entry in a table. The trading platform will have a dedicated user interface to gather the information required for creating a new fixing source, along with the omnipresent access rights check and the back-end database operations of creating the new entry.

The creation of fixing sources can be automatic as well. In other words, when the trader enters a trade with a hitherto unknown fixing source, it is automatically created (either explicitly in a fixing source table or implicitly by doing away with the fixing source table altogether). Such autogeneration is usually more trouble than it is worth because any errors in the trader's input would create new fixing sources. We can minimize the probability of erroneous inputs by type-ahead schemes in the user interface or confirmation dialogues. However, it is safer to delegate the fixing source management to its own table or, even better, to a dedicated static data management workflow.

During trade valuation, the past fixings and the history events are loaded and used. For trades such as swaps, the past fixings determine the past cash and realized P/L. The unrealized P/L is purely stochastic and does not depend on the past history of the trade. For path-dependent trades such as target redemptions and range accruals, the past history is important in pricing.

6.2.6 Settlement triggers or pathways

The basic objective behind trading is profit generation. Once the profit has been generated, it needs to be collected and 'realized'. In other words, the cash flow obligations arising from the trading activity need to be settled.

Due to the necessity of real cash exchanges, the settlement process is highly scrutinized. However, the process happens in the back office, far away from our spheres of influence or interest, which are mostly focused on the trading floor activities. This distance in functionality manifests itself in the architecture of the trading platform as well.

Unless the trading platform under consideration is an overarching, all-encompassing system that manages every aspect of trading and settlement, we do not usually try to make settlement triggering a part of it. This cautious reluctance is due to the complexities and details involved in generating settlement triggers and accounting entries. Settlement requires very detailed accounting rules to be set up and maintained. Important though it is, from a quantitative mathematical perspective it is just a tedious and meticulous bookkeeping effort. Besides, the tedium of setting up the settlement streams and accounts have already been carried out by the vended trading systems in use in the bank. It is best to ride on the existing implementation, in much the same way as credit replicates are handled.

Once we have decided to make use of the existing settlement stream of the vended system, we can adopt a push or a pull strategy in implementing the bridge from our trading system to it (see Figure 6.1). In the push implementation, we build a module in the trading platform that packages the trade parameters essential for settlement (cash flows, their schedules, counterparty details, etc.). The module sends the package to the vended system, which handles the settlement using a vendor-provided application programming interface (API). In the vended system, an image of the trade is created, which looks like a normal trade and is settled as such. The push module of our in-house trading system can update the trade details (cash flow amounts, for instance) as required.

Instead of having our trading platform do active pushing of the settlement data into an existing settlement system, we can adopt a pull strategy if we choose. In the pull mode, the vended trading or settlement system carries out the work of getting the settlement information. The pull module is something the quantitative developers put together, again using the vendor supplied API, but it is attached to the vended system. The in-house trading platform is largely unaware of the existence of the settlement pull module accessing its database to extract the daily profit and loss or cash flow information.

In both the pull and the push strategies of handling settlement, the trading platform generates trades in another system for carrying out some part of the processing. This mode of autocreating a trade can be regarded as an instance of

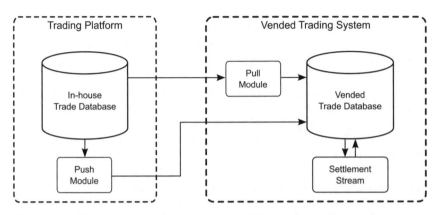

Figure 6.1   The management of settlement workflow in an in-house trading system using a vended platform. The trades as booked in the in-house system are settled through an existing vended trading platform, which takes care of all the accounting entry and settlement trigger generation, as well as bookkeeping. The in-house system can push its trades to the vended system or the vended system can pull the trades from the in-house system. Once the trades are in the vended system, they look like native trades and go through the settlement process

what the industry calls a straight-through processing (STP) operation. Indeed, the credit replicate generation is also an STP operation, and may share and reuse the implementation module. Straight-through processing has the advantage that it eliminates potential errors due to manual retyping of trade details. Besides, in manual processes involving operations that affect settlement, most banks employ a four-eye paradigm (one person does the work and a supervisor verifies), which the STP paradigm eliminates.

Big Picture 6.1:   Straight-Through Processing

'Straight-through processing' (STP) means different things to different people. The original idea behind STP was to minimize the amount of manual retyping involved as the trade moves from one business unit to another (or from one bank to another). It is in this sense that we use the term STP when we discuss credit replication and settlement integration and cash transactions.

In the industry, STP can also mean attempts to reduce the settlement delay, which indeed is an offshoot of getting computer systems to take on the task of moving the trade data among themselves. In most trade settlement transactions, there is a delay of two or three days (or more for certain asset classes like commodities). Straight-through processing aims to cut this delay to within one day or even to minutes.

In order to achieve such ambitious time targets, the level of interoperability required of the systems in various business units is high, and quite possibly unachievable. Besides, it may not be desirable to have this kind of unsupervised integration.

Despite our reservations about the lack of control, the advantages of STP are hard to resist. First of all, it reduces the settlement delay, thereby minimizing the settlement risk (that the counterparty may default during the allowed settlement period). Second, by eliminating manual input, STP improves the overall accuracy as the trade moves from system to system. This improved accuracy enables us to save on manpower costs as well. In the absence of STP, all operations that affect risk management or settlement go through a maker–checker (or four-eye) process taking up at least two headcounts.

Once a high level of STP is in place, it is possible to extend the idea to other processes like rate fixing, risky though it is. We can imagine grabbing the required rate source on a live feed at a predetermined time and entering it automatically into the appropriate fixing table in the central database. Again, this process improves efficiency, accuracy and operational costs, but sacrifices the intelligent assessment of the fixing rate going into the system. Although it is possible to devise all kinds of checks on the rate, they are no substitute for an experienced rates manager.

If there is one avenue that has taken STP to the extreme, it is the high-frequency trading (HFT) platform linked to the e-trading portals of many banks. Using the e-trading portals deployed on the Internet, clients enter FX spot trade requests on-line. These requests flow into the powerful HFT systems working behind the scenes to aggregate, risk-manage and carry out spot trades to realize them. The aggregated trades try to capitalize on tiny market advantages and, through the use of autonomous decision making algorithms, engage in a large number of trades to make profit. The whole chain from client trade request to eventual profit generation is automated, and takes place at a high frequency well beyond the realm of human intervention.

6.2.7   Batch processing and grid computing

A batch job is a computer program that runs without any user intervention. The user merely launches it, or causes it to be launched by a scheduler, and the batch program does its bit without further instructions. For instance, the humble 'Hello World' program that every developer writes in his computing kindergarten is a batch job in this sense. A slightly more advanced program that prints out 'Hello World' after you type in 'Hello PC' (or some other cute phrase) is not a batch program. A user interface (such as the GUI for trade booking or rate fixing) that responds to user actions is certainly not a batch program.

A trading system (whether in-house or vended) has to have a batch component to carry out a variety of regular processes:

- Mark-to-market. All trades are marked-to-market daily using the end-of-day rates to track the value of the banks book.
- Value at risk (VaR). Risk measures such as VaR are computed and monitored daily.
- Sensitivities. Market sensitivities of the trades (the Greeks) are computed daily both for front-office hedging purposes and for limits monitoring. They are used for P/L attribution (usually a product control job) as well.
- Scenario analysis. The front office often requires valuations on a matrix of scenarios in order to understand their exposure profiles with respect to possible market moves. They may need a matrix of their trade and portfolio valuations over a range of spot values and volatilities, for example.
- Time sensitivity measures. Traders and operations are interested in having an educated guess of what the portfolio characteristics would be like the next day. For this purpose, they want a rerun of most of the reports described above with the date rolled to the next day. This task is a bit involved because of possible fixings that may fall on that day, and will require the quant pricing models to support it.
- Trade ageing process. In some situations, the batch job will be designed to look ahead over a day or a predefined time horizon to record upcoming fixings and other trade events.

The batch is usually run on a scheduler. It may also be launched by an operator, typically middle-office staff, after getting the go-ahead from the end-of-day rates fixing. Since the batch job, in practice, consists of multiple jobs, they may run in parallel on multiple machines. Depending on the nature and urgency of the output reports, some of these jobs will have to finish before the start of business the next day. The concepts of close of business and start of business are complicated and challenging in today's globalized financial markets. If the close of business is in New York and the start of business is in Tokyo, the batch job has no time at all to produce the reports.

Because of the ever-increasing time pressure on batch jobs, we need to adopt some scalable strategy to speed it up. Parallelization suggests itself as an obvious choice. One type of parallelization popular among banks is the so-called grid architecture (see Figure 6.2). A grid is a large number of computers, usually rack-mounted in a datacentre, which acts as a reservoir of on-demand computing power. Grids are usually managed by commercial middleware, such as DataSynapse, or their open-source counterparts, such as Globus. The middleware will take care of dispatching the submitted job to the farm of computers and aggregating the output for the user. The grid usually services computationally intensive jobs like the EOD batch. However, the batch job is not the only customer for the grid. The grid may

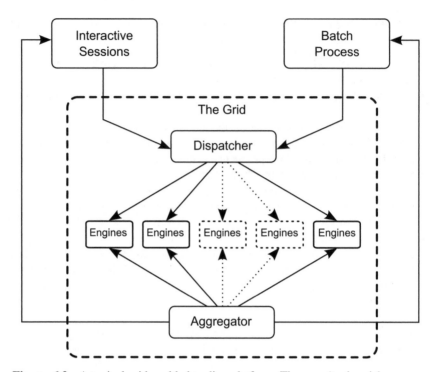

Figure 6.2 A typical grid-enabled trading platform. The user (trader, risk manager or the batch operator) interacts with a middleware that manages the grid. The grid middleware (represented by the dashed rectangles) will accept the submitted job, send it to a farm of computers, aggregate the output and send it back to the user

be called upon to serve interactive pricing requests from the traders or scenario analysis requests for hedging and risk assessment purposes.

Ideally, the grid would take the batch job as the trading platform submits it, divide it into roughly equal chunks, fan them out to individual engines, wait for the results, aggregate them and send the aggregated results back to the submitter. This ideal picture represents a clean separation between the grid and its user. In this picture, we can easily replace the grid with, say, a single computer, and expect to get the results transparently, although we may have to wait longer.

In reality, the interactions with the grid are not as transparent as the ideal picture in Figure 6.2 suggests. The trading platform plays an active role in segmenting the job and managing the data dependency. This involvement is hard to avoid because of the volume and nature of the data transmission between the trading platform and the grid. For instance, in the computation of value at risk (VaR), we may have one year's worth of market data (in what are known as scenarios) and, say, 1000 trades. We can segment the scenario data or the trade set, both of which amount to large quantities of data. However, an optimal segmentation may be in both of them. Segmentation decisions of this nature, and the subsequent aggregation, are difficult for a general purpose grid architecture to handle.

Big Picture 6.2:   Throwing the Baby out with the Bath Water

We can find a higher level parallel between any computationally intensive program and the interactive-batch processings of a trading platform. Let us take, for example, the Monte Carlo simulation of a high-energy physics detector. The high-energy physicists start with a carefully written simulation program with a painstakingly detailed description of their detector, and set it up with input parameters and conditions. They then launch the program (often in a batch, as it happens) and obtain simulated data, identical in form and content to the real data coming out of the detector. These data go through the same analysis program that consumes the real data and produces final results. Since the physicists know the input parameters in the simulated data, they can estimate the effect and efficiency of their detector and come up with correction factors in the analysis program. They then apply the same correction factors to the real data analysis and hopefully arrive at the unknown parameters of nature.

In our case, if we think of the trading platform with its interactive and batch components as similar to the Monte Carlo and analysis program of the high-energy physicists, we can see, albeit with a bit of stretching, several equivalences. The trade booking and market and reference data setup is like setting up the Monte Carlo simulation. The trading platform batch processing is equivalent to running the Monte Carlo simulator. The post-processing in a trading platform that generates and formats output reports is like the physicists' analysis program, which estimates nature's parameters.

I went through this comparison, contrived though it was, to point out one glaring absence in the way we do our batch processing. Unlike the high-energy physicists cranking Monte Carlo simulations, we do not store or cache the intermediate results of the computationally expensive batch process. At least, I have not seen it done in any systematic or serious way. This omission is a pity given the computational power and resources incurred in generating the values. Storing the intermediate data (like the present values of the trades and their Greeks) would afford an enormous amount of flexibility. In addition to being able to check the final reports on a later day, we would also be in a position to run new algorithms (a different kind of P/L attribution, for instance) retroactively.

An ideal way of storing the intermediate results would be in a database, with a reporting engine generating the final outputs that the traders and risk managers need. Of course, there is no such thing as a free lunch, and the intermediate storage does cost money. However, I believe it is a cheaper lunch than the potential loss of flexibility in throwing away the computed data. After all, you do not throw away a digital photo just because you have taken a print out.

6.2.8   Credit replication

Most vended trading systems have associated or well-integrated limits monitoring components to take care of risk management. The trade workflow through these systems is such that when a trade is booked, the information needed to manage its associated credit risks is automatically entered into these auxiliary components. An in-house trading platform, however, does not try to reproduce all these components, but it may have to talk to the same downstream systems to facilitate the same processing. For this communication, we may adopt the straight-through processing (STP) strategy we discussed in connection with settlement implementation.

Although these downstream systems and processes are specific to the bank, a representative example is useful in understanding the kind of programming flexibility we need to build into the trading platform architecture. Let us look at the credit replication process and the credit risk management system.

One standard method of managing credit risk is by estimating the potential future exposure (PFE) of each trade and comparing it against a pre-allocated credit limit of the counterparty we trade with. We compute the PFE using a Monte Carlo program, which simulates future market conditions (tens of thousands of them) and calculates how much the counterparty can end up owing us under each market condition. We then pick the credit exposure corresponding to a predefined confidence level – say, 95 % – and call it the PFE.

For simple trade topologies with closed-form pricing formulas, this method works well, but for structured and exotic products, a single trade pricing is already computationally intensive because we may use Monte Carlo or binomial tree algorithms to compute it. Simulating tens of thousands of pricing scenarios to estimate PFE, each of which involves a computationally expensive pricing module, is prohibitively time consuming. How do we compute the credit exposure then? We do it by approximating the payoff profile of our complex trades with simplified trade equivalents called credit replicates.

Given that the credit exposure computation does not have to be as accurate as profit and loss accounting, we can get away with some approximations. If we can replicate the payoff function of complex trade with a combination of plain vanilla options with closed-form pricing formulas, we can run them through the PFE simulation engine. The group of simple trades that approximate the credit exposure are called the credit replicates. We have to establish, however, that the credit replicates do not underestimate the exposure.

The credit replicate generation can be a standalone module feeding off the main trade repository of our in-house trading platform (see Figure 6.3). It can then read

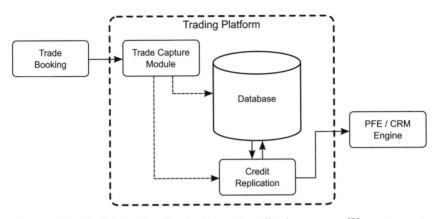

Figure 6.3 The information flow in the credit replication process. We can generate the credit replicates as a part of the trade capture module or we can have a replication module running on the trade records in the central trade depository. In either case, the replicates flow into a credit risk management (CRM) system that computes and manages the potential future exposure (PFE) of each trade

the trade data records, generate the replicates and send them to the (external) credit risk management engine. The replicate generator will have to set flags in the trade record so that we do not double-count credit exposures. Credit replication can also be a part of the trade capture module. Once the replicates are generated, they can merge with the downstream workflow.

Note that the generation of the credit replicates is only half the story. They have to be deleted when the underlying trade matures, or is cancelled. Worse, they have to be modified in tandem if the underlying structure is amended. Since each complex trade has multiple credit replicates, they have to be grouped together and tagged as belonging to one underlying real trade in order to facilitate the cancellation or modification operation.

6.2.9 Security and audit model

In a trading platform, the first level of security is usually implemented using the usual username/password access control to its user interface. In addition to granting and denying access, the trading platform also has to maintain multiple user profiles and assign each user a profile. The user profiles implement access levels such as:

- Front-office traders – book and amend trades
- Middle-office validators – validate and reject trades
- Middle-office verifiers – confirm or reject validations
- Trade control – static and reference data setup (portfolios, indices, etc.)

- Risk management – view trades and reports
- Rates management – fixing operations.

Note that the front-office traders can amend only those trades that are not in the validated or confirmed state. The state of the trade (booked, rejected, amended, validated, confirmed, cancelled, etc.) is represented by a status flag, or in a separate workflow engine. Thus, the user profiles are an implementation of access control on the transitions between different status flags attached to the trade.

Big Picture 6.3:   Access Control

The password access control to programs suffers from the drawback that it requires the end users to memorize many passwords and guard their secrecy. Besides, since each password controls only one program (unless the end user chooses to use the same password for access multiple programs and computers), the user does not take it very seriously. They may think that it is permissible to share the password to the trading platform, despite the policies and guidelines requiring them not to. When such sharing eventually leads to huge losses (as in the Société Générale fiasco of 2008), it is hard to hold any of the password sharing users fully accountable.

For all these reasons, it may be best to tie all access controls to the primary login identifier of the user to the computing environment of the bank. In this mode, once the user logs on to his computer, all the required access privileges are granted to him without further intervention on his part. It is similar to the email access on a typical personal computer these days. You do not have to supply the password every time you want to check your email on your computer.

While this scheme strongly discourages sharing of the password (for an employee may find it convenient to let others use his access rights to the trading platform, but he would not want public access to his email), it puts enormous pressure on the secrecy of a primary password.

Ranking as high as security in the operational risk management agenda of a bank is the notion of audit trails. They are historical records of who-did-what to the trade or market data that may affect the cash flows and the profit and loss position of the bank.

In a trading platform, we can anticipate audit trail requirements on trade modifications, such as changes in the notional amount, counterparty details or any other trade parameter. Audit trails are required on trade transformations as well – on fixings, triggering, cash flow generation, etc. Another avenue where audit trails are important is in market data modifications, which may affect the daily computations of marked-to-market prices or profit and loss computations.

An audit trail has a few technical requirements:

1. Ownership. The audit trail should be tightly linked to the access control scheme of the trading platform so that there is no ambiguity about who carried out the modification in the history it represents.
2. Timestamps. The audit trail should be timestamped to show the history.
3. Completeness. Given the audit trail and the end state of the object being audited, we should be able to reconstruct its earlier versions (and indeed its whole history).
4. Unmodifiability. The audit trail should not be exposed to any user interface through which it can be modified. In practice, this lack of interface access does not completely guarantee unmodifiability. An audit trail lives in a database and can always be tampered with therein. However, by appropriate access rights allocation to the database (only to a database administration team for the live, production database, for instance), we can minimize the likelihood of tampering.
5. Readability. We should have read-only access and an appropriate user interface to view the audit trail and modification history whenever needed.

A simple implementation of an audit trail scheme would be to create new records in the database for every amendment or operation. The original and the amended records will have timestamps and creator information, providing the necessary ingredients for audit trails. All records need to have a flag or a mechanism allowing us to determine which one is the active record.

Another scheme for implementing audit trails is to duplicate the existing record in the database before committing any user-requested change. The duplicated record is then saved into an audit trail table along with a timestamp and the user-identifying information. This duplication scheme will work well for fairly structured data confined to single records. When handling modifications to complicated data residing in multiple, interrelated records in several tables, the duplication strategy may prove inadequate. Even for simple data, when the volume increases, the size of the audit trail table becomes a concern.

One way to handle the volume scalability issue of the duplication strategy is to store only the differences between the two versions (before and after the modification being tracked) of the records in the database. In this scheme, the audit trail table consists of the relatively small difference records. This scheme works well and can be implemented close to the database layer of the trading platform. The trade-off is in reconstructing the modification history for display, which becomes more complicated.

Yet another implementation strategy is closer to the user interface layer of the trading platform. The user interface 'knows' the semantics and significance of various fields. Taking advantage of this semantic awareness, we can generate a rich audit trail if we decide to do it close to the user interface. However, if we adopt this scheme, we have to pay special attention to the completeness requirement and ensure that we do not discard information in the high-level semantic representation.

6.2.10   Documentation and support model

One unintended consequence of developing a trading platform in-house is a poorly defined support model for it. Once the trading platform is on-line, there will be a steady stream of new products and pricing models that need to be integrated into it. However, as the number of products and models in the system goes up, the level of the end-user support needed also increases. Unless planned in advance, this support load falls on the quantitative developer. As a result, the high-quality quantitative developer ends up responding to routine and unproductive support requests instead of focusing on his core value add, which is to deploy more products.

Big Picture 6.4:   Untenable Supports

It is easy to underestimate the level and nature of the support work needed in a trading platform development. During the design and initial implementation phases of the platform, the quantitative developers work closely with the traders and stakeholders who take a special interest in the project. Because of this close interaction and interest, the initial deployments go without a hitch. Besides, during this starting phase, the number of products and models is likely to be small.

During the second, production stage of the project, the usership is much wider, and the interest level of the newcomers may be of a job-necessity kind. Both of these factors increase the likelihood of support requests. In order to counter these factors, the user interface (especially the help and error messages part) will have to be robust.

Even with robust instructions, the support job is never easy. In a trading platform I previously worked on, the end users needed to have a database driver installed on their computers before they could run our in-house system. I therefore decided to have our program check for the existence of the driver on the client's machine and raise a warning if it was absent, asking them to get it installed. Soon, we started getting support requests saying, 'When I try to run your program, I get a warning message saying, "Please ask your local IT support to install the particular database driver." What should I do?!' To which the reply is, of course, 'Please ask your local IT support to install the particular database driver.'

In order to bring the quantitative developers back to their core activity, we have to decide on a post-installation support strategy early in the implementation phase.

One viable strategy is to divide the possible support tasks into different levels of severity in terms of developer involvement. For example, a list in the increasing order of severity can be as follows:

1. Installation instructions and update notifications. Ideally, the user documentation for installation and update is clear enough, giving step-by-step instructions to get the trading platform up and running so that the support calls arising from this step are minimal. In any case, these calls should be fielded by a front-line IT support team that is cheaper to maintain.
2. Prerequisites and first-run checks. If the client's computer does not have the prerequisite components, the trading platform should detect the deficiency at launch and provide clear error messages and instructions on how to rectify the problem. The calls arising from missing components should also be handled by a team other than the quantitative developers.
3. Common run-time queries. There is a need for an email group or chat room supporting common and oft-repeated questions when a novice end user tries to run the program. A collection of frequently asked questions (FAQs) may help in this regard, but, in practice, someone directing the end user to the right FAQ topic may be necessary, especially if the users are high-flying traders. This task also can be outsourced to a dedicated support team rather than the quantitative developers.
4. Special requests. At times, traders or risk managers may need special runs, such as a scenario analysis with special rates and volatilities or intra-day pricing runs in addition to the end-of-day batch runs. Such special requests may have to be handled by the development team, directly or indirectly. When special requests are repeated often, they become features of new versions of the trading platform.
5. Bug fixes. When the end users find bugs or errors in the trading platform, the development team, not the outsourced support group, will have to respond.
6. Feature requests. The development team has the ownership of managing end-user expectations and requests for new features in the trading platform.

The best option is to outsource as many types of requests as possible to a dedicated IT group for support. In the list above, for example, the first four types can be safely outsourced to a support team, who will field all such requests and forward the ones that require the developers' attention. In order for this strategy to work, the quantitative developers have to provide adequate documentation.

6.3   EXAMPLE ARCHITECTURE

We have looked at the various components that make up a trading platform. In fact, we looked at these components as business processes at first, focusing on their role in the trade life cycle. Later, we looked at the way in which various business units viewed these processes. Finally, in this chapter, we looked at them again as

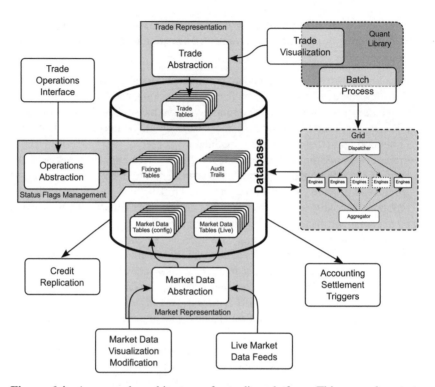

Figure 6.4 An example architecture of a trading platform. This example puts together all the facets of a basic trading platform that we have explored so far

program modules, exploring various implementation strategies, still staying at a level high enough to ensure generality.

We are now ready to put these modules together and look at the overall architecture of a typical trading platform, as in Figure 6.4. At first glance, this architecture may look dauntingly complex, but a closer inspection will reveal that every component in the architecture is, in fact, familiar. The top right corner, for instance, depicts the quant library, which forms the backdrop of the batch processing (computing mark to market values, value at risk, sensitivities, etc.) and the trade visualization (the interface that traders use to input trade parameters and inspect them). Indeed, it is the rapid deployment of the mathematical intelligence in the quant library that is the basic *raison d'être* of the in-house trading platform.

What may be surprising about the architecture diagram is that the quant library component is confined to a tiny corner in Figure 6.4. This smallness is not indicative of its lack of importance. It only serves to show that the trading platform is the domain of quantitative developers rather than model quants.

Looking at the rest of the architecture, the most dominant feature of the trading platform is the database that acts as the repository of trade data and market rates.

The trading platform is indeed a database application. The choice of the right database type, its access bandwidth, the hardware reliability, scalability, availability, etc., is of paramount importance to the success of the trading platform project.

As we saw, the database type and the trade and market data representations go hand in hand. In Figure 6.4, we have shown 'Trade Representation' near the top, influencing how trades are stored in the database and treated in the program. Similarly, the design decisions regarding how the market data is represented will determine its format in the database and its layout in the program memory.

On the left of Figure 6.4 we have depicted market operations, which create or modify records in the appropriate tables in the database. The database also holds audit trail tables, recording and historizing all modifications that may affect trade pricing or risk measures.

On the right is the batch process. The batch program, potentially a standalone GUI-less application, is built on the same quant library. It often has parallelization built in, and runs on a powerful farm of computers or a grid. The batch program, whether running on a grid or on an individual computer, communicates with the central database of the trading platform and reuses the trade and market representations that the interactive version uses. (We have not shown this reuse in Figure 6.4 for aesthetic reasons.)

Finally, we have other streams of data coming out of our central repository, feeding into the credit risk management or settlement workflows. They are depicted on either side of the figure, near the bottom. With all these components put together, the architecture shown in Figure 6.4 is that of a fully functional trading platform.

6.4 ADVANCED ARCHITECTURE

In the introductory chapter, we described four different implementation and deployment options for a trading platform. The third option there was to develop them in-house while using as much of the existing infrastructure as practical. The architecture described above is a complete in-house trading platform of this kind. However, the scope of the project may be more ambitious and overarching, as in the fourth option discussed in the introduction. Indeed, we have a wide spectrum of choices between these two implementation options, depending on the vision and resources of the bank.

In this section, we will take the design one step further with some of the ideas we discussed in the preceding chapters. Because this book does not aim to recommend any specific implementation strategy, we will present our scheme for this more complex and ambitious trading platform as a deliberately high-level picture of many database applications working in collaboration with each other. Any more details would risk giving the false appearance of a real architecture or implementation plan with recommendations that are beyond the author's intentions.

Figure 6.5 shows the architecture as a collection of database applications working in collaboration. It divides the software design into three tiers. The top-level

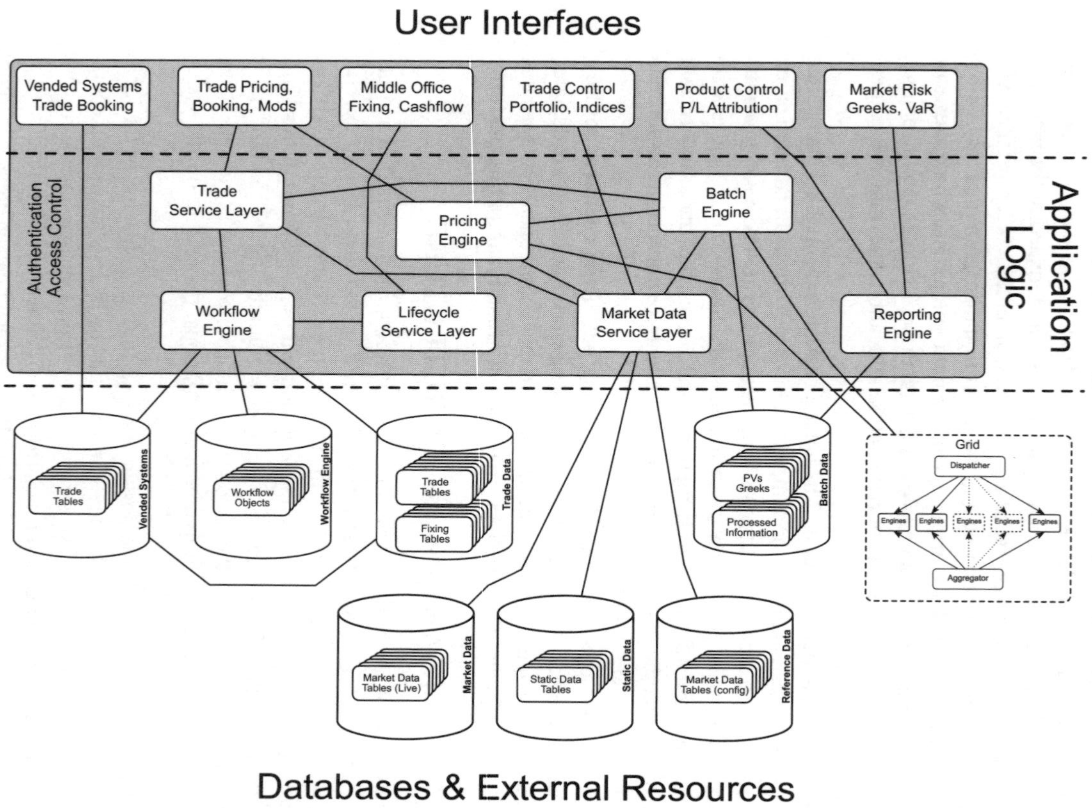

Figure 6.5 A high-level schema of a professional architecture of a trading platform. This design shows the architecture as a collection of database applications working in conjunction with each other to implement various aspects of the trading platform

presentation tier consists of various user interfaces. The middle logic tier is for the services and processes that implement the trading platform logic. The programs in this tier reside and run on separate machines. Providing storage and persistence to the logic tier are the databases, residing on servers in data centres, which are possibly spread out around the globe.

All the interactions between the users and the various components are authenticated and monitored by an appropriate access control mechanism. In Figure 6.5, the access control component is shown as an application logic entity encompassing both the presentation and logic tiers. In order to simplify this complex architecture to a manageable level, we have dropped the explicit depiction of credit replication and settlement triggering. However, they are implicit in the workflow engine activities.

Let us look at this picture from left to right. The first thing we see is a vended user interface for trade input for booking trades into its own database. This user interface and the database are not part of our trading platform architecture, but in an overarching deployment, we may want to access the trades on multiple vended systems and batch process them using our in-house pricing models. For this purpose, these trades may be channelled (straight-through processed or STPed) into our in-house trade database.

Talking to the vended database is a workflow engine. This engine may be an in-house application or, more likely, a commercial business process management system (BPMS). In either case, it is likely to have its own database where it creates and tracks its workflow objects, keeps audit history and generates MIS (management information system) data such as how long it takes to review/approve a trade, etc. It talks to the vended system potentially to export credit replicates for new trades and settlement triggers. Settlement (not shown in Figure 6.5) may take place either via the vended system, which is the preferred scenario, or via the in-house trading platform.

The workflow engine receives trade input from the trade booking user interface via a trade handling service layer, which takes care of trade representation. This service layer invokes the inception workflow (middle-office verification, rejection, amendments, etc.) and may delegate the database access to the workflow engine. The booking interface needs access to a static data repository (possibly mediated by a market data layer component) to present the right product, portfolio and counterparty selection options in accordance with the user's privileges.

Another major responsibility of the workflow engine is to manage the life-cycle events of the trades in the database. The life-cycle events (fixing, cash flows, option exercises, target/barrier breaches, etc.) are generated by a life-cycle engine, possibly aided by the trade pricing engine and the pricing models therein. The life-cycle events are handled in the middle office, using an appropriate user interface in the presentation tier, as shown in Figure 6.5.

The pricing engine is used in the trade booking user interface as well, for displaying inception pricing to sales and trading desk personnel. However, the primary consumer of the pricing engine is the batch process. The pricing engine is where our in-house mathematical intelligence resides. As with the simple architecture in Figure 6.4, the more advanced version in Figure 6.5 also confines the pricing engine to a tiny part in the overall design, highlighting the amount of details that we need to take care of before a pricing model can be deployed in a real trading scenario.

Pricing crucially depends on the market data, which are provided by a market data service component. This component talks to various databases – live data (generated out of the live feeds from data providers such as Bloomberg and Reuters), static data (approved products, portfolios, counterparties and their accounts, etc.) and configuration or reference data (index and curve definitions, rates and volatility pillars, stock, currency, bond information, etc.) Static and reference data are managed by an appropriate middle-office group (such as treasury control), which needs an interface on the presentation tier.

Because of the complexities involved in handling market data, some installations may choose to break up static and reference data management into independent components. Using the market and reference data, the pricing engine can actuate its quant models to price trades. The pricing engine may use a grid farm to perform computationally intensive pricing cases such as Monte Carlo models.

The pricing engine provides present value (PV) and sensitivity (the Greeks) computation services to the batch engine, which is usually launched by a scheduler or an operator after the end-of-day rates fixing. The batch job, with its quasi real-time requirement and the wide spectrum of users waiting for its output, is one of the most crucial aspects of a trading platform. It typically runs on a scalable grid farm. In the architecture shown in Figure 6.5, the batch engine uses its own database to store its output (PVs and the Greeks, the P/L vectors in VaR computation, etc.) The storage of its intermediate results helps the batch process enormously in its drill-down and rerun capabilities.

Finally, running on the batch database is a reporting engine, which may be a commercial application. It provides a means to design and roll out custom reports as needed based on the tables in the batch database. The final reports have presentation tier interfaces specific to other business units. For instance, the product control would want a P/L attribution and explainer, while market risk management would like the Greeks and VaR reports in accordance with their own needs.

The architecture shown in Figure 6.5 is only an example. Clearly, the databases and their tables may be combined or reorganized and the applications may be regrouped. In our example, we see natural fault lines developing in between groups such as vended systems, trade booking and services, workflow and life-cycle management, market data management with static and reference data, batch and reporting engines and so on. These groupings cut across the architecture vertically into fairly independent database applications.

This natural grouping is beneficial for a number of reasons. One is that we can deploy parallel development teams to work on them in a largely autonomous fashion, thereby reducing the overall turnaround time. Second, modularity of this kind makes it painless to add new services and to remove existing ones. They can be revamped and redeployed as needed. Finally, an architecture of this kind can be deployed incrementally in phases, while a monolithic design would be an all-or-nothing proposition.

6.5 SUMMARY

In this chapter, we have gone through the design considerations in building the architecture of a trading platform. We first discussed general software design principles like maintainability, scalability, security, etc., and saw how they meant a bit more in the context of financial software development.

We then went through various architectural components in a trading platform, including data representations, the need for robust audit trails, batch processing, etc. We saw that we needed to leverage on some of the existing computational workflow of the bank (for credit risk management and settlement, for instance) and explored possible strategies of achieving it.

In the latter part of the chapter, we put all the pieces together to come up with a full architecture that may actually be used to develop a working trading platform for exotics or structured products trading. Finally, we looked at a more advanced architecture as a complex group of fairly autonomous database applications working in tight collaboration to achieve the objectives of the trading platform.

An architectural design, however, is only a blueprint. In order to make it a reality, we need to flesh it out with material – bricks and mortar, as it were. We have already looked at the basic computational material we will need to use, in the last chapter, where we discussed the basics of programming languages. In the next chapter, we will expand on that theme and look at higher-level structures that will help us build our trading platform.

QUIZ

1. General software design principles mean a little more in the context of a trading platform. What do the following terms signify for us?
   (a) Maintainability and documentation
   (b) Scalability and extensibility
   (c) Security and access control.
2. List the main components of a trading platform in its software architecture.
3. Why does a trade representation call for serialization and deserialization?

4. Compare the following database choices for a trading platform:
   (a) Flat file database
   (b) Relational database
   (c) Object database.
5. What is different about the market data representation when compared to the trade data representation?
6. What are the common trade transformations that a trading platform has to support? From the perspective of software development, what are their components?
7. Why is it better to delegate settlement to an existing vended platform?
8. What is STP and how does it figure in credit replicates and settlement?
9. How does a grid work? Why is it difficult fully to automate dispatch and aggregation?
10. What are audit trails? How can they be implemented in a trading platform?
11. Describe a multilayered support model for a trading platform.

7

Computing Patterns for Trading

Design patterns in object-oriented programming (OOP) emerge from successful solutions to software architecture problems. They tend to recur in many design situations and suggest stereotyped solutions, much like the time-tested formulas that work for various genres of movies (such as family, sci-fi, slapstick etc.). Just as genres are not storylines or screenplays per se, the design patterns are neither source code nor language syntax/components. They are overarching themes of design.

Design patterns allow software architects and developers to reuse ideas that solve one problem and apply them to another problem. By promoting the reuse of ideas, patterns encourage code reuse as well. In addition, once a design pattern is chosen to address a certain problem, most of the design decisions follow naturally, ensuring completeness of the solution. Design patterns embody the expertise of master software architects in a readily applicable way and hold many advantages over starting from scratch, the least of which is time to deployment.

Big Picture 7.1: Paradigms in Computing

Paradigms in computing are not unlike the perspectives in trade processing that we talked about. Both computing paradigms and trade perspectives help the developers and users deal with the underlying concepts in an abstract and intuitive way. While the trade perspectives are not very esoteric, computing paradigms take the notion of abstraction to a whole new level. This proclivity is perhaps understandable because the use of paradigms, and the abstractions implied therein, fuel the phenomenal growth of the computing technology, both in hardware and software.

Paradigms permeate almost all aspects of computing. Some of these paradigms are natural. For instance, it is natural to talk about an image or a song when we actually mean a JPEG or an MP3 file. A file is already an abstraction evolved in the file-folder paradigm popularized in Windows systems. The underlying objects or streams are again abstractions for patterns of ones and zeros, which represent voltage levels in transistors, or spin states on a magnetic disk. There is an endless hierarchy of paradigms. Like the proverbial turtles that confounded Bertrand Russell (or was it Samuel Johnson?), it is paradigms all the way down.

Some paradigms have faded into the background although the terminology evolved from them lingers. The original paradigm for computer networks (and of the Internet) was a mesh of interconnections residing in the sky above. This view is more or less replaced by the World Wide Web residing on the ground at our level. However, we still use the original paradigm whenever we say 'download' or 'upload'. The World Wide Web, by the way, is represented by the acronym WWW that features in the name of all web sites. It is an acronym with the dubious distinction of being about the only one that takes longer to say than what it stands for, as Douglas Adams once pointed out. However, getting back to our topic, paradigms are powerful and useful means to guide our interactions with unfamiliar systems and environments, especially in computers, which are strange and complicated beasts to begin with.

Despite all the advantages of design patterns, not all situations may lend themselves to their use. Design patterns come at a price – they may make the code too complex and unreadable to those who are not familiar with them. Those who are in the know may stretch it too far when they try to force programming designs into patterns they know. Most patterns introduce multiple layers in the class hierarchy, esoteric abstractions and hard-to-follow virtual functions.

The art of programming lies in deciding how much of any design pattern is appropriate in a given project architecture. Being a large-scale software project, a trading platform will benefit from the right amount of the right patterns. In this chapter, we will review a few patterns that look particularly suitable for a trading platform. We will not try to be exacting and complete in our descriptions because many other books in the market (see the last chapter) treat the topic with the thoroughness it deserves. Our interest in this book is limited to what kind of design patterns we can use in our trading platform and how. Ultimately, the chief software architect of the trading platform will make the design decisions as to the patterns and styles, and other coding standards; the value of this chapter is only in providing a few options and serving as a source of reference should any of these patterns be chosen.

Big Picture 7.2:   Paradigms versus Patterns

While patterns are like recurring themes, paradigms are modes of thinking that shape and influence our perspectives. Nowhere is the dominance of paradigms more obvious than in object-oriented languages. Just take a look at the words that we use to describe some of their features: polymorphism, inheritance, virtual, abstract, overloading – all of them normal (or near-normal) everyday words, but signifying notions and concepts quite far from their literal meaning. Yet, and here is the rub, their meaning in the computing context seems exquisitely appropriate. Is it a sign that we have taken these paradigms too far?

Perhaps. After all, the 'object' in object-oriented programming is already an abstract paradigm, having nothing to do with 'That Obscure Object of Desire', for instance.

We do see the abstraction process running a bit wild in design patterns. When a pattern calls itself a visitor or a factory, it takes a geekily forgiving heart to grant the poetic licence silently usurped. Design patterns, despite the liberties they take with our sensitivities, add enormous power to object-oriented programming, which is already very powerful, with all the built-in features like polymorphism, inheritance, overloading, etc.

Patterns find most use in pure software projects such as a text editor or a word processor sporting features like alternate look and feel, internationalization, etc. In quantitative finance where the focus is more on mathematical expertise rather than programming wizardry, and performance is always more important than elegance, patterns are not often used. However, when we design a trading platform, with its user interfaces and database back-ends, we do get closer to a pure software challenge. In this chapter, we will touch upon a few patterns that we can use both in quantitative finance and platform development.

7.1 FAÇADE PATTERN

Although we formally call it a design pattern, a façade is really an aspect of good software design principles. The façade pattern presents a unified and simple interface that hides the complexities of the implementation. In object-oriented programming, the façade pattern provides most users with one façade object that can satisfy most of their requirements. Only advanced users may need to access the objects behind it to carry out tasks for which the façade does not provide methods.

As an example, consider the analyses we perform on a trade object. In addition to booking it, we may want to price it, visualize the output dependencies, compute the Greeks, set status flags to indicate life-cycle transformations, etc. In a trading platform, these actions may take place in different subsystem classes. If the client classes (or programming users) of the trading platform access the subsystem classes directly to carry out these tasks, we get into a messy architecture, as shown in Figure 7.1(a). On the other hand, if we abstract away all the subsystems and expose only a high-level interface to the clients through a trade façade, the whole architecture becomes much more manageable (Figure 7.1(b)).

We implicitly used this pattern in our three-tier architecture presented in the previous chapter as Figure 6.5. We have a trade services layer component, for instance, which abstracts away its database access and other implementation details from the users. (By 'users', we mean other developers whose programs consume the output of the trade service layer and not the end users of the trading platform.)

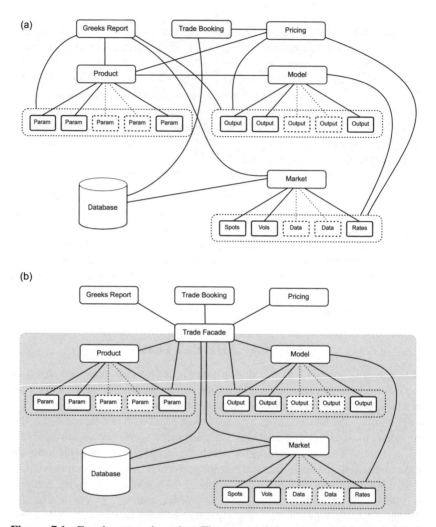

Figure 7.1 Façade pattern in action. The top panel shows some of the typical links between different classes in a trading platform. The bottom panel shows how the trade façade cleans up the communication

The access to the trade database may be via a workflow engine or direct – the implementation may be changed even after the deployment of the trading platform, if needed. Similarly, the pricing engine façade may or may not use a grid computing farm. Regardless of these implementation choices, the user classes always get a uniform and reasonably constant interface.

If, for some reason, we need to peek behind the façade (to study a particular market scenario, for instance), we can still access the subsystem classes. The façade

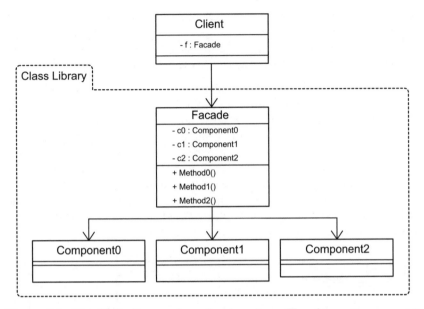

Figure 7.2 The UML diagram for a façade pattern. The classes `Component0`, `Component1` and `Component2` are behind the façade and the client class is not expected to access them directly, although it can if needed. All the common methods are implemented in the façade as `Method0()`, `Method1()` and `Method2()`

does not hide the internals from the clients; it merely provides a recommended interface that may prove sufficient to almost all general purpose users. Figure 7.2 shows a formal UML (Unified Modelling Language) diagram of a façade pattern implementation.

Closely related to the façade pattern is the adapter, which is a wrapper layer providing an interface between two classes that were not originally designed to work together. While the adapter pattern aims at compatibility, the façade focuses on simplicity. Both façade and adapter patterns occur in normal (non-object-oriented) programming as well, when we try to define application programming interfaces and the reuse code. In object-oriented programming, the patterns become more powerful and easier to implement and enforce.

7.2   VISITOR PATTERN

The visitor pattern is popular in financial software designs for two of its features:

1. It allows us to extend the functionality of classes without modifying their structure or interface.

2. It provides a viable solution to the lack of double dispatch in common object-oriented languages like Java and C++, which provide only single dispatch through virtual functions. In single dispatch, the compiler chooses the right function at run-time using the dynamic type of calling object.

In order to give us the flexibility of adding new operations to classes, the visitor pattern lets us separate their structure from their algorithms. We then list the operations (algorithms) in an aggregate visitor class, declaring them as all pure virtual, so that we need to implement them in the classes we derive from it. For customized operations, we derive a concrete visitor from the abstract visitor class, which has a call `accept()` that takes the object `this` as its argument. Knowing the type of the caller (through the this argument) and the function (through the virtual function resolution), the `accept()` call simulates double dispatch. Moreover, the derived visitor class is under our control, giving us the freedom to add functionality as we see fit.

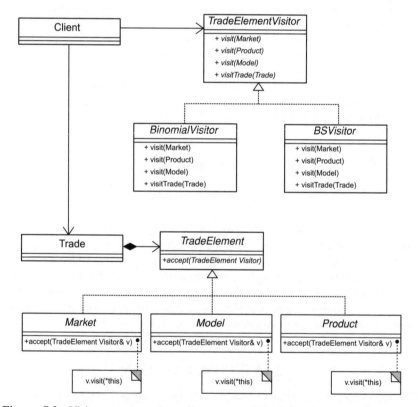

Figure 7.3 Visitor pattern as it applies to a trading platform. The UML diagram corresponds to the code listing below

As an example, we show how we can use the visitor pattern to implement multiple models for pricing a trade quickly. In this example (Figure 7.3 and the code listing below), we have a binomial tree model and a Black–Scholes model to price the trade. If we need to implement another model, we create another class deriving from TradeElementVisitor (called MyModelVisitor, say) and call its visitTrade method. Since all the code we write is under our control, we have managed to extend the platform without having to modify or pollute the underlying classes, their hierarchy or the overall architecture. It is the use of the visitor pattern that gives us this flexibility.

```cpp
#include <string>
#include <iostream>
#include <vector>

using namespace std ;

class Market ;
class Model ;
class Product ;
class Trade ;

// Interface to all trade components
struct TradeElementVisitor {
  virtual void visit(Market& market) const = 0 ;
  virtual void visit(Model& model) const = 0 ;
  virtual void visit(Product& product) const = 0 ;
  virtual void visitTrade(Trade& trade) const = 0 ;
  virtual ~TradeElementVisitor() { }
} ;

// Interface to any one of the trade components
struct TradeElement {
  virtual void accept(const TradeElementVisitor& visitor)
    = 0 ;
  virtual ~TradeElement() { }
} ;

// Market element, there are three market elements:
// Spots, Vols, Rates
class Market : public TradeElement {
public:
```

```
  explicit Market(const string& name) :
    name_(name) { }
  const string& getName() const {
    return name_ ;
  }
  void accept(const TradeElementVisitor& visitor) {
    visitor.visit(*this) ;
  }
private:
  string name_ ;
} ;


// Models
class Model : public TradeElement {
public:
  void accept(const TradeElementVisitor& visitor) {
    visitor.visit(*this) ;
  }
} ;


// Product
class Product : public TradeElement {
public:
  void accept(const TradeElementVisitor& visitor) {
    visitor.visit(*this) ;
  }
} ;


// A trade consists of a Product, Market ele-
ments and a Model
class Trade {
public:
  vector<TradeElement*>& getElements() {
    return elements_ ;
  }
  Trade() {
    elements_.push_back(new Market("Spots")) ;
    elements_.push_back(new Market("Rates")) ;
    elements_.push_back(new Market("Volatilities")) ;
    elements_.push_back(new Product()) ;
    elements_.push_back(new Model()) ;
  }
```

```
  ~Trade() {
    vector<TradeElement*>::iterator   it ;
    for(it = elements_.begin() ;
        it != elements_.end() ;
        ++it) {
      delete *it ;
    }
  }
private:
  vector<TradeElement*> elements_ ;
} ;

// BinomialVisitor and BSVisitor show how the trade can be
// priced using different models
class BinomialVisitor : public TradeElementVisitor
{
public:
  void visit(Market& market) const {
    cout << "Binomial Model: Getting the market data: "
         << market.getName() << "." << endl ;
  }
  void visit(Model& model) const {
    cout << "Binomial Model: Setting up the model."
         << endl ;
  }
  void visit(Product& product) const {
    cout << "Binomial Model: Setting up the product."
         << endl ;
  }
  void visitTrade(Trade& trade) const {
    cout << endl
         << "Pricing the trade using Binomial Model."
         << endl ;
    vector<TradeElement*>& elems = trade.getElements() ;
    vector<TradeElement*>::iterator it ;
    for(it = elems.begin() ;
        it != elems.end() ;
        ++it) {
      (*it)->accept(*this) ;
    }
    cout << "Binomial Model: Done setting up the trade."
         << endl ;
```

```
      cout << "Binomial Model: Can price it now." << endl ;
  }
} ;

class BSVisitor : public TradeElementVisitor {
public:
  void visit(Market& market) const {
    cout << "Black-Scholes Model: Getting the mar-
ket data: "
         << market.getName() << "." << endl ;
  }
  void visit(Model& model) const {
    cout << "Black-Scholes Model: Setting up the model."
         << endl ;
  }
  void visit(Product& product) const {
    cout << "Black-Scholes Model: Setting up the product."
         << endl ;
  }
  void visitTrade(Trade& trade) const {
    cout << endl
         << "Pricing the trade using Black-Scholes Model."
         << endl ;
    vector<TradeElement*>& elems = trade.getElements() ;
    vector<TradeElement*>::iterator it ;
    for(it = elems.begin() ;
        it != elems.end() ;
        ++it) {
      (*it)->accept(*this) ;
    }
    cout << "Black-Scholes Model: Done setting up
the trade."
         << endl ;
    cout << "Black-Scholes Model: Can price it now."
         << endl ;
  }
} ;

int main() {
  Trade trade ;
  BinomialVisitor binomialVisitor ;
  BSVisitor bsVisitor ;
```

```
  binomialVisitor.visitTrade(trade) ;
  bsVisitor.visitTrade(trade) ;
  return 0 ;
}
```

This sample program illustrates how new models can be added to trades without changing the underlying classes using the visitor pattern. It generates the following output:

```
Pricing the Trade using the Binomial Model
Binomial Model: Getting the market data: Spots
Binomial Model: Getting the market data: Rates
Binomial Model: Getting the market data: Volatilities
Binomial Model: Setting up the product
Binomial Model: Setting up the model
Binomial Model: Done setting up the trade
Binomial Model: Can price it now

Pricing the Trade using the Black-Scholes Model
Black-Scholes Model: Getting the market data: Spots
Black-Scholes Model: Getting the market data: Rates
Black-Scholes Model: Getting the market data: Volatilities
Black-Scholes Model: Setting up the product
Black-Scholes Model: Setting up the model
Black-Scholes Model: Done setting up the trade
Black-Scholes Model: Can price it now
```

However, nothing is for free, and the visitor pattern has serious disadvantages:

1. The visitor methods have predefined signatures, making modifications difficult. If the price() function in our example were to return a vector, we would need to define a new visitor class as well as new accept methods in each trade class.
2. The visitor pattern makes the code less readable. It also creates a tremendous overhead in implementing simple scenarios.

7.3   SINGLETON PATTERN

In designing a trading platform, we often come across objects that need to be instantiated exactly once. A live market data feed, for instance, needs to exist in the program memory as a single instance. Such single instances are implemented using the singleton pattern. Other singleton objects in a trading platform may include the aggregate of the market data or the trade data, where duplication may prove expensive in terms of computing resources. At a higher level, modern trading systems may adopt a market data server or a trade data server, which may be implemented as singletons on an application server on the network. More generally, the singleton pattern is used in the factory or virtual constructor patterns commonly used to implement software components.

We can use the concept of the singleton pattern in a non-OOP language as well, but we may have to resort to global variables and programming discipline to implement it. In other words, in the non-OOP world, the implementation for a singleton depends on developer discipline. We may be tempted to follow the same trick of declaring an object in the global namespace to implement the singleton idea in OOP as well. This trick will not work well because it does not enforce the condition that there should only be one instance of the object. However, it turns out that the singleton pattern is very easy to implement in an object-oriented language. In C++, we can define and enforce the singleton as in the code below.

```cpp
class Singleton
{
  public:
    static Singleton* Instance();

  protected:
    Singleton();

  private:
    static Singleton* m_instance;
};

Singleton* Singleton::m_instance = 0;
Singleton* Singleton::Instance ()
{
  if (m_instance == 0)
    {
      m_instance = new Singleton;
    }
  return m_instance;
}
```

Note that the constructor Singleton() is protected so that we cannot construct the singleton object. Instead, we use the Instance() method to access the object. The first time we call Instance(), it creates the singleton object. The next time onwards, it returns the reference to it, thereby enforcing its uniqueness.

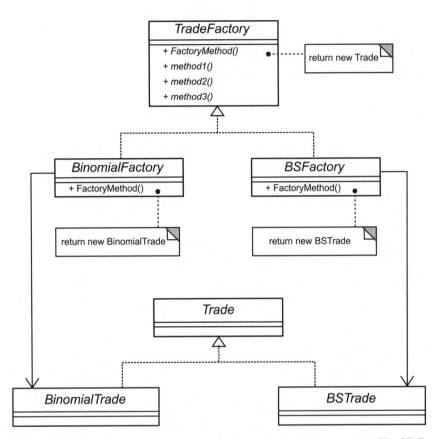

Figure 7.4 The factory method pattern in the trading platform context. The UML shown creates two kinds of trades – binomial and Black–Scholes. We can obviously extend it to any number of trade types

7.4 FACTORY PATTERNS

The factory method and abstract factory patterns are creational patterns that encapsulate the instantiation of objects so that their representation and configuration can be kept away from the overall system design. These patterns are useful when we need to create the object without knowing the exact subclass it belongs to. For instance, we may have to construct a generic trade object before we know that it is a plain vanilla option.

The factory method pattern shown in the UML diagram in Figure 7.4 uses inheritance to construct the right kind of trade objects. It can accomplish it also

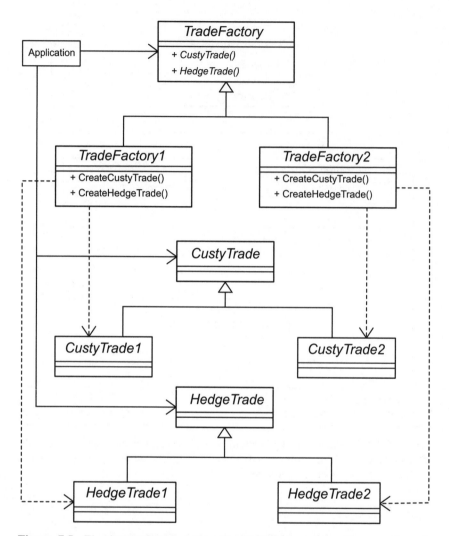

Figure 7.5 The abstract factory pattern. The UML diagram above illustrates its use in handling customer-facing trades and their hedging counterparts as parallel structures.

through a parameterized factory method, which gets the information about the kind of trade to manufacture through an input parameter.

The abstract factory pattern is useful when handling parallel class structures. For instance, suppose we have a set of customer-facing trades and their hedging counterparts. We may want to switch the pricing model of all the customer-facing trades to a new one in one go. At the same time, we may want to reprice the hedging trades using a compatible new model as well. Thus we have class parallelism – two sets of trades and two models – setting the stage for development using the abstract factory pattern.

In practice, the parallel nature may not be so obvious, but we may still find the abstract factory pattern useful and convenient. Figure 7.5 shows the UML diagram of the abstract factory pattern. This implementation lets us switch between two different trade factories implementing separate, parallel models for real and hedging trades.

In the factory method pattern, we write the trade factory class without knowing what trade it is supposed to create. It is the concrete subclasses (BSTrade and BinomialTrade) that provide the concrete factory method to create them. Thus, the factory method pattern may make it necessary for us to subclass every type of trade that we need, increasing the complexity of the resulting program. In the abstract factory pattern, the disadvantage is in having to modify the factory interface in response to new types of trades or models we implement. The flexibility that the patterns afford comes at the cost of increased obscurity, as it so often does in object-oriented programming.

7.5   COMPONENT OBJECT MODEL

Different from the patterns discussed so far is component object model (COM) programming. Patterns are themes or genres of solutions that may apply to the programming challenge that we are faced with. They help us reuse our programming skills and experience in an efficient manner across multiple projects or challenges. Within one project, the object-oriented paradigm encourages and facilitates source code reusability. What is assumed in reusing source code is that we stick to one programming language. In large-scale projects, this assumption may turn out to be too much of a constraint. We may indeed want to use multiple languages to leverage on the strong suits of each of them to tackle different aspects of the problem at hand.

A component object model provides a means of sharing the code at the binary level, as opposed to the source code level that we are used to. It defines a set of binary standards on how COM objects must be structured in the computer memory. Once it is compiled in accordance with the standards, COM objects can be shared regardless of the programming language in use. The object memory structure closely mirrors C++, and for that reason we find most of the COM development in that language.

In COM programming, the consumer of the COM object (another developer) accesses it exclusively through its interfaces. Interfaces are abstract classes (with only pure virtual functions) providing the consumer with various functions. The code that implements the interface functions resides in a component object class. The operating system (or the application managing the COM framework) keeps track of the various COM objects and interfaces using a central registry. In Windows, it is *the* registry. In order to help keep track of them, COM objects and interfaces have what are known as globally unique identifiers, or GUIDs.

One feature of COM is that all objects use their own reference counting. If an object finds itself no longer in use (meaning its reference count has reached zero), it is ready to be unloaded from memory during the next garbage collection.

The consumer of the COM object creates one using a generic 'create instance' call, requesting one of its interfaces. He then uses the functions provided by that interface. If he needs the functionality provided by a different interface, he can use a generic query interface to get it. Once done, he releases the interfaces (which will decrement the reference count of the object). Note that the COM methodology, in fact, makes use of the factory and singleton patterns discussed above.

The component object model is a powerful technology and has many books written on it. This meagre introduction is provided here merely to highlight its existence as a means of sharing binary code efficiently (albeit a bit ponderously), which may be called for in a large-scale trading platform implementation.

7.6 SUMMARY

Patterns are powerful tools in object-oriented programming. They solve most software problems that we may encounter in designing our trading platform. In them, we will find elegant and time-tested ideas that we can reuse. Unless we are aware of the existence of such a vast repository of design ideas, we may spend many days and months reinventing the wheel and figuring out new solutions to problems already solved. Design patterns are also likely to be more robust solutions than the ad hoc ideas we may come up with on our own.

To go one step further and to deploy solutions that can operate over the programming language barriers, we need to use powerful software technologies like the component object model (COM). In COM, the code reuse is at the binary compatibility level, where the component objects are dynamically shared at run-time. This mode of sharing gives the developers the freedom to choose implementation languages (within reason) specific and most appropriate to the task at hand. They may like to use C# for user interface designs, Java for web-based deployments, C++ for number-crunching situations, and so on.

Although we can improve the robustness of our software solutions through design patterns, we have to be careful in choosing the right pattern appropriate in solving the problem at hand. We have to evaluate the situation thoroughly from as many perspectives as we can anticipate before we choose the software solution, which is why we went through the myriad of trade perspectives and the minute details of the trade life-cycle management. Without such meticulous evaluation, the trading platform becomes an exercise in computer science wizardry, full of esoteric patterns and capabilities, but of limited use when it comes to prosaic operations like keeping track of a cash flow.

QUIZ

1. What are the differences between the adapter pattern and the façade pattern?
2. What is double dispatch and how does the visitor pattern implement it?
3. What are pure virtual functions?
4. How does the component object model implement binary level compatibility?
5. Compare the factory and abstract factory patterns.
6. What are the advantages and disadvantages in using patterns?

8

Flexible Derivatives Pricing Tool

The pricing tool in the attached CD is a companion program designed to illustrate the modular programming techniques described in this book, *Principles of Quantitative Development*. Although the pricing tool falls short of meeting all the requirements of a good trading platform, it illustrates many of the design and interface principles described in this book. In particular, the pricing tool provides excellent extensibility when it comes to defining and deploying new products and quantitative models. It also gives its users dynamic interfaces based on product or model definitions. The act of designing new products or models also takes care of putting together interfaces for them. Moreover, through a clean separation of various modules, the pricing tool can provide a rich toolkit (finite difference Greeks, visualization, etc.) to any newly developed products and models.

In this chapter, we will start with the design scope of the pricing tool and explain why it is not considered a trading platform. We will then go through some of its features and highlight the areas where they do meet the requirements of a good trading platform. We will follow it up a discussion on how these features are implemented, including the publicly available class libraries it uses. We will finish off by focusing on the often neglected documentation aspect. In the next chapter, we will discuss how the shortcomings of the pricing tool can be addressed so that it can become a true trading platform.

8.1 DESIGN SCOPE

The pricing tool is designed with one fundamental principle in mind – extensibility, which is scalability in terms of product and model definitions. Extensibility of this kind is achieved using a completely modular approach to model implementation. To the pricing tool, every pricing model is a dynamic link library (DLL) that exposes a set of functions with rigidly defined signatures. The only interaction between the pricing tool and the pricing model that evaluates a product is through these functions. Thus, the pricing tool simulates the façade pattern, although it is not implemented using the traditional object-oriented paradigm.

The rigid definition of the pricing function allows the pricing tool automatically to write a C++ file implementing the model and product as we define them interactively. Once the skeleton program is generated all we have to do is to insert the code implementing the pricing method and make a DLL out of it. The pricing tool will then load the DLL and use it as needed. Thus, we can extend the functionality of the pricing tool on the fly without even recompiling it. In fact, we do not even have to exit from the program to add a new product and/or model. Once added, the new product can be analysed using all the features in the pricing tool (the Greeks computation, plotting, etc.) without writing a single line of extra code for it.

The modular separation between the pricing method and the rest of the program in the pricing tool makes it easy to develop features (such as finite difference Greeks, scenario analysis, visualization tools, etc.) independent of the products and models. It also lets us devise dynamically self-adapting graphical user interfaces (GUIs) that match the product–model definition. In effect, the product–model definition becomes a macro that drives the behaviour of the program.

The pricing tool, therefore, responds well to the extensibility requirement that we demand of a trading platform. However, there are other requirements that the pricing tool does not address. It does not have the notion of a market. It treats market data on the same basis as trade parameters. Although this treatment may not be appropriate for complex, real-life trades, it is adequate for prototyping and proof-of-concept projects.

The pricing tool also lacks a database back-end. It does, however, store trades and scenarios in extensible mark-up language (XML) files, and can easily be adapted to save them in a database. Due to the lack of database support and the notion of a unified market representation, we cannot treat the pricing tool as a trading platform. We present it here as a working example that may aid in cementing the concepts we have explored so far in the book.

8.2 DESIGN GOALS AND FEATURES

The fundamental design goal of the pricing tool is a total separation between the user interface and the product–model modules of the program. This separation enables us to work independently on the functionality features of the program (data types, visualization, analysis, etc.) that apply to all the products and models we define.

8.2.1 Pricing tool features

Listed below are the main features of the pricing tool in its current version:

1. Interactive definition of new products. The pricing tool lets us define new products on the fly. It has a dedicated self-adapting GUI to define new products, which we can save for future use. We can also define a set of products that will be loaded at the program initialization.

2. Dynamic definition of models, and pricing functions. Once we define a product, the pricing tool helps us define and create one or more models that we can attach to it, and start pricing it. Like the product definition GUI, the model definition also uses its own dedicated GUI.

3. Autogeneration of a model template. The pricing tool can generate function templates to get us started in coding the model. The generated C++ code is ready to be compiled, and requires only minimal effort to integrate existing pricing model intelligence.

4. Ability to save and load product and model definitions. The program can save the products and models that we define, so that we can reuse them. In the current implementation, the pricing tool uses XML to save products and models.

5. Ability to save and load trades. Trade, in the context of the pricing tool, is an instance of a product–model pair with a given pricing scenario. The pricing tool can save trades or pricing scenarios in XML files and reload them.

6. Visualization. The pricing tool has built-in plotting tools to visualize the trade valuations. Given a product–model pair, the program gives us interfaces to plot any model output as a function of one or two product inputs, or one output versus another parametrically as we vary any one input. The plot ranges are customizable. We can make three-dimensional plots (output versus two inputs) as surfaces or colour charts. We can even slice and dice the three-dimensional plots. We can export all plots in PDF format for printing or presentation.

7. Scenario analysis. The plotting module works as a flexible scenario analysis tool as well because we can export the plots to Excel (as a CSV file) for further manipulations. A three-dimensional plot, for instance, will export to a three-column table with user-defined intervals and sampling on the X and Y axes.

8. Finite difference computation of the Greeks. Using the pricing tool, we can interactively compute all possible sensitivities (first and second derivatives) of any output with respect to any input. We can specify the interval (bump size) to shock the input in a variety of familiar ways. All finite difference computation scenarios can be exported to Excel.

9. Extensive data types support. The pricing tool supports a rich set of data types for product parameters and model outputs, as described below in the next subsection.

10. Import from Excel. For complex data types (like dates, vectors or matrices) the pricing tool lets us cut and paste from an Excel sheet.

11. Context-sensitive help. Almost all the buttons and fields in the pricing tool have tool-tips associated with them. These tool-tips are dynamically generated and give a quick indication of the actions to be taken or the values expected. In addition, all the different GUI modules have a 'Help' button, which will bring up a context-sensitive help specific to the window the user is working with. The user can also access the help window using the standard Windows help shortcut – the F1 key.

8.2.2   Data types support

We need a rich set of types for financial analysis. For this reason, the pricing tool supports various data types both for inputs (product parameters) and outputs (model outputs). The required type of parameters and outputs can be chosen while defining the product or model. Once the parameter type is chosen, the user interface will adapt to accommodate the right kind of data entry. This self-adapting interface makes it easy for the end users to enter data in their preferred manner.

The various data types available in the pricing tool are described below along with the special features implemented for the way in which we input them into the GUI elements:

1. Double (double) is the basic float type in the pricing tool. Almost all scalar quantities fall into this category. Examples are spot price, constant interest rate, etc. The data entry box of a double number adapts itself to display it using comma-separated thousands (as 9,999,999, for instance). It also accepts input shortcut notations to facilitate data entry:
   - n% which translates as $n/100$;
   - nk (or nK) for $1000*n$;
   - nm (or nM) for n million;
   - nb (or nB) for n billion.
   We can input 3,000,000 as 3m. In fact, any combinations of the shortcut notations are permitted as well. If we type in 3m10k into one of the data entry boxes that take a double, it will be translated to 3,010,000.
2. Integer (int) is the basic integer type. Although we do not usually come across integral values in the number-crunching world of quantitative finance, we do have, for example, quantities like the number of iterations in a Monte Carlo simulation. We also have a large number of selection flags (like European/American/Bermudan exercise types for an option), which are usually implemented as integers in the program.
3. Vector is a simple array of doubles. Vectors are a fairly common data type. For example, we may come across a rate vector once in a while.
4. Matrix is a two-dimensional array of doubles. They are used to represent two-dimensional surfaces, which are again a common data type in quantitative finance. An example would be a volatility surface.
5. Date is internally stored as doubles (the Excel date equivalent), but shown to the user in the DD/MM/YYYY format. The data entry box for a date (and the edit interface for DateVecs and the date part of a Curve) takes the mnemonics and formats as follows:
   - (n)d/w/m/y (for n days, weeks, months or years from today, with n a positive integer);
   - DD-MM-YYYY;
   - DD/MM/YYYY;

- YYYYMMDD;
- Excel date (Excel date is a number, such as 39851 to represent 7 February 2009).

We come across dates all the time in any kind of trade definition, such as the trade start date, maturity date, etc. A flexible and intuitive date entry facility is therefore important in a trading platform.

6. A date vector (DateVec) is a vector of dates. DateVecs are internally stored as simple vectors, but have the special user interface to support the input mnemonics and output formatting. An example of a date vector is the fixing schedule of an interest rate swap.

7. A Curve represents a time-dependent quantity. It is internally stored as a matrix of two columns, again supporting the date mnemonics and formatting for the first column and the double mnemonics for the second. From the end user perspective, the curve data type comes up more frequently than a simple vector. Examples include a yield curve or a volatility term structure.

8. The pricing tool supports Menus that the end user can interactively create as a part of his product or model definitions. The menu selection is internally stored as an integer within the program. They are saved in the XML definition of the product with all the information needed to render it as a nice menu. An example would be a menu showing the option exercise types of a product as, say, European/American/Bermudan. If the end user selects European in the menu the program may get an integer value of one, for instance.

8.3 USER INTERFACE

Since the pricing tool is a graphical user interface (GUI), the program flow we choose to follow is not predetermined and we have a plethora of choices. In Figure 8.1, we illustrate a typical sequence where we define a new product, add a model to it and process it (price it, visualize it, compute its Greeks, etc.), saving the product/model definitions along the way.

When we launch the program, it reads in an init file called PricingTool.ini. This file contains a list of product/model definitions, which are XML files themselves describing the names, types and default values or function names of the product and model parameters. They also specify the DLL implementing the model. Once the pricing tool reads in these XML files, it populates its list of products in its main control interface titled 'Product Pricing/Plotting/Analyzing Tool'. We have the option of editing an existing product or creating a new one. Either way, we move on to the 'Create/Edit Product' window.

Editing a product is an interactive and intuitive way of modifying its parameters and saving the product definition back to its XML file. We can change the number and types of its the parameters as well as their default values. Note that we can

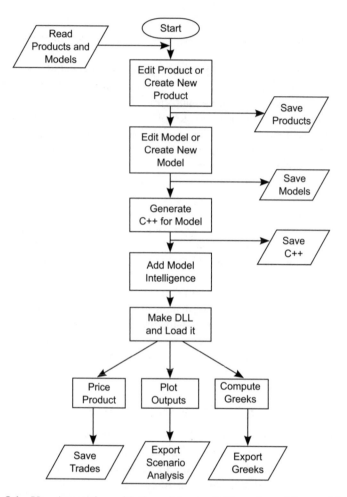

Figure 8.1 User interaction with the pricing tool. Since the pricing tool is a GUI application, the program flow is not predefined; it depends on the user actions. This figure shows the steps involved in starting from a product, creating or editing a model, attaching the model DLL, pricing, plotting, analysing the product, etc.

use any XML or plain text editor to make the product modifications directly on the saved file as well, although the pricing tool interface is more natural.

Once we have defined a product, we can define a model for it using a 'Create/Edit Model' interface. This interface is launched either from the product creation window or directly from the main control interface. The interface to edit a model is similar to the one for product modification. However, since model parameters are considered outputs, they have function names associated with them.

The next step is to generate a function template for the model based on our product and model definitions. The function template is the skeleton C++ code that the pricing tool generates for us using the function names we give to the output parameters. After inserting the necessary model intelligence into this skeleton code, we compile it and make a DLL out of it that we can load into the pricing tool, completing the product–model definition process.

With the new product and its model defined, we can use the pricing tool to study the product–model pair. We can price the product, plot the dependencies of its outputs to various inputs, study the sensitivities of its outputs and so on. We will go through the user interfaces for these activities in this chapter, before looking at the implementation details in the next.

8.3.1 Main control interface

When we start the program, we get a screen, shown in Figure 8.2. On the left, we have a product selection list box. We can add new products by clicking on the 'New' button below this selection box. We can also edit or delete an existing

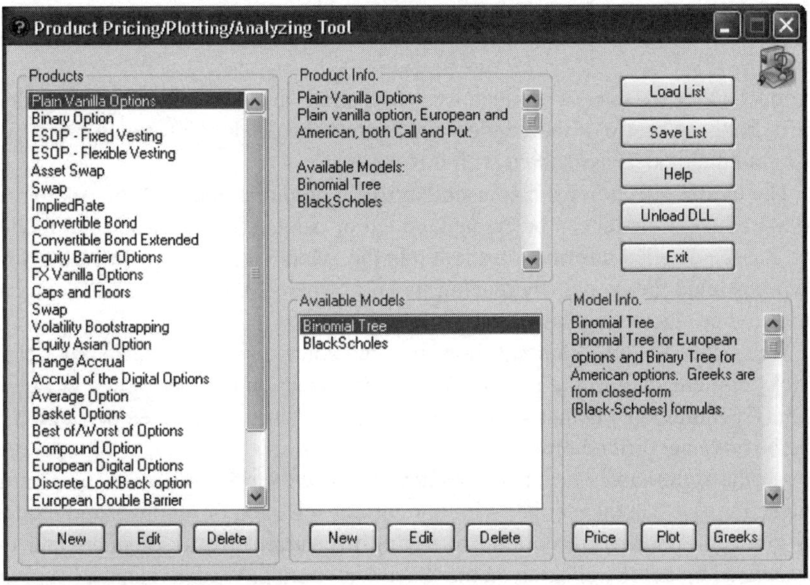

Figure 8.2 The main control interface of the pricing tool. The tall list box on the left contains the products defined in the pricing tool. The middle column shows the models defined for the selected product. New products and models can be added at will and the existing ones can be edited. The buttons on the right show the actions the user can perform

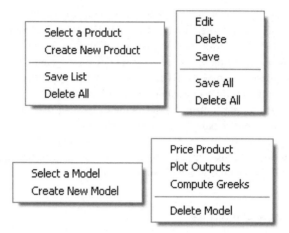

Figure 8.3 Context menus in the main control interface of the pricing tool. In the top left is the context menu on the empty region of the Products selection box. Top right shows the context menu on a specific product. Similarly, bottom left is the context menu on the empty region of the Models selection box, while the bottom right shows the context menu associated with a specific model

product. Once we select a product, we see its name and description in the 'Product Info' box, top centre of the window. Just below the product information box, we can find the models associated with this product.

The model selection list box is similar to the product selection box. Analogous to a product, a model can be created, edited or deleted. Once we select a model, we can see detailed information about it in the 'Model Info' box to the right. If we have installed the model (by placing its DLL where we have specified), we can price the product using the selected model.

We can access the common actions through context menus (revealed by a right click) implemented in the product and model selection box, as shown in Figure 8.3. Depending on whether we right-click on a product or on an empty region of the box, we get different menus.

On the right-hand side of the window, we have various buttons representing the actions we can take, either with our current selection of products and models or globally. We have the option of saving the current list of products and the associated models by clicking on the 'Save List' button. We can reload a list saved previously by clicking on the 'Load List' button. Note that the 'Load List' action is cumulative – it adds new products to the list of products without clearing the existing ones. The saved lists are stored in XML format, fully compliant with the XML standards. We can edit them using normal text editors or dedicated XML editors. We can also view them conveniently using Internet Explorer.

The pricing tool implements rigorous error checks on user actions on its interfaces. For instance, if we have no product selected, the 'Edit' and 'Delete' buttons are not active. If no model is selected for a particular product, in addition to the edit and delete options, the pricing tool disables the product pricing, plotting and Greek computation buttons. Since the pricing tool knows the model module details (the location of the model DLL and its name), it can check for their validity. If it cannot find the DLL, load it successfully or resolve all the model output functions, it does not allow us to attempt pricing and other processings.

8.3.2   Create/edit product

Figure 8.4 shows the interface that lets us define (create or edit) a product. In the example in the figure, we are defining plain vanilla options. The interface shows the name and description fields of the product and the list of parameters. Each parameter, in turn, has a name and a description. In addition, it can be of different types: double, int, Vector, Matrix, Date, DateVec (Date Vector, such as a list of fixing dates), Menu (which will be rendered as options) or Curve (such

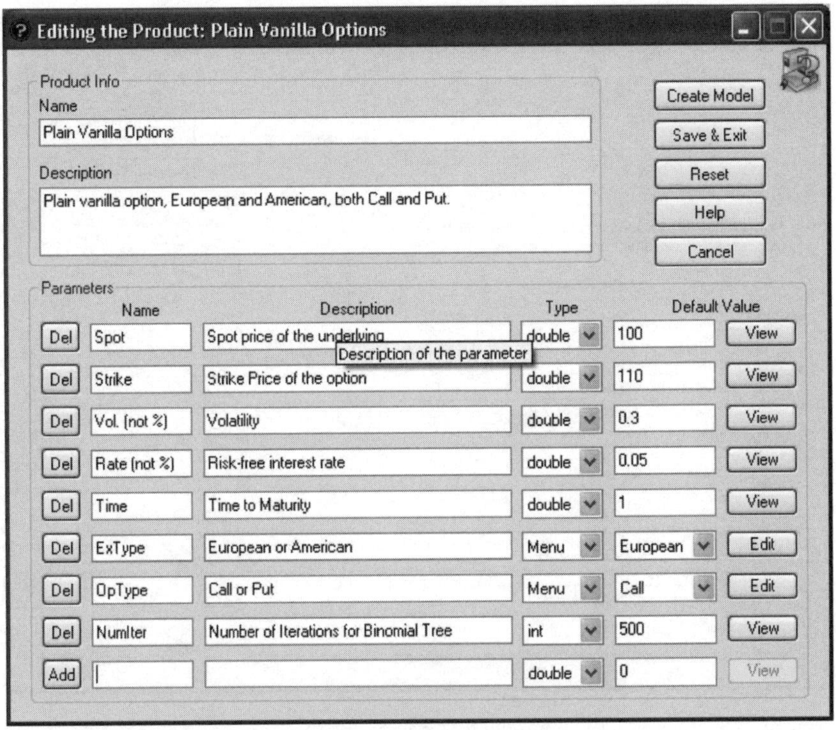

Figure 8.4 Defining a plain vanilla option in the pricing tool

as interest rate curves, which are special matrices with two columns – dates and values). In Figure 8.4, we can see that the exercise type (American or European) and the option type (Call or Put) are menus. Each parameter has a default value, which can be seen in the interface or viewed at full precision by clicking on the 'View' button. On complex types like vectors and matrices, the text box that shows the default value becomes an 'Edit' button. For menus, the 'View' button becomes an 'Edit' button to help us define the menus interactively.

The product definition interface is dynamic. If we add one more parameter after Rho, for instance, the interface will grow by one row to allow us to define another parameter, if needed. It is also aware of modifications and warns us about discarding changes if we attempt to close the window without saving changes.

8.3.3   Create/edit model

The interface to edit a model looks similar to the product editing window. Figure 8.5 shows the user interface where we are defining a binomial tree model for pricing our plain vanilla options. Analogous to the product definition window, this

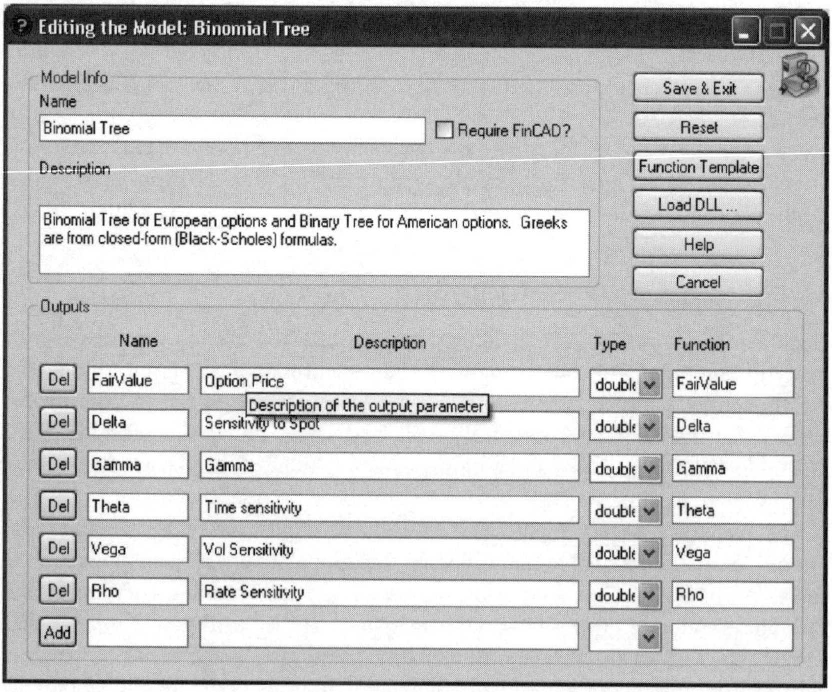

Figure 8.5   Defining the binomial tree pricing model for plain vanilla options in the pricing tool

interface also shows a model name and description, and a list of outputs from the model. In setting up the outputs, the model definition interface shares many features of the process of constructing the product parameters. Like the product editing window, the model window is aware of modifications and is dynamically sized. The outputs can also be of any of the generic types (`double` or `int`) or the complex types (`Vector`, `Matrix`, `Date`, `DateVec` or `Curve`). The type `Menu` does not make any sense in the context of an output parameter and is therefore omitted.

Outputs do not have default values, but they have function names attached to them (which are autoconstructed from the output names, if omitted). These function names are used in generating the model implementation code when we click on the 'Function Template' button. Once the model implementation is compiled into a DLL, we can load it into the pricing tool using the 'Load DLL' button. Note, however, that in WinAPI, there is no sure way of unloading a DLL, which creates a problem if we try to rebuild the DLL. The original DLL stays loaded and therefore locked by the system, preventing us from overwriting it with a new version. The recourse in that case is to close the pricing tool, rebuild the DLL and restart. The location of the loaded DLL is also saved along with the product/model definition so that it is automatically loaded the next time we load the product.

Next to the 'Model Name' text box, we see a check box titled 'Require FinCAD?' This check box is to inform the program that the model implementation uses FinCAD libraries. FinCAD is a commercial program with its own pricing and licensing terms, and is not distributed with *Principles of Quantitative Development*. If the model is marked as requiring FinCAD, the program will look for the appropriate run-time files and refuse to load the model if it cannot find them.

8.3.4   Generating a function template

Once a product–model pair is defined, we can ask the pricing tool to generate ready-to-compile C++ code using the product and model definition by clicking the 'Function Template' button. Figure 8.6 shows the interface (a built-in text editor) that displays, and optionally edits and saves, the generated code. Note that the parameter names and the output function names from the product–model definition are used in the code generation process.

The skeleton C++ code generated uses global inputs and outputs to carry out pricing. All the product parameters become the global inputs, as seen in Figure 8.6, and all the model parameters become the global outputs. The names of these global variables are derived from the sanitized versions of the corresponding parameter names. The task of the function implementing the model (the name of which is derived from the model name) is to compute, within its body, the global outputs using the global inputs. In Figure 8.6, this function is `void Binomial()`, which can be implemented as follows using a public-domain quant library.

```
? Edit Pad                                                          [_][□][X]

[ Save ] [ Reset ] [ Undo ] [ Select ] [ Cut ] [ Copy ] [ Paste ] [ Done ] [ Help ]

#include <windows.h>
#include <linal.h> // for Vector and Matrix
#ifdef __cplusplus
     #define cppfudge "C"
#else
     #define cppfudge
#endif

#ifdef BUILD_DLL
     // the dll exports
     #define EXPORT extern cppfudge __declspec(dllexport)
#else
     // the exe imports
     #define EXPORT extern cppfudge __declspec(dllimport)
#endif
#define MAXSTR 2048

// Global Inputs
static double g_Spot ;
static double g_Strike ;
static double g_Vol ;
static double g_Rate ;
static double g_Time ;
static int g_ExType ;
static int g_OpType ;
static int g_NumIter ;

// Global Outputs
double g_FairValue ;
double g_Delta ;
double g_Gamma ;
double g_Theta ;
double g_Vega ;
double g_Rho ;

// Provide this function implementing the model
void Binomial()
{
     // Make sure that this function computes all the Global Outputs above
     // from the Global Inputs above.  You can call other functions from here
}

//==============================================================//
// DON'T CHANGE ANYTHING FROM HERE TO THE END OF THIS FILE //

// See if any of the inputs have changed
EXPORT bool InputChanged(double d[], int n[], Vector* v[], Matrix* m[])
{
     bool changed =
          (g_Spot  != d[0]) ||
          (g_Strike != d[1]) ||
          (g_Vol   != d[2]) ||
          (g_Rate  != d[3]) ||
          (g_Time  != d[4]) ||
          (g_ExType  != n[0]) ||
          (g_OpType  != n[1]) ||
          (g_NumIter != n[2]) ;
     return changed ;
}
```

Figure 8.6 Generating model implementation and pricing functions (C++ code) using the pricing tool. This skeleton code generated by the pricing tool needs to be 'fleshed out' with the pricing model intelligence, which we will put in place of the two highlighted lines in the figure above. The pricing model will use the 'Global Inputs' to compute the 'Global Outputs'. Once the outputs are programmed, the model implementation is complete

```
void Binomial()
{
  if (g_ExType == 0) // European
    if (g_OpType == 0) // Call
```

```
{
    g_FairValue = option_price_call_european_binomial
        (g_Spot, g_Strike, g_Rate, g_Vol, g_Time, g_NumIter)
    option_price_partials_call_black_scholes
        (g_Spot, g_Strike, g_Rate, g_Vol, g_Time,
        g_Delta, g_Gamma, g_Theta, g_Vega, g_Rho) ;
}
else if (g_OpType == 1) // Put
{
    g_FairValue = option_price_put_european_binomial
        (g_Spot, g_Strike, g_Rate, g_Vol, g_Time, g_NumIter)
    option_price_partials_put_black_scholes
        (g_Spot, g_Strike, g_Rate, g_Vol, g_Time,
        g_Delta, g_Gamma, g_Theta, g_Vega, g_Rho) ;
}
else
    mb("Vanilla-Binomial.dll",
        "What the heck is this European option?rn"
        "Not Call, not Put?") ;
else if (g_ExType == 1) // American
    if (g_OpType == 0) // Call
    {
        g_FairValue = option_price_call_american_binomial
            (g_Spot, g_Strike, g_Rate, g_Vol, g_Time, g_NumIter)
        option_price_partials_american_call_binomial
            (g_Spot, g_Strike, g_Rate, g_Vol, g_Time, g_NumIter,
            g_Delta, g_Gamma, g_Theta, g_Vega, g_Rho) ;
    }
    else if (g_OpType == 1) // Put
    {
        g_FairValue = option_price_put_american_binomial
            (g_Spot, g_Strike, g_Rate, g_Vol, g_Time, g_NumIter)
        option_price_partials_american_put_binomial
            (g_Spot, g_Strike, g_Rate, g_Vol, g_Time, g_NumIter,
            g_Delta, g_Gamma, g_Theta, g_Vega, g_Rho) ;
    }
    else
        mb("Vanilla-Binomial.dll",
            "What the heck is this American option?rn"
            "Not Call, not Put?") ;
}
```

Take a close look at the function templates generated.
Each Output parameter needs a unique pricing function, as shown in the template.
If the function names are not unique, fix the function names of the output parameters.
Then regererate the function templates and copy them to your editor.
You can then edit this template file, paying particular attention to the 'real' function that does the work.
This real function is at the return statement.
You should worry about its prototype, return type, calling argument sequence etc.
Once all this is done, generate a dll and load it.
Use the following commands (or equivalent) to generate the DLL
    g++ -DBUILD_DLL -I. /share/src -c -o <module>.o <module>.cc
    dllwrap --output-def <module>.def --dllname <module>.dll <module>.o <libs>
    g++ -shared --entry _DllMain@12 -o <module>.dll <module>.o <module>.def <libs>
where the function templates file name is <module> (like funcs.cc) and
any functions that the function refers to are defined in <libs> (like libRecipes.a)

Buttons:
    Save: Save the template to a .cc file,
    Reset: Discard all changes and restart,
    Undo: Single level undo facility,
    Select: Select all text,
    Cut, Copy, Paste: If you have to ask ...,
    Done: Accept changes and exit,
    Help: How you got this window.

Figure 8.7 The help text of the code generation display, detailing the steps needed to create a DLL

Everything outside the body of this function computing the global outputs is not to be modified. It includes the functions assigning the global outputs to expose them to the pricing tool, which will be accessed using function pointers resolved during run-time.

The code skeleton has a function (called `bool InputChanged()`) to test if any of the user inputs have changed. If no input has changed, there is no point in recalculating the outputs, and it merely returns the results from the previous computation. Therefore, if we click on the 'Price' button twice without changing any of the inputs, the second time around we will see that the pricing tool returns the values with no delay.

Once we edit the generated code to implement the model intelligence, we have to compile it into a dynamic link library (DLL). We can find the instructions for doing that by clicking on the 'Help' button of the code editor, as shown in Figure 8.7. These instructions apply to a Windows PC running Cygwin. The companion CD that comes with this book contains a Visual Studio project `MakeDLL`, which can be used to generate a DLL.

The text editor that displays the code is reused in the pricing tool, for instance, in editing complex parameters like menus, vectors and matrices.

8.3.5 Complex parameter visualization

During pricing and processing trades, we want to view and modify the input parameters, such as the trade inputs and market variables. For basic types like

Table 8.1   Yields of Singapore Sovereign bonds on 10 February, 2009, as an example of `Vector`, `DateVec` and `Curve` data types in the pricing tool. The first column is the date pillars, which can be defined as a `DateVec` called `pillars`. The second column is the yield in percentage, which can be represented in a `Vector` (called `rates`). The two columns (pillars and rates) put together form a `Curve`, which we call `sgsyld`

Pillars	Rates (%)
11/02/2009	0.21
10/05/2009	0.29
10/02/2010	0.39
10/02/2011	0.57
10/02/2014	1.31
10/02/2016	1.72
10/02/2019	2.07
10/02/2024	2.7
10/02/2029	3.09

`double` and `int`, we can easily display and edit the parameters in a simple edit box control. However, the pricing tool supports complex data types (like `Vector`, `Matrix`, `Curve`, etc.) as well. In order to facilitate data entry for these data types, the pricing tool gives us a flexible interface.

While defining the parameter during product creation, if we choose `Vector` or `Matrix`, the edit box that shows the default value transforms into an 'Edit' button. Clicking on the button, we can bring up the same edit pad shown in Figure 8.6. For a `Matrix`, we enter the elements separated by space, comma or tab, and the rows delimited by a line-feed. We can either input the numbers directly or load a text file, or cut and paste from other applications such as Microsoft Excel. We get the edit pad interface for `Vector`, `Matrix`, `DateVec` or `Curve`.

As an example, let us consider a `Vector`, a `DateVec`, a `Curve` and a `Matrix`. We tabulate a sample yield curve in Table 8.1. The first column contains the date `pillars` (a `DateVec`) and the second column holds the `rates` (a `Vector`), and together they form a `Curve` called `sgsyld`. To illustrate how we can visualize a surface, we also define a `Matrix` that we call `vol`, representing a hypothetical volatility surface.

The pricing tool makes it easy for us to enter double and date values by recognizing mnemonics (such as %, k, m, b for doubles and d, m, y, etc., for dates). It also guesses the date format (YYYYMMDD, DD/MM/YYYY, etc.). The pricing tool maintains these convenient features in its edit pad interface for the complex data types as well.

Table 8.2 Illustration of the flexible date input formats supported in the pricing tool. The date vector `pillars` can be given in any of the formats above or in any combination of them. The delimiters between two dates can be a line break, space, comma or a tab

DD/MM/YYYY	Excel date	YYYY-MM-DD	YYYYMMDD
11/02/2009	40119	2009-11-02	20091102
10/05/2009	40091	2009-10-05	20091005
10/02/2010	40453	2010-10-02	20101002
10/02/2011	40818	2011-10-02	20111002
10/02/2014	41914	2014-10-02	20141002
10/02/2016	42645	2016-10-02	20161002
10/02/2019	43740	2019-10-02	20191002
10/02/2024	45567	2024-10-02	20241002
10/02/2029	47393	2029-10-02	20291002

In order to create the date vector `pillars`, we can type into the input edit pad the dates in various formats, as shown in Table 8.2. We can mix and match the formats as well and give any possible combination, with a wide choice of delimiters between the values. This flexibility gives us the freedom to cut and paste values from multiple spreadsheets or other sources without much editing and formatting. Similar to the flexibility in the date input format, the `rates` vector also can be entered as 0.21 % or 0.0021.

When entering the values for the `Curve sgsyld` as two columns in its edit pad data entry interface, this flexibility is maintained. Any combination of the various input facets is automatically recognized and translated into the pricing tool memory.

Data entry errors in complex types are best identified through visualization, which is why the pricing tool gives us plotting options for all complex data types. By clicking on the 'View' button, we can inspect the data in two steps. First, we will see a dialog box with the data structure pretty-printed, with the option of plotting it, as shown in Figure 8.8.

If we choose to plot it, depending on the data type and our choice, we get different plots. In Figure 8.9 top left, we have plotted the `Vector rates`, and next to it, on the right, we have the `Curve sgsyld`. Note that these two plots are different. A `Vector` is plotted on the Y axis with its indices (equally spaced) on the X axis. A Curve, on the other hand, is plotted with the date vector on the X axis. The bottom part of Figure 8.9 shows two different ways of visualizing our hypothetical volatility surface `vol`.

Menus are a special data type in the pricing tool. It is used to indicate our options during pricing – we can select one of the menu items, but we cannot modify the menu items themselves while pricing or analysing a trade. However,

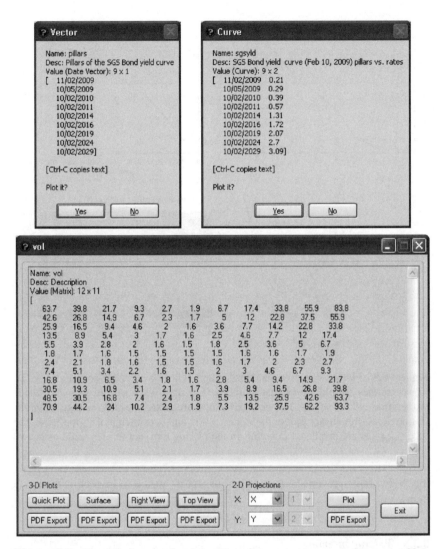

Figure 8.8 Viewing the complex data types of `Vector`, `Curve` and `Matrix`. Note that, for a `Matrix`, we have multiple visualization options. We can also export the `Matrix` plots in PDF format for printing

while defining a product, we need to be able to define or modify the menu items. In order to accomplish this split behaviour, the pricing tool transforms the default edit box into the menu itself when we set a parameter type to menu. We can edit the menu items by clicking on the 'Edit' button, which is what the 'View' button transforms into, when we set the parameter type to menu. While pricing, however,

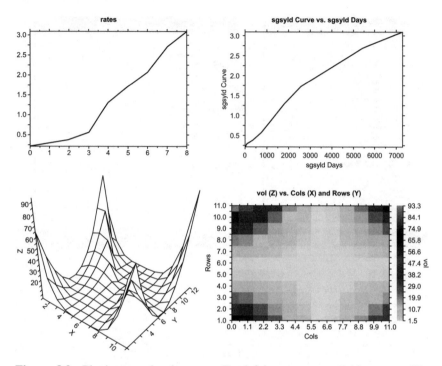

Figure 8.9 Plotting complex data types. Top left is a `Vector` variable: `rates`. The values in rates are plotted against its index. Top right is the `Curve` `sgsyld`, made of the same `rates` values. The `sgsyld` values are plotted against the date intervals. Bottom left is the surface plot of the `Matrix` `vol` and bottom right is its top view. The `Matrix` plots are displayed in colour in the pricing tool, not in grey scale as shown here

the 'View' button reverts back and gives us an easy means of inspecting the menu items.

8.3.6   Pricing interface

In a regular trading system, the pricing interface is the same as the trade booking screen, or has a direct link to it. In our pricing tool, however, we do not have a database to store the trades. In fact, the concept of a trade is only loosely implemented as pricing scenarios arising from the pricing interface.

Figure 8.10 shows the pricing window of our program, launched for plain vanilla options using a binomial tree pricing model. The window is dynamic in its size, appearance and properties. The window title identifies the product and the model – a useful feature because we may open multiple windows thanks to the

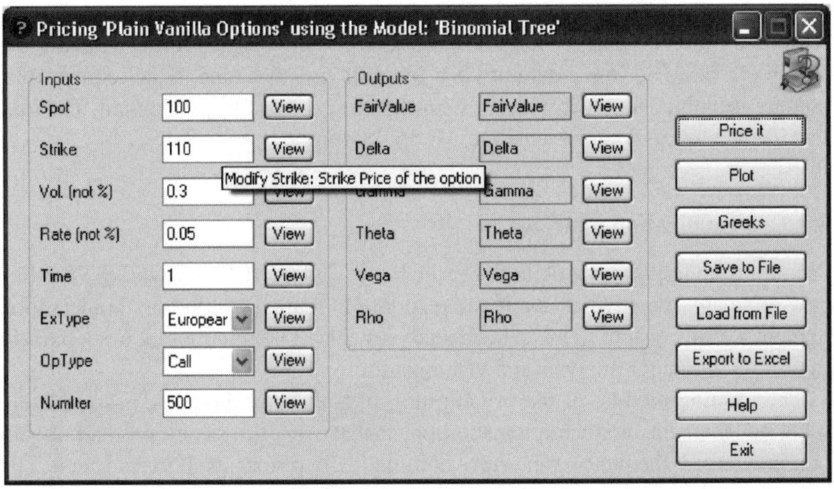

Figure 8.10   The pricing interface of the pricing tool. Note that we can launch the plotting or sensitivity computation windows by clicking on the 'Plot' or the 'Greeks' button. We can also save the pricing scenario (along with the product–model information) serialized into an XML file, or load an existing scenario. This save/load facility loosely simulates trade booking and retrieving

asynchronous nature of the GUI. The window size depends on the number input and output parameters, so that we can define as many of them as we need without worrying about the interface size, which is limited only by our monitor screen size.

The interface is context-sensitive in terms of the help it provides us. The 'Help' button (or the F1 key) brings up a help window specific to the pricing window. Moreover, each input field and button in the interface has a tool-tip specific to the parameter it is linked to. The tool-tip is generated out of the name and description of the parameter.

In the pricing interface, the group box on the left contains the input trade parameters (including market values). The group box in the centre is for the outputs. Note that each input and output has a 'View' button, which we can use for inspecting or visualizing the parameter (for complex data types).

On the right, we have a set of action buttons. In addition to the expected 'Price' button, we also have shortcuts to plotting and the finite difference Greeks computation windows. We can save the pricing scenario (which is our poor equivalent of the notion of a trade) or load an existing scenario. The scenarios are saved in XML format and the loading part has built-in error checking to ensure product–model compatibility. For a text representation of the pricing scenario, we can click the 'Export to Excel' button, which instructs the pricing tool to generate a text version and bring it up in an Edit Pad (the same window as in Figure 8.6, reusing it with different content). The pricing tool generates the text version in a reasonably aligned and readable fashion using white space padding. Saving the text in the Edit Pad into a default CSV file will give us a nice, Excel-compatible, comma-separated text file, with the extra white space paddings trimmed. The Edit Pad has the usual, context-sensitive, 'Help' button.

8.3.7 Visualization interface

Plotting is an important tool, both for the trader and the risk manager, to visualize how price and sensitivities change in response to market conditions. Traders look to their trading system to make such analyses easy. The pricing tool has a built-in plotting window for analysis and visualization.

The plotting module of the pricing tool, like all other modules, is completely separated from the model implementation, so that every time a new product–model pair is selected, the plotting interface automatically primes itself to analyse it. The analysis of the input–output dependence can be carried out in three modes:

1. We can study the variation of one model output (such as the fair value or Delta) as the function of a product input (such as the spot or volatility) in a simple two-dimensional plot. Figure 8.11 shows the plotting interface in two-dimensional mode and the plot output showing the dependence of the fair value of an American call option on the spot price of the underlying.

   Similar to the pricing screen, the plotting interface also sports tool-tips that are sensitive to the parameter the mouse cursor is hovering on, giving us its name and description. We can change the value of any parameter so that the plotting analysis is centred about that pricing scenario defined by the parameter values on the interface. Furthermore, when we change the plotting property of a parameter (such as its range, number of points or the kind of range specification), the interface automatically selects that parameter as an argument to vary for plotting.

2. We can generate a complex three-dimensional surface plot of the variation of one output as a function of two inputs. By clicking on the '3-D' radio button selection, we go to the plotting interface in three-dimensional mode, as shown in Figure 8.12. The figure also shows the plot output showing the dependence of the fair value of an American call option on the spot price as well as the volatility of the underlying.

   In three-dimensional plots, we can choose any of the product input parameters as the X or Y coordinate. For Z, we choose any of the model outputs. In Figure 8.12 top, we can see that the inputs under the group boxes 'X' and 'Y' refer to the same product parameter. This repetition gives rise to a curious problem – we end up with two interfaces to modify each parameter. The plotting window resolves this problem by ganging the two sets of controls together,

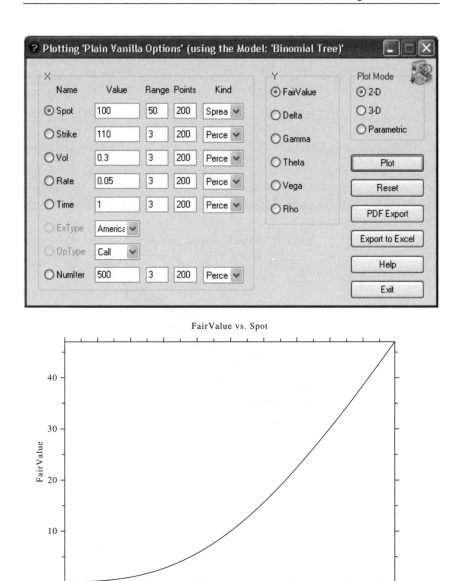

Figure 8.11 Plotting the fair value of an American call option against the spot price of the underlying. The plotting interface is shown at the top and the output at the bottom

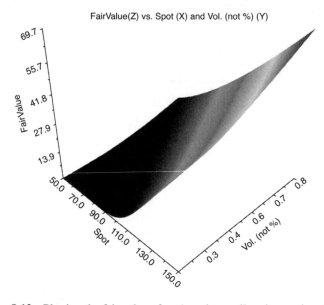

Figure 8.12 Plotting the fair value of an American call option against the spot price and the volatility of the underlying. The plotting interface is shown at the top and the output at the bottom

such that if we modify the parameter using any one of the interfaces, the other one immediately picks up the modification even before we commit the changes.

We can visualize a three-dimensional plot in a variety of ways, similar to the options shown in Figure 8.8 for Matrix plotting. In fact, the underlying code for plotting is the same, and the three-dimensional plotting options window reuses the Matrix visualization interface.

3. We can also study parametric variations in the pricing tool. The parametric plotting option is a tool not commonly found in traditional trading systems. In this mode, we can study the variation of one model output against another. A parametric plot depicts the relationship between two outputs as one input is changed.

   For example, we can study how the fair value and the Gamma vary as we change the spot over a range. Figure 8.13 shows the plotting window in 'Parametric' mode. The Gamma of an American call option is plotted against its fair value (both outputs of the binomial tree model) as we vary the spot price of the underlying over a range.

Common to all plotting windows are the buttons and controls on the right. The 'Plot Mode' lets us switch between the three different modes described above. As we switch from one mode to another, the interface adapts itself in tandem. Below the mode selector, we find the following action buttons:

- The 'Plot' button launches the plot in the current mode.
- The 'Reset' button puts all the parameters back to their default values.
- The 'PDF Export' button creates a printable output of the plot that would be plotted if the 'Plot' button was clicked.
- The 'Export to Excel' generates a CSV (comma separate value) text file of the plot that can be read by spreadsheet programs. This export feature simulates a scenario analysis. For instance, by exporting the plot in Figure 8.12, we get a spot-vol scenario analysis of an American call option prices over the ranges and number of points as specified in the interface.

   The export function reuses the Edit Pad (introduced in Figure 8.6), customized for CSV editing so that the contents are formatted for readability in the window, but trimmed when saved in a file.
- The 'Help' button brings up a context-sensitive help screen describing how to use the plotting interface.

Also common to the three modes are the ranges over which the inputs are changed for plotting purposes, which can be specified in three different ways for a given parameter value V and Range R:

1. Percentage spread. Input V is varied between $V(1 \pm R/100)$.
2. Mid $\pm$ spread. Input is varied between $V \pm R$.
3. Minimum and maximum. Input is varied between $\min(V, R)$ to $\max(V, R)$.
4. The number of points at which the output is computed can also be specified by the user. The default is 200 points for two-dimensional plots, 100 for parameter plots and 15 for three-dimensional plots.

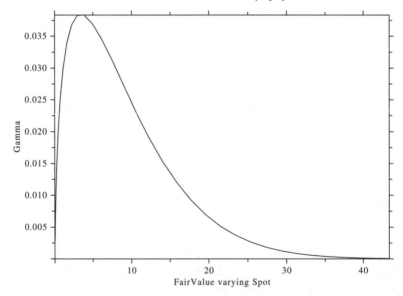

Figure 8.13 Plotting the Gamma of an American call option against its fair value as the spot price is varied as shown. The plotting interface is shown at the top and the output at the bottom

8.3.8   Finite difference engine

The pricing tool has a built-in finite difference sensitivities calculator. The self-adapting finite difference engine, thanks to the clean separation of product–model interface modules, is independent of the product–model pair. The user interface of the finite difference engine adapts itself to the product and model definitions, as we have come to expect.

We can compute the sensitivities of any output parameter from the model with respect to any (continuous) input parameter of the product. Discrete parameters (like option menus) are excluded, but we can compute 'derivatives' with respect to integers (number of iterations, for instance) and complex types (Vectors). For continuous types of input parameters, we get mathematical derivatives defined as

$$\frac{\partial f}{\partial x} = \frac{f(x + \Delta x) - f(x - \Delta x)}{2\Delta x}$$

$$\frac{\partial^2 f}{\partial x^2} = \frac{f(x + \Delta x) + f(x - \Delta x) - 2f(x)}{(\Delta x)^2}$$

where f is an output parameter of the model and x is an input parameter of the product. We can specify the step size Δx either as an absolute increment or as a fractional, relative change. The pricing tool computes the sensitivities around the parameter scenario as specified in the finite difference interface, as shown in Figure 8.14. The finite difference engine does both the first and second derivatives in one go and caches the results so that, if we ask for them again without changing the inputs of the product, we get them with no delay.

This mathematical definition of the sensitivity may run into trouble with market conventions. For instance, Vega is usually defined as the change in the derivative price for 1 % change in the volatility of the underlying (or $\partial f / \partial \sigma$, where σ is the volatility in percentage). If, in the pricing tool, we define the volatility as a fraction rather than as a percentage, we will have to scale the resulting Vega by a factor of 100.

8.4   SUMMARY

In this chapter, we looked at the user interface part of the companion program, the pricing tool. Among its significant strong points are the clean separation between the GUI elements and the mathematical finance libraries, and self-adapting interfaces. In fact, a fully functional, compiled version of the pricing tool contains no mathematical finance intelligence other than some day-count conventions and the notion of the finite difference Greeks (which may be considered too generic to be called 'quant' intelligence). Thanks to this rigorous fire-walling, the pricing tool is able to generate a code template for model implementation and adapts

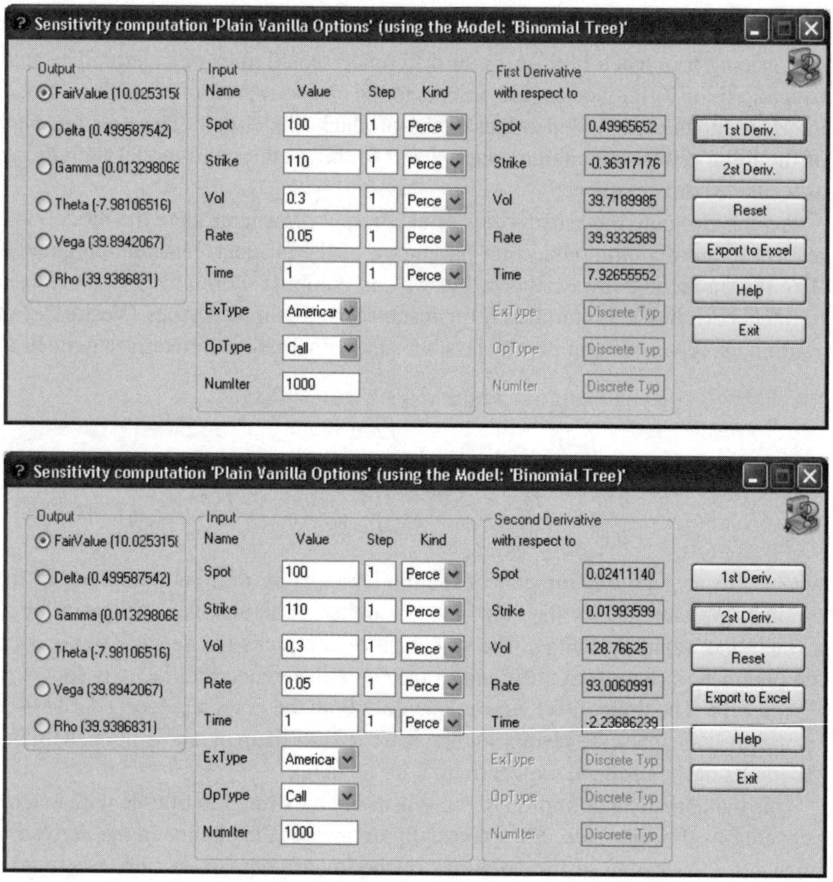

Figure 8.14 Computing finite difference sensitivities of an American call option using the binomial tree pricing model in the pricing tool. The top figure shows the results for first-order derivatives, while the bottom one shows the second order. Note that the input and outputs of types for which the derivatives do not make sense are excluded by the interface

its interfaces and behaviour to any valid product–model combinations, and can 'render' and manipulate them. One can see the similarity between the pricing tool and any document-handling programs (such as a word processor, HTML renderer, image editor, etc.) that are generic and agnostic to the semantics of the document under consideration. They can work with the document through its syntactical validity.

This indifference to the semantics of the product–model combination is highly desirable from a time-to-market perspective. If the pricing tool can grow into a full-fledged trading platform (which is the theme of the next chapter), the mere act of defining a product and its model is all that is needed to provide a validated booking and analysis interface. The generic, agnostic GUIs that work for all products cut down at least one validation step in rolling out a new product or a pricing model.

QUIZ

1. Why is it desirable to keep the GUI 'dumb' by moving the quantitative intelligence away from it?
2. How does the pricing tool resemble a generic word processor?
3. Define an interest rate swap (IRS) using the pricing tool.
4. Edit the IRS using the pricing tool and generate a 'model' to price it.
5. Edit the IRS in its XML form using a text editor and add a new parameter. Study its behaviour in the pricing tool. (You will have to recompile the 'model' DLL.)

9
Pricing Tool to Trading Platform

In the last chapter, we went through the features of the pricing tool from a user's perspective. Despite all its user interface niftiness and its modular design, the pricing tool is not close to being a trading platform. In this chapter, we will first look at some its implementation details and briefly outline how we can add the necessary features to make it a viable trading platform.

In both these topics, we will be brief, and for good reasons. The implementation details, though interesting from a software design and development point of view, may not appeal to all readers. For this reason, we have delegated the detailed source code documentation to the accompanying CD. On the requirements of a real trading platform, we have already spent quite a bit of time (in Chapter 6) highlighting the shortcomings of the pricing tool where applicable. We will, therefore, limit ourselves to high-level descriptions of these topics in this chapter. Such a description may serve as a 'to-do' list of the pricing tool, as well as an introduction to the detailed source code documentation on the CD.

9.1 PRICING TOOL: INTERNALS

The pricing tool uses C++ as its chosen programming language to implement its logic. Its presentation layer is written using simple WinAPI functions. Although it does not have a database layer, it saves product and model information and pricing scenarios in XML format. It can also save and load certain information in comma-separate values, thus creating an easy bridge to spreadsheet applications popular in trading and risk management.

Figure 9.1 shows the high-level user interactions of the pricing tool as a UML use case diagram, where we have depicted the user as the usual stick man. Our initial interactions with the pricing tool fall into four categories:

1. Definition. Our first order of business is to define products and associate models with them. The product and model creation interfaces allow us to save the definitions into XML files that we can read later for future use, further fine tuning or manipulation.
2. Modification. We use the same product/model creation interfaces to edit them. The XML read and write extensions exist in this use case as well.
3. Configuration. We define a model that takes the product parameters as its input to compute a set of outputs that we specify. Once we have defined a

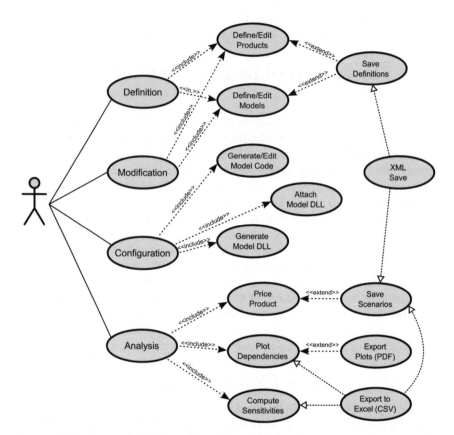

Figure 9.1 Use case depiction of the pricing tool showing how a user interacts with it. The user has the option to define, modify or analyse a product–model pair. He can also configure and edit various products and models already defined and saved

product–model pair, it is time to configure the model implementation. For this, we let the pricing tool create a skeleton implementation and add our quantitative and finance intelligence to it. We them compile it into a DLL and attach it to the product definition. This is the only programming step we need to do while using the pricing tool.

4. Analysis. With the product–model pairs defined and configured, the pricing tool automatically gives us a rich set of analysis tools. We get pricing and plotting interfaces, and a finite difference engine for Greeks calculations.

In order to describe these user interactions, we can divide the pricing tool implementation code into three parts:

1. Common quantitative finance processing that applies to all pricing models.
2. The main graphical user interfaces (GUI) that control and guide the user interaction.
3. Common service windows and controls implementing a consistent look and feel of the program.

Let us start with the common classes and functions implementing the quant finance processing that forms the backbone of the program. We can then move on to understanding how these modules talk to the GUI elements. This sequence gives us the best advantage in terms of lucidity.

9.1.1 Common quant classes

Figure 9.2 describes the program design that supports the quantitative aspects of the pricing tool. As this UML class hierarchy diagram illustrates, we try to refactor the source code to the extent possible by implementing the required functionality early in the base classes. As a result, all the objects in the pricing tool derive from a `Thing` class, whose main job is to provide identification methods – a name and a description. It also provides a basic implementation of the XML input/output methods so that every object knows how to save itself to a file and load itself back.

Parameters are common to both products and models. We make use of this commonality to design a base class `Base` for them, inheriting from `Thing`. This `Base` class has a vector of parameters and utility functions to manipulate them. It also has specific XML input/output methods that handle the parameters. The parameters belong to the `Param` class, which is again derived from `Thing`. The `Param` class provides type information, stores plotting specifications (which we use when we try to plot an output against an input parameter) and service methods to view, export to CSV, plot and edit parameters. These service methods expose GUI functionalities of parameters and outputs.

Deriving from the `Base` class is `BaseProduct`, which contains one or more models as a vector, and methods to manipulate them. It also has methods that provide GUI functions like editing itself.

The `Product` and `Model` classes are essentially the same as their `BaseProduct` and `BaseModel` variants. They exist for historical reasons and provide another layer of abstraction should we ever need it. We will need this layer when we implement a batch job that loops over the trades and processes them.

An object of the class `BaseProduct` evaluates itself using its default model, which is of the type `BaseModel`. We derive `BaseModel` also from the `Base` class. The main difference between the model and product classes is that the models contain a vector of outputs and methods associated with model editing and DLL assignment.

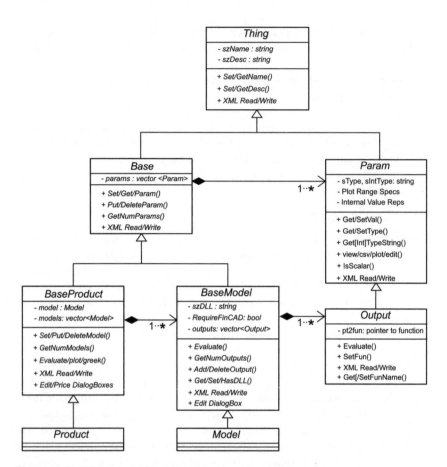

Figure 9.2 UML class hierarchy of the quant part of the pricing tool

A model output belongs to the Output class, which derives itself from the Param class. In addition to the methods and members of a parameter, the output also has a function pointer to the DLL entry point that can evaluate it and service methods specific to it.

In Figure 9.3, we have the class hierarchy of the Param and Output classes. The Param class holds any input and output of the types supported in the pricing tool. The type is stored in every class instance as a string as well as an enumerated integer. The type of a Param object can be scalar (int or double) or a Vector or a Matrix.

The nonscalar types also include date vectors (a vector of dates, internally represented as a normal Vector) and curves (a matrix of order $[r \times 2]$, where the first column contains dates, implemented as a normal Matrix). The scalar

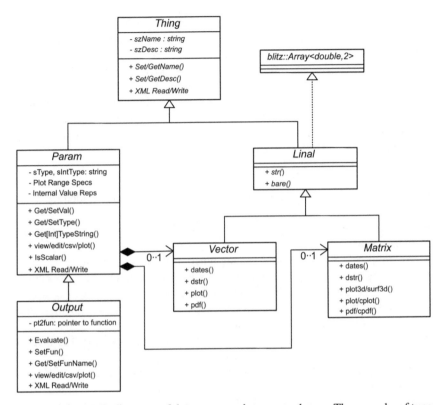

Figure 9.3 UML diagrams of the `Param` and `Output` classes. They may be of type `Vector` or `Matrix`, which are based on Blitz arrays

parameters can also masquerade as special types such as menus (internally stored as an `int`) or date (stored as a `double`). These special types, despite their reused internal representation, have dedicated input and output handlers. For instance, we can specify a date in its input GUI as 1m, which the pricing tool interprets as today + one month. For a normal `double` input, on the other hand, 1m would mean one million (and be translated as 1,000,000).

Common to all types of parameters are a few methods: view (a message box containing a pretty-printed version of the parameter), edit (an interface to modify its value), plot (quick visualization for vectors, matrices and their variants as curves and date vectors): and CSV (an export function, if applicable).

The nonscalar types (`Vector` and `Matrix`) are derived from `blitz::Array<double,2>` (which implements a two-dimensional array as a part of the freely available Blitz++ library), thereby inheriting a large set of tools and memory management functionality. The inheritance is done in two stages – through a LinAl (Linear Algebra) class, which implements a string export function for the derived classes, both as a bare string and a decorated string appropriate for pretty-printing and display.

A Vector is an $[r \times 1]$ array, while a Matrix is an $[r \times c]$ array. These classes implement visualization methods, such as various plotting options as well as export functions. A Matrix, if it holds a date vector, can export and pretty-print it. It can also plot and export the plot (both as a CSV file and in PDF format). It uses a common GUI element Plotter to provide the user with the possible plotting and export options. The Vector object also has similar methods.

We can summarize the class hierarchy as follows:

- Every object in the program is a Thing, which knows how to identify itself, set its name and description.
- A Param inherits those properties and adds information about its type and default value.
- An Output is a Param with a pricing function associated with it.
- A Param can be of type integer (typically for keeping track of user selections and options), double (scalar values), Vector or Matrix, or Date or a Date Vector. Of these, Vector, Date Vector and Matrix are classes inherited from LinAl (linear algebra object), which in turn is a Thing.
- A Base encapsulates the methods common to a Model or a Product, and it knows how to add or delete a Param.
- A Product knows how to add and delete a Model, how to price itself and how to get edited.
- A Model knows how to set its DLL and get edited.
- The BaseProduct and BaseModel classes are strictly not necessary in the current implementation of the pricing tool, but may become necessary when we start defining more complicated products and developing batch processing.
- All objects know how to write themselves out in XML and read back from a file.
- A Model, when read back from an XML file, will look for its pricing functions in its associated DLL. If not found, it will disable the associated analysis actions (pricing, plotting and finite difference Greeks).

9.1.2   Main interfaces

The six main windows are all instances of WinAPI DialogBox. Such windows are easy to implement in any modern integrated development environment (IDE). In the pricing tool, however, they are implemented 'by hand,' manually specifying the window dimensions and handling the WinAPI call-backs.

In WinAPI, all windows have a message handling call-back function. (In some languages such as C#, the message passing interface is hidden behind an event-driven paradigm.) The call-back function receives messages whenever an 'event' takes place on the window. By responding to these messages, and by posting or sending other messages, a developer can customize the appearance and behaviour of the window.

In addition to the call-back function, the window also requires a static layout definition, called its resources in WinAPI. The resources may use constants that are usually held in a corresponding resource header file. Thus, each window in the pricing tool comes with three files. For the main control interface, these files are:

1. The call-back function in a C++ file, with names like `SelectProc.cc`.
2. The resource file, e.g. `SelectProc.rc`.
3. A resource header file, e.g. `SelectProc.rh`.

All the user interfaces in the pricing tool incorporate tool-tips, context-sensitive help and an 'About This Program' button on the top right corner that brings up a splash screen. Before going through the specifics of these GUI windows, let us look at how we implement these common features.

The tool-tip implementation uses the fact that all windows (including controls like buttons and text edit boxes) have a resource identifier, which we declare as constants in the resource header (`.rh`) file. The resource header file then finds itself included in the resource (`.rc`) and the source code (`.cc`) files, which gives us a clever mechanism for associating tool-tip strings with GUI controls. In WinAPI, we can specify resource strings in a string table and associate them with numbers. By using the same constant identifier name for the resource string as the GUI controls (see `tooltip.rc` for the string table), we can easily keep track of which string goes with which control.

Context sensitive help pops up when we hit the F1 key (Windows default key for help) or the 'Help' button on the GUI window. The help window that comes up knows the window from which we invoke it, which is why we consider it sensitive to the context. We use the HTML help library to generate the help file (`PricingTool.chm`), which is a compiled HTML file. This CHM file contains the HTML source files within and can display the page that we request. When we invoke the help from `SelectProc`, for instance, we request `SelectProc.htm`, thereby implementing the context sensitivity. In addition, we keep the handle to the help window (`g_Hlp`) in our global namespace `pqd` so that we can reuse it.

The last common feature is the 'About This Program' button and the associated splash screen. We use it for showing the user some information about the website of *Principles of Quantitative Development* and for branding. We also display the same window as the splash screen upon program launch. The splash screen and the 'About This Program' windows are a `DialogBox` (implemented as `AboutProc` with its associated `.cc`, `.rc` and `.rh` files) like all other GUI windows, but with special characteristics. The tiny icon is, in fact, the program icon inserted into the

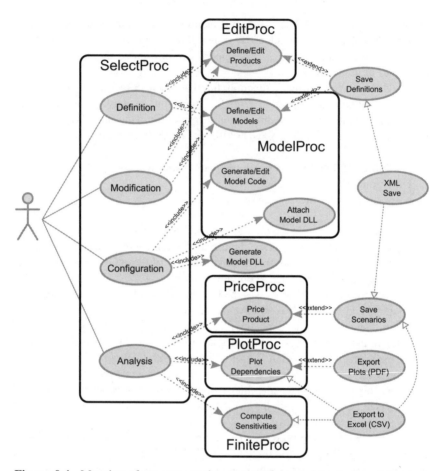

Figure 9.4 Mapping of use cases to the user interface modules in the pricing tool. Each of the user interface modules handles one or more use cases

resource file as CTEXT (text box) control, but with the icon resource as the default text.

In the pricing tool, we have six interfaces, each of which corresponds to their three (.cc, .rc and .rh) files. These interfaces respond to various aspects of the user case diagram, as shown in Figure 9.4. We will go through the six interface modules one by one. In addition to the standard windows message handling, these interface modules also handle the quantitative finance tasks. Much of the intelligence behind these tasks is abstracted away from the user interface call-back functions, although a complete separation is neither possible nor perhaps advisable.

SelectProc

`SelectProc` implements the main control GUI and gives us the ability to save and load product/model definition files in XML, as well as an initialization file, which is a list of XML files to be loaded at start-up. The products thus loaded are kept in a `std::vector` of a `Product`. Each product read in also has a model definition, internally stored as a `std::vector` of a `Model` member of the `Product` object. The model, in turn, may have an associated DLL implementing it.

`SelectProc` module handles the four categories of use cases in the first layer of Figure 9.4, where we can create new products or models, edit existing ones, configure a DLL implementation of the model or perform various analyses.

In order to enhance user experience, `SelectProc` has context menus and other context-aware features. Context menus are the options we present to the end users when they click the right mouse button on the product and model list boxes in the GUI. We implement context menus by responding to the WM_CONTEXTMENU message in the call-back function. We have to find the location of the mouse click and give different menu items depending on whether the user clicks on a product name, model name or in the empty region within the list boxes. Figure 9.5 illustrates how `SelectProc` segments the GUI window.

Also active in the list boxes are the keyboard shortcuts that are natural for inserting, deleting and editing (namely the insert, delete and enter keys) a product or a model. We implement this functionality by responding to the WM_VKEYDOWN message.

By responding to the LBL_SELCHANGE message and identifying the originating window control as the product selection list box, we can populate the model selection box with the pricing models available for that product. Once the user has selected a model as well, we provide some information about the product–model pair in the information area. Figure 9.5 illustrates the various hot regions in the `SelectProc` interface.

From the `SelectProc DialogBox`, we provide the user with single-click access to various actions that map the use cases in Figure 9.4:

1. Product creation, editing and deletion.
2. Model (for the selected product) creation, editing and deletion.
3. Loading an XML list of product and model definitions.
4. Saving the current definitions to a file.
5. Help specific to the `SelectProc` window.
6. Analysis options such as price, plot and the Greeks, once the user selects a product and a model.

Note that the product/model editing, pricing, plotting and Greek computation windows are all of a singleton kind. If the user clicks on the button to launch

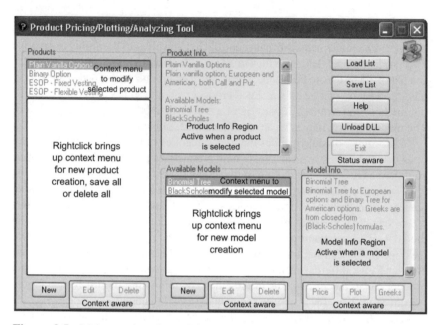

Figure 9.5 Main user interface of the pricing tool and its active regions, showing the regions where the product or model-specific context menus are present, status sensitivity of buttons and the information regions

the interface, we first look for its existence by following global variables (in the pqd namespace) corresponding to their window handles. Furthermore, as shown in Figure 9.5, the various action buttons on the interface are context and status sensitive. Such painstaking attention to detail is crucial to the success of the program in term of its eventual acceptance or rejection by the end users.

EditProc

The first use case included in 'Definition' (referring to Figure 9.4) is to define a new product. We use the GUI module EditProc to handle this case. This module can also edit an existing product, which is part of the second use case. In this module, we have implemented a dynamic behaviour – as the user adds a parameter, the interface grows in anticipation of another one. Figure 9.6 shows this dynamic behaviour. The interface is also aware of its modification status so that it can enable the save button only if the user changes some part of the definition and warn the user of potential loss of data on unintentional exits.

Common to all interfaces in the pricing tool are edit boxes that are aware of the data type so that they exhibit behaviour appropriate to the variable under modification. Ubiquitous tool-tips and a context-aware help window guide the user further.

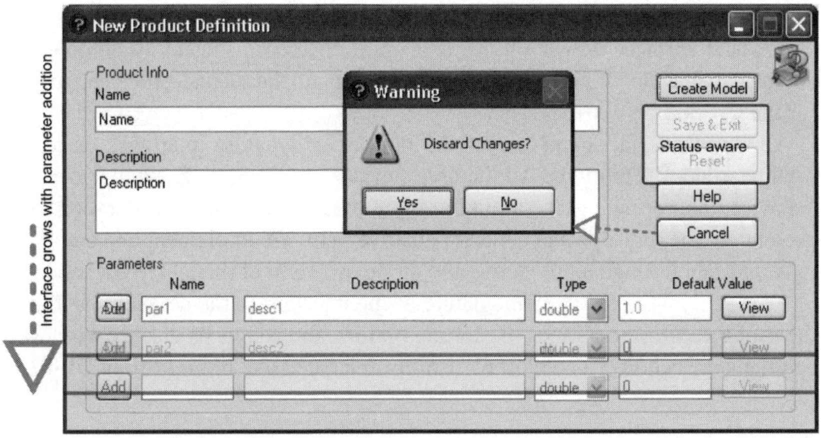

Figure 9.6 Product editing interface showing its dynamic nature and status sensitivity

The user can launch a model creation `DialogBox` directly from `EditProc` by clicking on the 'Create Model' button.

ModelProc

`ModelProc` overlaps the first, second and third use cases in Figure 9.4. The user can define a model (after having defined a product) using this GUI element. He can also generate and edit the model implementation code from the same interface, and, after creating a DLL for his pricing model, he can configure the product–model pair to use it.

`ModelProc` is also a dynamic window like `EditProc`. We can think of the concept of dynamic user interfaces as the rendering process of a script or mark-up driven product and model description, much like a web browser rendering an HTML page. In the pricing tool, we use XML to store product and model descriptions. After we construct the product–model objects in the program, whether read-in from an XML file for editing or created based on user inputs, we use its characteristics to drive the user interface. This method makes the GUI modules thin and agnostic to the product–model details and the program very modular and scalable. A new product development, for instance, does not call for a dedicated GUI development effort and its validation.

Analysis interfaces

The three user interfaces facilitating the analysis use cases depicted in Figure 9.4 are `PriceProc`, `PlotProc` and `FiniteProc`. `PriceProc` implements the product pricing interface, while `PlotProc` is for plotting various dependency curves and surfaces. `FiniteProc` is a finite difference sensitivity computation engine capable of computing both the first-order and the second-order sensitivities (or the Greeks).

All three interfaces implement the notion of dynamic interfaces driven by product–model definitions. All the user controls are again type-aware and extend behaviour appropriate to the input or output parameter under consideration. Also present are the tool-tips and context-sensitive help. We implement this consistent look and feel through ample reuse and modularization of the underlying code.

`PlotProc` takes the dynamic nature of the interface to the next level – it gives the user three different kinds of plotting options and adapts its display window to suit the user's choice. The plotting itself is delegated to a library called DISLIN.

9.1.3   Pluggable pricing models

One of the other major features of the pricing tool is its ability to generate a template for model implementation. We can also view this feature as a rendering of the in-memory product and model objects. In other words, we generate the template code based on the product parameters as the inputs and model outputs as the results. Once the pricing tool writes out the template for a model implementation, the end user edits it to impart the quantitative intelligence to it. He then compiles it into a DLL and attaches it to the model from the `ModelProc` interface. Thus, the end user can augment the pricing tool at will without ever having to recompile the main program.

We achieve this clear separation between the quant model and the rest of the pricing tool through a rigid definition of the interface. The model interacts with the pricing tool through a set of evaluator functions, one for each output. All these evaluator functions have the same signature.

```
template<class T>
void pfunc(double d[], int n[], Vector* v[],
           Matrix* m[], T* out) ;
```

All of the evaluator functions are available in the DLL that the user attaches to the model. During the process of attaching the DLL, `ModelProc` looks up the evaluator function (whose name it knows from the model definition) and holds the function pointer in the output object. If not found, `ModelProc` issues a warning.

Later, when the pricing tool asks an output to evaluate itself, it uses the function pointer to reach the evaluator in the DLL. The DLL code (the code that the pricing tool generates) localizes all the computational logic in one function and sets up all the input parameters and output variables as global in the scope of the file. The task of this single intelligent function is to compute all the outputs based on the inputs. Since the outputs are global, the evaluator functions merely pick them up and dispatch the requested outputs back to the caller. In order to save time, the evaluator checks if any of the inputs have changed before embarking on computing the outputs.

9.1.4 Reusable components

All these GUI modules make use of a set of service windows and helper functions. Reusing such building blocks, a basic principle in software engineering, gives us maintainability because any potential mistakes need to be corrected in one basic unit. Such modular reuse also ensures a consistent look and feel, enhancing the user experience.

EditPad

We use `EditPad` as the user input or modification interface for complex data types (`Vectors`, `Matrix`, menus, etc.) as well as for presentation and output operations such as DLL template generation. The edit pad is a simple notebook-like control that can operate both in 'save' and 'load' modes. In other words, it can either display information to the user, let him modify and save it, or allow him to load a file from disk to view it. In either mode, the text that he loads into `EditPad` is available in the calling function when he exits from it.

In addition to the standard Undo, Select, Cut, Copy and Paste buttons, `EditPad` also features a Help button that brings up a help window. The help also shows up when the user presses the Windows shortcut key F1. We can customize the text that the help window displays, making `EditPad` very versatile.

We pass all the inputs to `EditPad` (including the help text) through an array of `std::string`. However, to do that, we have to disguise its memory pointer as a WinAPI-specific `LPARAM` pointer because `EditPad` is also a `DialogBox` with its own call-back function `EditPadProc`. Among the parameters we pass to it is a flag indicating whether the text is a CSV (comma-separated value) file content, in which case `EditPad` will use appropriate formatting and aligning techniques to present the text in a user-friendly fashion.

Plotter

In quantitative finance, we often need to visualize three-dimensional data, such as volatility surfaces or the price dependence, as the underlying spot and its volatility vary over some range. In order to give the user as much flexibility as possible in visualizing such three-dimensional data, we designed an independent interface, `Plotter`, which we reuse for all such plotting.

Like `EditPad`, `Plotter` is also implemented as a `DialogBox` with a call-back function. We pass the memory pointers to the matrix and X and Y vectors to plot through the LPARAM argument. Once we have all the information to plot, we present the interpolated, ready-to-plot matrix in an uneditable text box and offer the user various options to plot. The user can export the plots in PDF format from the Plotter interface. We also provide ways of projecting and visualizing various views and splices of the matrix.

Message boxes

WinAPI gives us message boxes that we can use to grab a user's attention and get his feedback. In order to make the message boxes more robust and developer-friendly, we overload and template them in the pricing tool.

```cpp
//! messagebox that shows anything
template <class T>
void mb(const T& val)
{
  MessageBox (NULL, ToString(val).c_str(),
              "Information", MB_OK|MB_TASKMODAL);
}
template <class T1, class T2>
void mb(const T1& title, const T2& val)
{
 MessageBox (NULL, ToString(val).c_str(),
             ToString(title).c_str(),
             MB_OK|MB_TASKMODAL);
}
```

We also use similar templating techniques to pretty-print vectors of any type. The ToString() function is an example of a templated type converter.

Type converters

ToString is a utility function (inspired by the corresponding C# method of the same name and purpose).

```cpp
//! returns the string value of any class
template <class T>
std::string ToString(const T& val)
{
  std::ostringstream os ;
  os << val ;
  return os.str() ;
}
```

With templated message boxes and anything-to-string converters, we have easy means to manage the communication between the pricing tool and its end user in a consistent manner. We use such type converters and overloaded functions throughout the implementation of the pricing tool, especially at the utility and service functions layer, improving readability and maintainability.

9.1.5 Source code documentation

Also crucial to enhancing maintainability, and hence the longevity of the program, is exhaustive source code documentation. In the CD accompanying this book, we have included `PricingTool-source.chm` – a fully cross-referenced compiled HTML help file that contains its source code documentation.

This documentation is generated by Doxygen from the source code itself, and hence kept current. Details including hierarchies (both forward and backward) are also pictorially represented in the source code documentation, which will allow code maintenance and help prevent bugs.

9.1.6 External packages

The companion CD that comes with this book contains the pricing tool installation package (as a folder to be copied to the reader's computer) and the source code. The following packages are used in the implementation of the pricing tool:

1. Cygwin. Linux-like environment for Windows, with all the tools necessary to compile and maintain a software project. The pricing tool was originally developed and deployed from a Cygwin platform. More information at: http://www.cygwin.com/.
2. Visual Studio Express. The pricing tool can be built using the Visual C++ Express Edition – the free version of the popular Visual Studio development environment from Microsoft. More information about the Express edition at: http://www.microsoft.com/express/vc/.
3. TinyXml, a simple, small, C++ XML parser that can be easily integrated into other programs. More information and documentation can be found at: http://sourceforge.net/projects/tinyxml, http://www.grinninglizard.com/tinyxml.
4. Blitz++, a C++ class library for scientific computing that provides performance on, a par with Fortran 77/90. Vector and Matrix are implemented using the Array class in Blitz++. See: http://sourceforge.net/projects/blitz/.
5. DISLIN, a high-level plotting library for displaying data as curves, polar plots, bar graphs, pie charts, three-dimensional colour plots, surfaces, contours and maps. More information at: http://www.dislin.de/. Note that DISLIN is not free for commercial use.
6. Boost, for Date support. More information at: http://www.boost.org, under Date-Time: http://www.boost.org/doc/html/date_time.html.

9.2   FUTURE ENHANCEMENTS

Despite all the good things going for it, the pricing tool is still quite far from being a trading system because it lacks a few crucial features. We discussed these shortcomings earlier. We may be able to add on the missing features and call the pricing tool a full-fledged trading platform, but it may not be a wise course of action. A far wiser modus operandi would be to start from scratch, by talking to the business units in order to understand and document their requirements and by designing a robust and scalable architecture to support them.

Many of the ideas and concepts in the pricing tool architecture are useful, and we should keep them in mind as guiding principles. In particular, a user interface that stays agnostic to the intricacies of the structure it is displaying is a powerful idea. Such script-driven GUIs can greatly improve time-to-market and make release cycles short and painless. Another powerful concept is the clean separation of the pricing logic so that the end user can augment the program without touching its core components. This feature, if implemented well, also cuts down the time-to-market – one of the basic motivations behind embarking on an in-house trading solution.

For the sake of completeness and at the risk of repeating ourselves, we will go over the missing features of the pricing tool once more. The most basic missing feature is user authentication and security. Then comes the ability to manage the trade life cycle and maintain its history. From an architecture perspective, what is missing is a trade database and a market data representation.

9.2.1   Trade database

The database is the central component of a trading platform. In fact, a trading platform is essentially a database application. Once we have a good data representation schema and a table structure, we can decide and implement the database layer. In our pricing tool, we use flat XML files for persistence, which are a flexible, yet highly structured, storage medium. If we want to deploy a real database layer, we can either translate the XML schema into a relational database structure or decide to store the entire XML string in a database, leaving the deserialization up to the program.

Regardless of which database strategy we adopt, we have to build on it to handle adequately the trade inception workflow and status management. Without the workflow (where the front office can save a trade and forward it to the middle office for verification, and the middle office can either approve or reject it, etc.) the pricing tool cannot claim to be a trading platform. Inception workflow also includes the appropriate user interfaces to carry out the approval/rejection tasks. Along with this trade status management, we also need to build audit trails and devise an adequate mechanism to access and display it.

9.2.2   Market data

Just as we separated the quantitative logic from the rest of the plumbing in the pricing tool, we have to modularize the market element also. As we saw earlier, handling the market data is a large-scale undertaking in its own right. Although the pricing tool has a trade representation in terms of XML serialization, it does not attempt to deal with market data in any meaningful fashion. If we want to incorporate market data into the pricing tool, we have to spend considerable effort designing it based on the principles we described earlier.

In particular, we have to support static data (portfolio, approved products, staff names, their access privileges, etc.) and reference data (index setup, rates/curves/currency/bond/equity configurations, etc.) in addition to live market data. This support will include appropriate user interfaces, along with access checks, to manipulate static and reference data, interfaces to live market data, storage, end-of-day rates fixing – all those features that we discussed earlier in the book.

Big Picture 9.1:   Market Data – Quantization Errors

To illustrate the intricacies of market data and rates management we describe one particular problem in rates computation and a possible solution. The problem is in the way the market quotes NDF prices in terms of swap points and how it propagates to offshore interest rates.

Traders have trouble constructing yield curves for currencies that have exchange restrictions. For such currencies, over-the-counter markets for forwards usually develop in the form of nondeliverable forwards (NDF). From these markets, one can deduce an offshore rate using interest rate parity against a liquid currency, typically the US dollar. These rate calculations are affected by liquidity issues in the NDF market as well as numerical problems. One such numerical problem is the round-off errors inherent in the way the market quotes the NDF price in terms of swap points. Let us take a close look at this quantization error and examine a solution to improve the accuracy of the implied yield curve. Improved accuracy stabilizes the implied yield curve between consecutive days and, consequently, improves the stability of profit and loss figures of the associated portfolios.

The principle of interest rate parity gives us a method of implying the interest rate of a (possibly offshore) currency from the forwards market. Interest rate parity between two currencies can be easily derived by requiring no-arbitrage between two investment options, as shown in the figure above (Exhibit A):

1. Start with \$1. Deposit it in a USD account bearing an interest rate r_u for a duration T. At time $= T$, convert the principal of \$1 and the accrued interest at the exchange rate \$1 $= n$ MYR. The current estimate of the exchange rate is the forward rate. Assume that the resulting sum is A (in MYR).

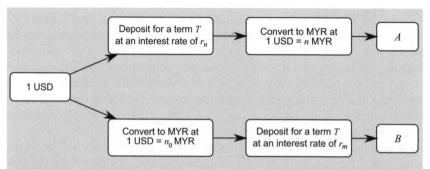

Exhibit A   Two investment options for 1 USD. By the no-arbitrage argument, both options should yield the same returns

2. Start with \$1. Convert it into MYR at the spot exchange rate of \$1 = n_0 MYR. Deposit it in an MYR account bearing an interest rate of r_m for a duration T. Assume that the resulting sum is B (in MYR).

If the sum resulting from the first route is not the same as the one from the second one, risk-free arbitrage opportunities exist. Efficiency of the market ensures that the exchange rates and the interest rates vary in such a fashion as to eliminate arbitrage opportunities. Therefore, $A = B$:

$$A = \left(1 + r_u \frac{T}{N_u}\right) n$$

$$B = \left(1 + r_m \frac{T}{N_m}\right) n_0$$

where

$$
\begin{array}{rl}
n_0 = & \text{spot rate MYR/USD} \\
n = & \text{forward rate MYR/USD} \\
r_u = & \text{interest rate in USD} \\
N_u = & \text{day count factor in USD} \\
r_m = & \text{interest rate in MYR} \\
N_m = & \text{day count factor in MYR}
\end{array}
$$

With $A = B$, we get the MYR implied rate as

$$r_m = \left[\frac{n}{n_0}\left(1 + r_u \frac{T}{N_u}\right) - 1\right] \frac{N_m}{T}$$

Thus, knowing the forward rates between USD and MYR and the yield curve in USD, we can imply a yield curve in MYR. If we get the forward rates from the NDF market, the implied curve is the offshore curve.

We can further simplify this relationship by assuming the same day count convention in USD and MYR for convenience (implying $N_u = N_m = 1$):

$$r_m = \left[\frac{n}{n_0}(1 + r_u T) - 1\right]\frac{1}{T}$$

In the market, the forward rates are typically quoted in terms of swap points. Thus, n can be expressed as

$$n = n_0 + \Delta$$

where Δ represents swap points. Since Δ is usually quoted with a step size of 5 or 10 basis points, there is an inherent error of half the step size in the market quotes. Such quantization errors lead to significant errors when T is small. We can see this by rewriting the equation for r_m in terms of Δ:

$$r_m = \left[\frac{n_0 + \Delta}{n_0}\left(1 + r_u\frac{T}{N_u} - 1\right)\right]\frac{N_m}{T}$$

$$= \left[\frac{\Delta}{n_0} + r_u\frac{T}{N_u}\left(1 + \frac{\Delta}{n_0}\right)\right]\frac{N_m}{T}$$

If the quantization error on Δ is $\delta\Delta$, then the error on r_m is

$$\delta r_m = \frac{\partial}{r_m}\partial\Delta\delta\Delta = \left(\frac{\delta\Delta}{n_0} + r_u\frac{T}{N_u}\frac{\delta\Delta}{n_0}\right)\frac{N_m}{T}$$

Since T is expressed in years, the second term in the parenthesis is about two orders of magnitude smaller than the first one, and can be neglected:

$$\delta r_m \approx \frac{\delta\Delta}{n_0}\frac{N_m}{T}$$

Thus, for the same quantization error in quoted swap points, the error on the implied rate is more significant for shorter maturities.

From the equations for A and B, we can derive an expression for swap points Δ:

$$A = \left(1 + r_u\frac{T}{N_u}\right)n = B = \left(1 + r_m\frac{T}{N_m}\right)n_0$$

$$\Delta = n_0\left(\frac{1 + r_m T/N_m}{1 + r_u T/N_u} - 1\right)$$

Assuming same day count conventions to simplify the algebra, one gets

$$\Delta = n_0\left(\frac{1 + r_m T}{1 + r_u T} - 1\right)$$

Using Taylor series expansion, we approximate Δ as

$$\Delta \approx n_0 \left[(1 + r_m T)(1 - r_u T + r_u^2 T^2) - 1 \right]$$

which can be simplified as

$$\Delta = n_0 \left[(r_m - r_u)T + r_u(r_m - r_u)T^2 + r_m r_u^2 T^3 \right]$$

or

$$\frac{\Delta}{T} = n_0 \left[(r_m - r_u) + r_u(r_m - r_u)T + r_m r_u^2 T^2 \right]$$

If the coefficient of T^2 is small for typical values of interest rates and maturities, Δ / T can be considered linear.

Typically, r_u and r_m are within a factor of two of each other. Taking the values $r_u \sim 0.05$, $r_m \sim 0.05$ and $r_u - r_m \sim 0.03$, we get

$$\Delta = n_0(0.03T + 0.0015T^2 + 0.000\,125T^3)$$

The quadratic term is two orders of magnitude smaller than the constant term and can be safely ignored. Even the linear term is an order of magnitude smaller than the constant term, so that Δ / T is almost constant.

We have shown that the transformed variable Δ / T is linear as a function of the maturity T. In the following discussion, we will use this fact to our advantage.

Note that Δ is constrained to be zero when the maturity $T = 0$. This constraint merely reiterates the trivial fact that spot transactions are carried out at the spot rate. Though trivial, this fact provides an anchor point in the regression fitting described below.

From the market, we get a set of swap points Δ_i corresponding to maturities T_i. We define a variable

$$y_i = \frac{\Delta_i}{T_i}$$

Let the quantization error on Δ_i be δ, which is independent of i because the step size is independent of the tenor for which the swap point is quoted. The error on y_i is, therefore, inversely proportional to T_i:

$$\delta y_i = \frac{\delta}{T_i}$$

This is illustrated in the figure below (Exhibit B).

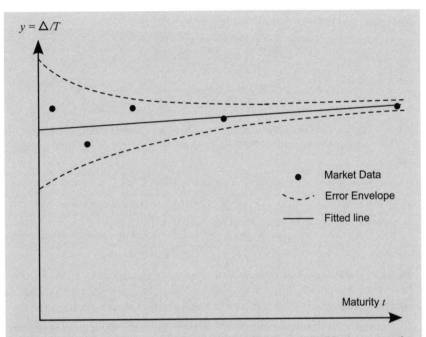

Exhibit B Expected error envelope in the variable $y = \Delta/T$. The errors are inversely proportional to maturity, so that, at short maturities, the error is large

Since we expect a linear relationship between y and t, the function used for fitting is

$$y = at + b$$

In order to account for the error envelope, we use a χ^2 minimization for fitting:

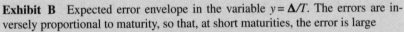

$$\chi^2 = \sum \left(\frac{y_i - aT_i - b}{\delta y_i} \right)^2$$
$$= \frac{1}{\delta^2} \sum (y_i - aT_i - b)^2 T_i^2$$

At the minimum of χ^2,

$$\frac{\partial \chi^2}{\partial a} = 0 \Rightarrow \sum (y_i - aT_i - b)T_i^3 = 0$$
$$\frac{\partial \chi^2}{\partial b} = 0 \Rightarrow \sum (y_i - aT_i - b)T_i^2 = 0$$

Note that

$$\frac{\partial^2 \chi^2}{\partial a^2} = 2 \sum T_i^4 > 0$$

$$\frac{\partial^2 \chi^2}{\partial b^2} = 2 \sum T_i^2 > 0$$

Thus, when the first derivatives are zero, χ^2 is guaranteed to be a minimum.

The two equations setting the first derivatives to zero can be solved for a and b:

$$a = \frac{\sum T_i^3 y_i \sum T_i^2 - \sum T_i^2 y_i \sum T_i^3}{\sum T_i^2 \sum T_i^4 - (\sum T_i^3)^2}$$

$$b = \frac{\sum T_i^3 y_i \sum T_i^3 - \sum T_i^2 y_i \sum T_i^4}{(\sum T_i^3)^2 - \sum T_i^2 \sum T_i^4}$$

Though the solutions look complicated, they are computationally efficient. The form of the solutions is different from normal linear regression because we have assigned a lower weight to points with larger errors. Linear regression (as applied to straight-line fitting) typically assigns equal weights to all the (x, y) pairs.

Once we have a and b, we recompute the swap point for any maturity T as:

$$\Delta_i^{(f)} = T_i(aT_i + b)$$

As expected, $\Delta^{(f)} = 0$ for $T = 0$, enforcing the spot rate for spot transactions.

Using the fitted swap points, the implied rate can be recomputed as

$$r_m = \left[\frac{n_0 + \Delta}{n_0} \left(1 + r_u \frac{T}{N_u} - 1 \right) \right] \frac{N_m}{T}$$

$$= \left[\frac{\Delta}{n_0} + r_u \frac{T}{N_u} \left(1 + \frac{\Delta}{n_0} \right) \right] \frac{N_m}{T}$$

Note that the second form offers better numerical stability because of smaller round-off errors.

While the approximation of linearity and the fitting methodology presented above are theoretically sound, we need to take into account certain considerations before we can apply this method in practice. When we accept the fitted swap points as real and use them for profit and loss calculations and risk analysis, we are using more information than the market is actually providing. This implicit extrapolation can be troublesome from a control point of view. How do we ensure that the fitted values are not too far away from the market values? On what basis do we judge the acceptability of the difference between the fitted values and market values? These considerations prompt us to set a conservative limit on the allowed movement in the values.

Using our notations earlier, we can express the quantization errors in swap points as

$$\text{Swap points} = \Delta \pm \delta/2$$

For instance, the market quoted swap points for USD/MYR NDF are quantized at 0.0010. This means that if the market quotes a swap point of 1 month NDF at 0.0020, the 'real' value could be anywhere between 0.0015 to 0.002 499. In other words, all the values in the range $0.0015 \le \Delta < 0.0025$ are quantized to $\Delta = 0.0020$.

Therefore, we can constrain our fitted values to within the range of $\Delta_i \pm \delta/2$ without compromising the practioner's dictum of never disregarding a market quote. Taking this constraint into account, we can write our equation for a constraint-fitted swap point as follows:

$$\Delta_i^{(c)} = T_i(aT_i + b) \quad \text{if} |\Delta_i^{(f)} - \Delta_i| < \frac{\delta_i}{2}$$

$$= \Delta_i + \frac{\delta_i}{2} \quad \text{if} \Delta_i^{(f)} > \Delta_i + \frac{\delta_i}{2}$$

$$= \Delta_i - \frac{\delta_i}{2} \quad \text{if} \Delta_i^{(f)} < \Delta_i - \frac{\delta_i}{2}$$

The effect of this constraint on the fitted implied rate is shown in the illustration below.

Let us consider the generation of a yield curve for MYR from the USD/MYR spot rate, the USD yield curve and the NDF swap points quoted in the market for USD/MYR nondeliverable forwards. The data used in the following example are for 18 October 2006.

The spot rate (n_0) used in this illustration is 1 USD = 3.67 MYR. The USD yield curve as of 18 October 2006 is given in the table in Exhibit C. Market quoted swap points Δ_i for USD/MYR NDF transactions are given in the table in Exhibit D. (We use only bid swap points in this illustration.)

Maturity T_i (days)	Rate $r_u(\%)$
1	5.260
10	5.275
31	5.280
60	5.305
91	5.340
181	5.370
272	5.370
364	5.300

Exhibit C   USD yield curve as of 18 October 2006

Maturity T_i	Raw Δ_i	Fitted $\Delta_i^{(f)}$	Constrained $\Delta_i^{(c)}$
7	0.0000	−0.0015	**−0.0005**
31	−0.0050	−0.0065	**−0.0055**
61	−0.0120	−0.0128	**−0.0125**
94	−0.0200	−0.0196	−0.0196
182	−0.0380	−0.0373	**−0.0375**
367	−0.0730	−0.0732	−0.0732

Exhibit D   Swap points for USD/MYR NDF as of 18 October 2006. Raw (Δ_i) – market quoted swap points. Fitted $(\Delta_i^{(f)})$ – resulting from the linear regression fit as described in the methodology above. Constrained $(\Delta_i^{(c)})$ – fit is restricted to the quantization errors. Bold font indicates the cases where the constraint made a difference

Note that the step size (or the quantization error δ) of the market quotes is 0.0010. For the maturity of seven days, the market quoted bid swap rate is zero. This zero quote has a drastic impact on the implied yield curve for MYR.

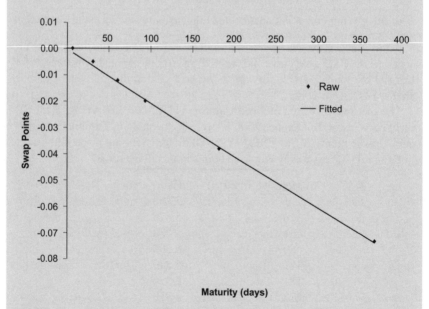

Exhibit E   Swap points (Δ_i) fitting Δ_i/T_i to a line. The difference between the points and the fitted curve is very small

The 'Fitted' column in the table lists the results of the fit as described earlier. The market quoted numbers and the fitting are shown in the figure in Exhibit E. Note that the fit is constrained to go through zero as explained previously. This constraint and the lower weight that we assign to the swap points at shorter maturities (because of the larger errors, as described above) have the effect of smoothing out the implied curve. The 'Constrained' column of the table refers to the fitted swap points restricted to be within the quantization error, as described above.

Note that the difference between the market quoted ('Raw') values and the fitted values is very small. However, such small shifts have large impacts in the implied rate, as shown in the table in Exhibit F.

Maturity (days)	MYR Rate (raw)(%)	Error (raw)(%)	MYR Rate (fitted)(%)	MYR Rate (constrained)(%)	Error (fitted)(%)
7	5.3195%	1.4222%	3.2213%	4.6084%	0.0042%
31	3.7166%	0.3223%	3.2300%	3.5555%	0.0039%
61	3.3805%	0.1645%	3.2568%	3.2982%	0.0035%
94	3.2442%	0.1073%	3.2923%	3.2923%	0.0031%
182	3.2816%	0.0561%	3.3182%	3.3096%	0.0021%
367	3.3083%	0.0286%	3.3038%	3.3038%	−0.0003%

Exhibit F   Implied interest rates in MYR using raw swap points and fitted swap points as of 18 October 2006

In this table, the 'error' is the change in the implied rate for a shift of 0.0010 (the market quote step size or the quantization error) in the corresponding swap point. In other words, for a maturity of 7 days, if we change the swap point from 0.0000 (as quoted in the market) to 0.0010, the raw implied rate in MYR will change from 5.3195 % by an amount 1.4222 %. However, the fitted implied rate would change only by an insignificant 0.0042 %.

The yield curves from raw swap points and fitted swap points are shown in the figure in Exhibit G. The error bars represent the variation in the implied value for a shift of 1 step size (0.0010) in the swap points. Note that for the fitted implied yield curve, the error bars are too small to be seen in the figure.

The constrained fit is when the fitted swap points are restricted to be within the quantization errors of the market quotes. The constrained curve moves in the same direction as the fitted curve. However, as expected, the range of movement is restricted to half the size of the error bars representing the quantization errors. While the resulting yield curve still has the unrealistic look of the original implied curve, this is the largest deviation from the market quote that one is permitted in a typical financial institution. If one accepts the 'Fitted' curve as the implied rate, one may be extracting more information

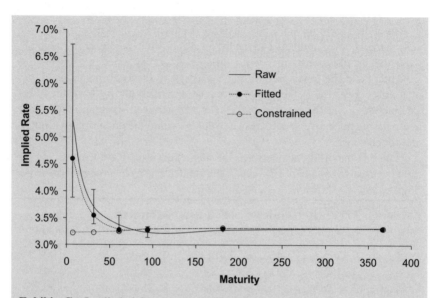

Exhibit G Implied yield curve for MYR using raw swap points and fitted swap points as of 18 October 2006

than what the market implies with potential unpleasant consequences in one's profit and loss estimates or risk analysis. The difference between the 'Raw' and 'Constrained' yield curves may be good enough to ensure stability in the profit and loss numbers.

9.2.3 Life-cycle management

Trade transformations and historization are aspects that even experienced quantitative developers tend to ignore, or at least underestimate. These aspects go hand-in-hand with the trade database, security model and audit trail design. We have discussed their show-stopper importance and intricacies earlier.

The pricing tool lacks the notion of time and of rolling days. Again, if we want to work it into the pricing tool, we have to spend many hours and days designing and implementing it. As we saw earlier, in a real trading platform, some of the life-cycle events may be managed by a workflow engine (or a commercial business process management system, or BPMS). If such a system is called for, we need to develop the interfaces between the target BPMS and the pricing tool.

9.2.4 Security and access control

Security and entitlements are the cornerstone of a trading platform because of the sensitive nature associated with financial transactions. Every action on a trade has real-world consequences in terms of money. Therefore, we take access control, security and audit trail logging very seriously. We worry not only about the password access and entitlements but also about the on-transit integrity of trade and market data. Because of its importance, authentication and access control technology is beyond the design scope of most in-house pricing platforms these days. They tend to adopt a proven vended technology to implement it.

The pricing tool, however, has no security model or access control. If we ever need to think of the pricing tool as a minitrading platform, we have to implement some technology to authenticate various users to perform the tasks they are entitled to do.

9.2.5 Batch process

In the pricing tool as it is now, the 'trades' are merely saved pricing scenarios. Once we implement a database back-end to save the trades, and have a collection of them, we need to worry about the end-of-day processing for risk management and other downstream processing. This facility, perhaps the most crucial feature in a trading platform, is sorely lacking in the pricing tool.

Because of the modularity with which the pricing tool is designed, it will not be difficult to put together a batch program. We can imagine the trades in the database having (or being) XML-serialized pricing scenarios that can be read into the batch-program memory. We then iterate over them with our pricing and finite difference functions, potentially on a grid farm, to arrive at the desired reports.

9.3 SUMMARY

In this chapter, we went through the details of the design philosophy and the implementation tactics behind the piece of software accompanying this book. We highlighted its advantages and spent some time on its shortcomings. The imbalance between the amount of time we spent on each may have given the reader a skewed idea about the relative balance between the good and the bad of the pricing tool. However, we should not underestimate the enormity of the missing features and the effort required to implement them. This point indeed is the crux of the whole book. Despite their apparent lack of glamour, these details really do make or break a trading platform.

QUIZ

1. Study the pricing tool code and redesign the parameter types. In other words, rewrite `Double`, `Int`, `Date`, `DateVec`, `Curve` and `Menu` as classes deriving from Param.
2. While the pricing tool can load a DLL to implement a new model on the fly, it cannot unload a DLL. If you cannot unload the DLL, you cannot replace

it without exiting from the program, and hence you cannot modify the model easily. Extend the pricing tool to be able to unload model DLLs.
3. Review the shortcomings that make the pricing tool unsuitable for trading.
4. Separate the market parameters and define a `Market` class parallel to a `Product` or a `Model` class, with XML persistence.
5. Implement a database layer on the pricing tool to store products, models and market objects.

10

Summing Up

10.1 EPILOGUE

If the financial crisis of 2008 taught us anything, it is the need to view the process of trading in its entirety, often expanding our perspective even beyond the boundaries of one financial institution. Had we had the benefit of such a big perspective, we could have appreciated the unsustainable levels of over-leveraging that crept up behind our credit risk management methodologies using credit ratings. In hindsight, we now know that credit rating is perhaps inadequate. It is similar to issuing credit lines on a customer's credit rating. In Singapore, our regulatory authority (Monitory Authority of Singapore) allows banks to issue a credit limit up to twice the customer's monthly salary, which it believes to be a reasonable leverage. However, we have no limit on how many banks can issue credit lines and cards to one customer based on this limit. So you can end up having a net credit limit that amounts to many times more than what would be a reasonable leverage. Similarly, banks and corporate counterparties may have unsustainable levels of leveraging against their credit rating. As we all know now, over-leveraging is never a problem during boom times. It comes back to haunt us only when markets begin to shrink.

Another benefit of hindsight is our knowledge and appreciation of how credit and market risks have merged into a new kind of risk that we have no defence against. When credit instruments like CDS became tradeable and speculative products rather than insurance policies for credit risk management, they needed to come under the umbrella of market risk. When market pressures widen the credit spread and affect credit ratings and CDS prices as a consequence, we have all the ingredients for positive feedback loops and vicious circles. We saw this in action during the 2008 credit meltdown.

At an even higher level, we perhaps could have appreciated the depths of globalization that made even the most stringent of regulatory frameworks ineffective and the kind of global operational risks of the whole financial system that slowly emerged and caught us unawares. As knowledge workers in the globalized financial industry, our sole weapon is our knowledge, and knowledge is ineffective when we divide it up into isolated silos of narrow proficiency.

The nasty effect of fragmented knowledge was brought into sharp focus by the gullibility with which some of the top management embraced the notion of debt securitization based on CDO (Collateralized Debt Obligation) pricing. The

Gaussian copula pricing model for CDO uses a single correlation number to encapsulate the intricacies of credit markets and their interdependence. Despite the copious warnings from the quant who originally developed the model, it was adopted by the finance world with an alarming eagerness and astonishingly scant understanding. It did not matter that this magic correlation number was neither a market observable not easily estimated. Even the effect of this number on the prices was poorly appreciated. The idea that low-quality debt could be packaged and sold to investors with risk appetite was an opportunity too good to pass up.

Although at a smaller scale compared to global financial markets, the architecture of a trading platform also calls for a more horizontal understanding and knowledge. In designing and deploying a trading platform, we have to pay particular attention to such a big picture view, lest our efforts should be rendered null and void by unforeseen requirements, policies or risks. The inspiration behind this book is the enormity of the caution we need to exercise in appreciating the whole trade workflow, life cycle and the perspectives held dear in various business units.

The big picture view is often lost while designing a trading system, and there are always good reasons for it. A trading platform is the end result of the collaboration among three distinct fields of endeavour:

1. Quantitative finance, which provides the mathematical intelligence behind the pricing models. Darlings of the pre-meltdown era, the quants still make product innovation possible by telling us how to price and risk-manage novel structures and instruments.
2. Computer science, which brings in the technology in rolling out a robust solution. But for the hard work of computer scientists (such as software architects and quantitative developers), the mathematical intelligence of the bank would never see the light of day. Only on robust systems can new innovative pricing models be rolled out.
3. Business knowledge that specifies the requirements around trading. Falling through the cracks between the other two highly technical fields is the world of business analysts, with their people skills, incessant meetings and never-ending lunches. Their contribution is essential to the success of the trading platform. However, in a technical challenge such as the trading platform development, it is best for the technically savvy to pick up the business knowledge, for it is always easier than getting the business savvy to understand the technical details.

Since each one of these fields is a deep specialty in its own right, the experts in any one of them tend to be irreverent of the other two. It is this lack of respect and awareness that I intended to rectify through this book.

As a book targeting the overlap among three specialized fields, *Principles of Quantitative Development* may not have gone deep into any one of them. However, I had to write it in the manner I did because a deeper exploration into any one field would have alienated the practitioners of the other two. My hope is that I have managed to strike the right balance, inspiring interest among all three of them. I am convinced that the book will serve as an eye opener to those embarking on this exciting field of quantitative development and as a checklist to the experts designing and managing large-scale trading platform programs.

Although this book may seem overarching in its breadth, it is only a tiny subset of banking and finance activities, seen through the eyes of a quantitative professional. A bank is a collection of a staggering array of endeavours strung together with an underlying purpose of increasing its customers' wealth or access to credit. It encompasses such disparate and specialized fields as relationship management to database administration.

Quantitative development, although an all-consuming passion for those engaged in it, is only a small part in the bigger scheme of all things financial. Such a niche field as it is, quantitative development is still a confluence of multiple domains of expertise and calls for highly specialized books such as this one. However, it is important to see our role (and indeed that of the various business units) in the organization in its bigger picture context. The lack of such awareness can cause meltdowns and fiascos of global proportions.

10.2   FURTHER READING

10.2.1   Quantitative finance

The main entry barrier for a quantitative professional with a nonfinance background, when he ventures into the intriguing world of options and derivatives, is one of argot. The language used in quantitative finance is so different and the jargon so profuse that his foray looks like a daunting task. However, this difficulty is only on the surface. The mathematical and quantitative aspects, though exacting and full of painstaking details, are not intrinsically difficult, but the new campaigner has to cut through the large amount of jargon and verbiage before getting to it. He can find help in the right kind of introductory books.

Big Picture 10.1:   Effect of Modelling on Models

Mathematical finance is built on a couple of assumptions. The most fundamental of them is the one on market efficiency. It states that the market prices every asset fairly, and the prices contain all the information available in the market. In other words, you cannot glean any more information by doing any research or technical analysis, or indeed any modelling. If this assumption does not pan out, then the quant edifice we build on top of it will crumble. Some may even say that it did crumble in 2008.

We know that this assumption is not quite right. If it was, there would not be any transient arbitrage opportunities. Even at a more fundamental level, the assumption has shaky justification. The reason that the market is efficient is that the practitioners take advantage of every little arbitrage opportunity. In other words, the markets are efficient because they are not so efficient at some transient level.

Mark Joshi, in his well-respected book, *The Concepts and Practice of Mathematical Finance*, points out that Warren Buffet made a bundle of money by refusing to accept the assumption of market efficiency. In fact, the weak form of market efficiency comes about because there are thousands of Buffet wannabes who keep their eyes glued to the ticker tapes, waiting for that elusive mispricing to show up.

Given that the quant careers, and literally trillions of dollars, are built on the strength of this assumption, we have to ask this fundamental question. Is it wise to trust this assumption? Are there limits to it?

Let us take an analogy from physics. I have this glass of water on my desk now. Still water, in the absence of any turbulence, has a flat surface. We all know why – gravity and surface tension and all that. However, we also know that the molecules in water are in random motion, in accordance with the same Brownian process that we readily adopted in our quant world. One possible random configuration is that half the molecules move, say, to the left and the other half to the right (so that the net momentum is zero). If that happens, the glass on my desk will break and it will make a terrible mess, but we have not heard of such spontaneous messes (from someone other than our kids, that is).

The question then is: Can we accept the assumption on the predictability of the surface of water although we know that the underlying motion is irregular and random? (I am trying to make a rather contrived analogy to the assumption on market efficiency despite the transient irregularities.) The answer is a definite yes. Of course, we take the flatness of liquid surfaces for granted in everything from the useless lift-pumps and siphons of our grade school physics books all the way to dams and hydroelectric projects.

So what am I quibbling about? Why do I harp on the possibility of uncertain foundations? I have two reasons. One is the question of scale. In our example of surface flatness versus random motion, we looked at a very large collection, where, through the central limit theorem and statistical mechanics, we expect nothing but regular behaviour. If I was studying, for instance, how an individual virus propagates through the bloodstream, I should not make any assumptions on the regularity in the behaviour of water molecules. This matter of scale applies to quantitative finance as well. Are we operating at the right scale to ignore the shakiness of the market efficiency assumption?

The second reason for mistrusting the pricing models is a far more insidious one. Let me see if I can present it rather dramatically using my example of the tumbler of water. Suppose we make a model for the flatness of the water surface, and the tiny ripples on it as perturbations or something. Then we proceed to use this model to extract tiny amounts of energy from the ripples.

The fact that we are using the model impacts the flatness or the nature of the ripples, affecting the underlying assumptions of the model. Now, imagine that a large number of people are using the same model to extract as much energy as they can from this glass of water. My hunch is that it will create large-scale oscillations, perhaps generating configurations that do indeed break the glass and make a mess. Discounting the fact that this hunch has its root more in the financial mess that spontaneously materialized rather than any solid physics argument, we can still see that large fluctuations do indeed seem to increase the energy that can be extracted. Similarly, large fluctuations (and the black swans) may indeed be a side effect of modelling.

Options, Futures, and Other Derivatives offers a perfect launching pad for a physicist or an engineer considering a career as a quantitative finance professional. For someone switching from another quantitative field to finance, the main difficulty is in the lingo used in banking and finance. *Options, Futures, and Other Derivatives* does a remarkable job in introducing the terms and concepts (and jargon and conventions) at the right pace so that the reader is neither overwhelmed nor bored.

An introductory book to the lucrative and fast-paced world of quantitative finance, *Options, Futures, and Other Derivatives* does not go very deeply into any one asset class or to the level of detail and specialized knowledge a serious professional will need to hold under his hat. For that, we will have to look at other books. Whatever this book has to offer is necessary knowledge, but not sufficient, both from a mathematical finance perspective and from that of a quantitative developer.

A remarkably successful book with at least seven editions to date, *Options, Futures, and Other Derivatives* is considered a bible to a quant. For that reason, you may find it hard to borrow a copy of Hull's book, even if you can find many with your colleagues.

Full Title:	*Options, Futures, and Other Derivatives with Derivagem CD* (7th edition)
Author:	John C. Hull
ISBN:	978-0136015864
Publisher:	Prentice Hall; 7th edition (May 2008)

Stochastic Calculus for Finance, Volumes I and II, augments your foundation in stochastic methods for pricing. Written with an adequate amount of mathematical rigour, without losing lucidly in its exposition, the first volume, *The Binomial Asset Pricing Model*, deals with discrete time models, while the second one, *Continuous-Time Models*, builds on it to move to more abstract treatment of the subject.

Full Title:	*Stochastic Calculus for Finance I: The Binomial Asset Pricing Model* (Springer Finance)
Author:	Steven E. Shreve
ISBN:	978-0387249681
Publisher:	Springer; 1st edition (28 June 2005)

Full Title:	*Stochastic Calculus for Finance II: Continuous-Time Models* (Springer Finance)
Author:	Steven E. Shreve
ISBN:	978-0387401010
Publisher:	Springer; 2nd edition (April 2008)

The Concepts and Practice of Mathematical Finance is another book well suited to a newcomer in the field of quantitative finance. It goes into more mathematical details than the venerable Hull book. Joshi emphasizes mathematical rigour and intuition, but assumes that the reader knows the argot of the domain. For this reason, his book, *The Concepts and Practice of Mathematical Finance*, may be better read as a second or third book, and as a foundation to a mathematical foray into quantitative finance.

Full Title:	*The Concepts and Practice of Mathematical Finance (Mathematics, Finance and Risk)*
Author:	Mark S. Joshi
ISBN:	978-0521514088
Publisher:	Cambridge University Press; 2nd edition (November 2008)

Paul Wilmott on Quantitative Finance is a three volume set in which the well-known mathematician-turned-quant Wilmott teaches quantitative finance from a practitioner's perspective. The emphasis is on practical problems and solutions rather than mathematical purity and completeness.

Full Title:	*Paul Wilmott on Quantitative Finance* (three volume set)
Author:	Paul Wilmott
ISBN:	978-0470018705
Publisher:	Wiley; 2nd edition (March 2006)

10.2.2   Computing

Software engineering and programming is a field with so many textbooks and so much reference material that it would be silly to give a conventional list here. Even in the niche filed of how to program in C++ for mathematical finance, we can find several good books. The books that we would need while deploying a trading system would depend on the chosen programming platform, language and technologies. Here are a couple of books that stand outside this narrow focus, giving interesting and time-tested concepts and ideas that apply to all software projects.

Big Picture 10.2:   Group Dynamics

When researchers and academicians move to quantitative finance, they have to grapple with some culture shock. Not only does the field of finance operate at a faster pace, it also puts great emphasis on teamwork. It cuts wide rather than deep. Quick results that have immediate and widespread impact are better than perfect and elegant solutions that may take time to forge. We want it done quick rather than right. Academicians are just the opposite. They want to take years to mull over deep problems, often single-handedly, and come up with solutions that are elegant and perfect.

Coupled with this perfectionism, there is a curious tendency among academic researchers towards creating a 'wow' factor with their results, as opposed to finance professionals who are quite content with the 'wow' factor in their bonuses. This subtle mismatch generates interesting manifestations. Academics who make the mid-career switch to finance tend to work either alone or in small groups, trying to perfect an impressive prototype. Banking professionals, on the other hand, try to leverage on each other (at times taking credit for other people's work) and roll out potentially incomplete solutions as quickly as possible.

As a consequence of this corporate need to show results, a good people manager in a bank is an effective and valuable asset. In academia, however, the emphasis is often on individual excellence in technical knowledge, which is not always good for you in a modern financial institution. Unless you are careful, others will take advantage of your expertise and dump their responsibilities on you. You may not mind it as long as they respect your expertise, but they often hog the credit for your work and present their ability to evade work as people management skills.

Gang of Four, as it is popularly known, or *Design Patterns: Elements of Reusable Object-Oriented Software*, enjoys a near legendary esteem among experienced object-oriented programmers. It deals with design patterns that tend to recur. More accurately, it describes programming situations that can be massaged into known patterns, thereby vastly reducing the designing effort and possibility of bugs.

Design Patterns: Elements of Reusable Object-Oriented Software, however, is not for beginners, nor is it an exhaustive treatise on patterns. It is merely a cookbook that you can refer to whenever you think you need the implementation details of a particular pattern. Every serious developer should have access to it.

Full Title:	*Design Patterns: Elements of Reusable Object-Oriented Software*
Authors:	Erich Gamma, Richard Helm, Ralph Johnson and John M. Vlissides
ISBN:	978-0201633610
Publisher:	Addison-Wesley (1994)

Exceptional C++ is a book targeting experienced C++ developers, illustrating subtleties in programming through a number of engaging puzzles. Although it may be geeky to call a book on C++ a page-turner, this book of brain-teasers comes very close. Together, the original *Exceptional C++* and its sequel *More Exceptional C++* teach their readers valuable lessons in all sorts of interesting tit-bits, for instance, on the subtleties of temporary objects, pre- or post-incrementing and so on.

Exceptional C++ is a collection of 47 case studies (or puzzles based on what could be case studies) that cement the concepts of object-oriented programming in the reader's mind. The second volume serves up another 40 puzzles.

Full Title:	*Exceptional C++: 47 Engineering Puzzles, Programming Problems, and Solutions*
Author:	Herb Sutter
ISBN:	978-0201615623
Publisher:	Addison-Wesley (1999)

Full Title:	*More Exceptional C++: 40 New Engineering Puzzles, Programming Problems, and Solutions*
Author:	Herb Sutter
ISBN:	978-0201704341
Publisher:	Addison-Wesley (2001)

10.2.3 Economics

The 'Big Picture' of quantitative finance, as I strive to demonstrate in this book, is the whole banking and financial system. What is indeed bigger is economics. Spending some time on economic history is really a rewarding exercise. It will give you interesting insights into the boom-and-bust cycles, the rationales behind the various and differing perspectives held dear in today's flattening world. Economics is a vast field in its own right and encompasses the vagaries of financial markets in much the same way that philosophy envelops scientific concepts. Here are some books that enhanced my understanding and appreciation of how the world works and, more importantly, provided ample entertainment in doing so.

The Commanding Heights recapitulates the economic history of various countries during the second half of the twentieth century. Although opinionated, this book is a must-read if you want to appreciate the economic schools of thought that form the backdrop of financial activities and regulations.

Full Title:	*The Commanding Heights: The Battle for the World Economy*
Authors:	Daniel Yergin and Joseph Stanislaw
ISBN:	978-0684835693
Publisher:	Free Press (2002)

Confessions of an Economic Hit Man reads more like a thriller than a book on economics. Although many established entities refute the veracity of its claims, this book paints a picture of how corporate greed strives to control the natural resources of the developing world. According to Perkins, big corporate players, hungry for resources, subject the Third World to unredeemable monetary obligations through development loans and unrealistic growth forecasts. Perkins, who says he was one of the economists (or 'economic hit men') generating such irrational growth forecasts, decides to denounce such practices in this book.

Full Title:	*Confessions of an Economic Hit Man*
Author:	John Perkins
ISBN:	978-0452287082
Publisher:	Plume (2005)

Big Picture 10.3:   Philosophy of Money

Underlying all financial activity are transactions involving money. The term 'transactions' means something philosophically different in economics. It stands for exchanges of goods and services. Money, in economic transactions, has only a transactional value. It plays the role of a medium facilitating the exchanges. In financial transactions, however, money becomes the entity that is being transacted. Financial systems essentially move money from savings and transform it into capital. Thus money takes on an investment value, in addition to its intrinsic transactional value. This investment value is the basis of interest. Given that the investment value is also measured and returned in terms of money, we get the notion of compound interest and 'putting money to work'. Those who have money demand returns based on the investment risk they are willing to assume. The role of modern financial system becomes one of balancing this risk–reward equation.

We should keep in mind that this signification of money as an investment entity is indeed a philosophical choice that we have made over the past few centuries. Other choices do exist – Islamic banking springs to mind, although this practice has been diluted by the more widely held view of money as possessing an investment value. It is fascinating to study the history and philosophy of money, but it is a topic that calls for a full-length book in its own right.

Appendix

A.1 CD CONTENTS

The CD that comes with this book contains the companion program 'Pricing Tool', which illustrates the principles discussed. The CD will auto-play in most Windows-based computers and give you instructions on how to install and use the program. It is organized as follows:

- The PricingTool folder contains the executable image of the program. In order to install the pricing tool on your PC, you can create a new folder (suggested name: PricingTool) in your Windows programs folder (usually in C:\Program Files) and copy the entire contents of the PricingTool folder there. If needed, you can create a shortcut to the program (C:\Program Files\PricingTool\PricingTool.exe) on your desktop or start menu for easy access.

  In addition to the pricing tool executable (PricingTool.exe), its on-line help file (PricingTool.chm) and initialization file (PricingTool.ini), the PricingTool folder also contains the dynamic link library (DLL) for plotting support using the DISLIN package (dislnc.dll). The init file (PricingTool.ini) is a list of products to be loaded when the program initializes, and refers to the XML product definition files in the xml subfolder. The subfolders in the PricingTool folder are:

  - xml: meant to contain the product/model definitions in XML format. These XML files can be edited to modify the definitions either using any text or XML editor, or from the PricingTool interface.
  - dll: holds the dynamic link libraries implementing models, based on the product–model definitions created interactively in the program.
  - pars: holds the pricing scenarios in XML format.

  These subfolders can be moved around or renamed as needed.

- The `Source` folder contains the source code of the pricing tool. The interested reader will find the solution and project files that can be accessed with Visual Studio 2008. These files are available in the `Source\VS2008` subfolder.

  The main solution file the reader should start with is `pqd.sln`, which contains the projects `PricingTool.vcproj` and `MakeDLL.vcproj`. As their names indicate, `PricingTool.vcproj` will build the pricing tool program and `MakeDLL.vcproj` will help build a dynamic link library implementing any pricing model that the reader defines interactively using the pricing tool. Both of these projects make use of the utility functions organized in `MyCode.vcproj`. The solution and project files are so configured that all the intermediate and output files generated by the Visual Studio build process will be confined to the `Source\VS2008` subfolder.

  The subfolders of Source are:
  - `VS2008`: contains the Visual Studio project and solution and the associated, generated files. It also houses the subfolder `Libs`, containing the output of `Mycode.vcproj`, as well as other libraries used by the pricing tool.
  - `PricingTool`: contains all the source code files needed to build the pricing tool. It has subfolders `xml`, `pars` and `dll`, which are the same as the ones found in the `PricingTool` folder with the same names.
  - `MyCode`: contains the utility functions used in the solution `VS2008\MyCode.sln`. It also has subfolders containing the `blitz`, `boost`, `tinyXML` and `DISLIN` packages.
  - `MakeDLL`: contains the model implementation of a large number of vanilla and exotic products that are defined in the pricing tool by default. These source files implementing the product–model pairs are meant to be consumed by `VS2008\MakeDLL.vcproj`

The detailed source code documentation (generated by Doxygen) can be found in the Source folder. It is called `PricingTool-source.chm` and contains graphical class hierarchies and includes file dependencies to help the reader.

A.2   HISTORICAL PERSPECTIVE

This book has its origins in an article that appeared in my regular column in *Wilmott Magazine*. It is the enthusiastic response to this article that inspired me to suggest this topic for a full-length book, where I could develop these ideas much further. Here is the slightly edited version of the original article, reproduced with permission (*Wilmott Magazine*, November 2009, pp. 35–37). In addition to providing a historical perspective on the origin of the book, this article also gives you an interesting and readable summary of the ideas presented.

Big Picture A.1:   Software Nightmares

To err is human, but to really foul things up you need a computer. So states the remarkably insightful Murphy's law. Nowhere else does this ring truer than in our financial workplace. After all, it is the financial sector that drove the rapid progress in the computing industry – which is why the first computing giant had the word 'business' in its name.

The financial industry keeps up with the developments in the computer industry for one simple reason. Stronger computers and smarter programs mean more money – a concept we readily grasp. As we use the latest and greatest in computer technology and pour money into it, we fuel further developments in the computing field. In other words, not only did we start the fire, we actively fan it as well. However, it is not a bad fire; the positive feedback loop that we helped set up has served both industries well.

This interdependency, healthy as it is, gives us nightmarish visions of perfect storms and dire consequences. Computers being the perfect tools for completely fouling things up, our troubling nightmares are more justified than we care to admit.

Models versus Systems

Paraphrasing a deadly argument that some gun aficionados make, I will defend our addiction to information technology. Computers do not foul things up; people do.

Mind you, I am not implying that we always mess it up when we deploy computers, but at times we try to massage our existing processes into their computerized counterparts, creating multiple points of failure. The right approach, instead, is often to redesign the processes so that they can take advantage of the technology. This is easier said than done. To see why, we have to look beyond systems and processes and focus on the human factors.

In a financial institution, we are in the business of making money. We fine-tune our reward structure in such a way that our core business (of making money, that is) runs as smoothly as possible. Smooth operation relies on strict adherence to processes and the underlying policies they implement. In this rigid structure, there is little room for visionary innovation.

This structural lack of incentive to innovate results in staff hurrying through a new system rollout or a process re-engineering. They have neither the luxury of time nor the freedom to slack off in the dreaded 'business-as-usual' to do a thorough job of such 'nonessential' things.

Besides, there is seldom any unused human resource to deploy in studying and improving processes so that they can better exploit technology. People who do it need to have multifaceted capabilities (business and computing, for instance). Being costly, they are much more optimally deployed in the core business of making more money.

Think about it; when is the last time you (or someone you know) got hired to revamp a system and the associated processes? The closest you get is when someone is hired to duplicate a system that is already known to work better elsewhere.

The lack of incentive results in a dearth of thought and care invested in the optimal use of technology. Suboptimal systems (which do one thing well at the cost of everything else) abound in our workplace. In time, we will reach a point where we have to bite the bullet and redesign these systems. When redesigning a system, we have to think about all the processes involved and we have to think about the system while designing or redesigning processes. This cyclic dependence is the theme of this article.

Systems do not figure in a quant's immediate concern. What concerns us more is our strongest value-add, namely mathematical modelling. In order to come up with an optimal deployment strategy for models, however, we need to pay attention to operational issues like trade workflow.

I was talking to one of our top traders the other day and he mentioned that a quant, no matter how smart, is useless unless his work can be deployed effectively and in a timely manner. A quant typically delivers his work as a C++ program. In a rapid deployment scenario, his program will have to plug directly into a system that will manage trade booking, risk measurements, operations and settlement. The need for rapid deployment makes it essential for the quants to understand the trade life cycle and business operations.

Life of a trade

Once a quant figures out how to price a new product, his work is basically done. After coaxing that stochastic integral into a pricing formula (failing which, a Crank–Nicholson or Monte Carlo), the quant writes up a program and moves on to the next challenge.

It is when the trading desk picks up the pricing spreadsheet and books the first trade into the system that the fun begins. Then the trade takes on a life of its own, sneaking through various departments and systems, showing different strokes to different folks. This adventurous biography of the trade is depicted in Exhibit A in its simplified form.

At the inception stage, a trade is conceptualized by the front-office folks (sales, structuring, trading desk – shown in shaded ovals in the figure). They study the market need and potential, and assess the trade viability. Once they see and grab a market opportunity, a trade is born.

Even with the best of quant models, a trade cannot be priced without market data, such as prices, volatilities, rates and correlations, and so on. The validity of

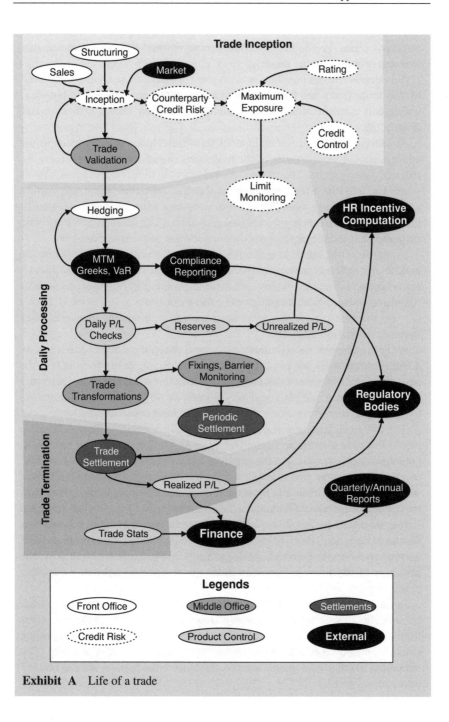

Exhibit A Life of a trade

the market data is ensured by product control or market risk people. The data management group also needs to work closely with information technology (IT) to ensure live data feeds.

The trade first goes for a counterparty credit control (the grey bubbles). The credit controllers ask questions like: if we go ahead with the deal, how much will the counterparty end up owing us? Does the counterparty have enough credit left to engage in this deal? Since the credit exposure changes during the life cycle of the trade, this is a minor quant calculation on its own.

In principle, the front office can do the deal only after the credit control approves of it. Credit risk folks use historical data, internal and external credit rating systems and their own quantitative modelling team to come up with counterparty credit limits and maximum per trade and netted exposures.

Right after the trade is booked, it goes through some control checks by the middle office. These people verify the trade details, validate the initial pricing, apply some reasonable reserves against the insane profit claims of the front office and come up with a simple yea or nay to the trade as it is booked. If they say yes, the trade is considered validated and active. If not, the trade goes back to the desk for modifications.

After these inception activities, trades go through their daily processing. In addition to the daily (or intra-day) hedge rebalancing in the front office, the market risk management folks mark their books to market. They also take care of compliance reporting to regulatory bodies, as well as risk reporting to the upper management – a process that has far-reaching consequences.

The risk management folks, whose work is never done, as Tracy Chapman would say, also perform scenario, stress test and historical value at risk (VaR) computations. In stress tests, they apply a drastic market movement of the kind that took place in the past (like the Asian currency crisis or 9/11) to the current market data and estimate the movement in the bank's book. In historical VaR, they apply the market movements in the immediate past (typically last year) and figure out the 99 percentile (or some such predetermined number) worst loss scenario. Such analysis is of enormous importance to the senior management and in regulatory and compliance reporting. In the figure of Exhibit A, the activities of the risk management folks are depicted in bubbles of another shade of grey.

In their attempts to rein in the ebullient traders, the risk management folks come across in their adversarial worst. However, we have to remind ourselves that the trading and control processes are designed in that way. It is the constant conflict between the risk takers (front office) and the risk controllers (risk management) that implements the risk appetite of the bank as decided by the upper management.

Another group that crunches the trade numbers every day from a slightly different perspective are the product control folks, shown in the figure. They worry about the daily profit and loss (P/L) movements both at the trade and portfolio level. They also modulate the profit claims by the front office through a reserving mechanism and come up with the so-called unrealized P/L.

This P/L, unrealized as it is, has a direct impact on the compensation and incentive structure of the front office in the short run – hence the perennial tussle over the reserve levels. In the long term, however, the trade gets settled and the P/L becomes realized and nobody argues over it. Once the trade is in the maturity phase, it is finance people who worry about statistics and cash flows. Their Big Picture view ends up in annual reports and stakeholder meetings, and influences everything from our bonus to the CEO's new Gulfstream.

Trades are not static entities. During the course of their life, they evolve. Their evolution is typically handled by middle-office people (grey bubbles) who worry about trade modifications, fixings, knock-ins, knock-outs, etc. The exact name given to this business unit (and indeed other units described above) depends on the financial institution we work in, but the trade flow is roughly the same.

The trade flow that I described so far should ring alarm bells in a quant heart. Where are the quants in this value chain? Well, they are hidden in a couple of places. Some of them find a home in the market risk management, validating pricing models. Some others may live in credit risk, estimating peak exposures, figuring out rating schemes and minimizing capital charges.

Most important of all, they find their place before a trade is ever booked. Quants teach their home banks how to price products. A financial institution cannot warehouse the risk associated with a trade unless it knows how much the product in question is worth. It is in this crucial sense that model quants drive the business.

In a financial marketplace that is increasingly hungry for customized structures and solutions, the role of the quants has become almost unbearably vital. Along with the need for innovative models comes the imperative of robust platforms to launch them in a timely fashion to capture transient market opportunities.

In our better investment banks, such platforms are built in-house. This trend towards self-reliance is not hard to understand. If we use a generic trading platform from a vendor, it may work well for established (read vanilla) products. It may handle the established processes (read compliance, reporting, settlements, audit trails, etc.) well. But what do we do when we need a hitherto unknown structure priced? We could ask the vendor to develop it, but then they will take a long time to respond. When they finally do, they will sell it to all our competitors or charge us an arm and a leg for exclusivity, thereby eradicating any associated profit potential.

Once a vended solution is off the table, we are left with the more exciting option of developing an in-house system. It is when we design an in-house system that we need to appreciate the Big Picture. We will need to understand the whole trade flow through the different business units and processes as well as the associated trade perspectives.

Trade Perspectives

The perspective that is most common these days is trade-centric. In this view, trades are the primary objects, which is why conventional trading systems keep track of them. Put a bunch of trades together and you get a portfolio. Put a few portfolios together and you have a book. The whole global market is merely a collection of books. This paradigm has worked well and is probably the best compromise between different possible views.

However, the trade-centric perspective is only a compromise. The activities of the trading floor can be viewed from different angles. Each view has its role in the bigger scheme of things in the bank. Quants, for instance, are model-centric. They try to find commonality between various products in terms of the underlying mathematics. If they can reuse their models from one product to another, potentially across asset classes, they minimize the effort required of them. Remember how Merton views the whole world as options! I listened to him in amazement once when he explained the Asian currency crisis as originating from the risk profile of compound options – the bank guarantees to corporate clients being put options, government guarantees to banks being put options on put options.

Unlike quants who develop pricing models, quantitative developers tend to be product-centric. To them, it does not matter too much even if two different products use very similar models. They may still have to write a separate code for them depending on the infrastructure, market data, conventions, etc.

Traders see their world from the asset-class angle. Typically associated with a particular trading desk based on asset classes, their favourite view cuts across models and products. To traders, all products and models are merely tools to making profit.

IT folks view the trading world from a completely different perspective. Theirs is a system-centric view, where the same product using the same model appearing in two different systems is basically two different beasts. This view is not particularly appreciated by traders, quants or quant developers.

One view that all of us appreciate is the view of the senior management, which is narrowly focused on the bottom line. The big bosses can prioritize things (whether products, asset classes or systems) in terms of the money they bring to the shareholders. Models and trades are typically not visible from their view – unless, of course, rogue traders lose a lot of money on a particular product or by using a particular model, or, somewhat less likely, they make huge profits using the same tricks.

When the trade reaches the market risk folks, there is a subtle change in the perspective from a trade-level view to a portfolio or book-level view. Though mathematically trivial (after all, the difference is only a matter of aggregation), this change has implications in the system design. Trading systems have to maintain a robust hierarchical portfolio structure so that various dicing and slicing as required in the later stages of the trade life cycle can be handled with natural ease.

The busy folks in the middle office (who take care of trade validations and modifications) are obsessed with trade queues. They have a validation queue, market operation queue, etc. Again, the management of queues using status flags is something we have to keep in mind while designing an in-house system.

When it comes to finance people and their notions of cost centres, the trade is pretty much out of the booking system. Still, they manage trading desks and asset classes as profit and cost centres. Any trading platform we design has to provide adequate hooks in the system to respond to their specific requirements as well.

Quants and the Big Picture

Most quants, especially at junior levels, despise the Big Picture. They think of it as a distraction from their real work of marrying stochastic calculus to C++. Changing that mindset to some degree is the hidden agenda behind this column.

As my trader friends will agree, the best model in the world is worthless unless it can be deployed. Deployment is the fast track to the Big Picture – no point denying it. Besides, in an increasingly interconnected world where a crazy Frenchman's actions instantly affect our bonus, what is the use of denying the existence of the Big Picture in our neck of the woods? Instead, let us take advantage of the Big Picture to empower ourselves. Let us bite the bullet and sit through a 'Big Picture 101'.

When we change our narrow, albeit effective, focus on the work at hand to an understanding of our role and value in the organization, we will see the potential points of failure of the systems and processes. We will be prepared with possible solutions to the nightmarish havoc that computerized processes can wreak. And we will sleep easier.

Glossary of Terms

Accrual accounting
In finance, accrual accounting is an accounting method that includes future expected cash flows in order to arrive at an accurate estimate of a company's current financial condition. This method is to be contrasted with a cash accounting scheme. For example, if the only transaction a bank makes is a loan, then it has a net negative position in terms of cash. However, when considering the future revenue stream, through an accrual accounting method, the bank is likely to have a positive position using accrual accounting.

API
In computer science, API stands for the application programming interface. It is a collection of functions, tools and conventions that will make it easy for a developer to use a library or a system. It formalizes the interaction between a program library or module (or hardware platform) and the software developed based on it, by hiding the complexities of implementation behind the façade of the API. For instance, the Windows operating system 'exposes' an API (WinAPI, for short) which we used in developing the user interface of a pricing tool. Since we used the API, we did not have to worry about how to draw a window on the screen or handle scrollbars and mouse events. Similarly, we used the API of the DISLIN package for plotting and visualization.

Asset liability management (ALM)
In a bank or a financial institution, ALM refers to the management of assets and liabilities in such a way as to maintain its capital liquidity within prescribed risk limits. Typically, the assets and liabilities tend to be large, and the capital liquidity is the difference between these large quantities. The liquidity is therefore subject to large fluctuations for relatively small variations in the market values of the assets or liabilities.

Asset-backed security (ABS)

An asset-backed security is an instrument whose payoff depends on the performance or value of a basket of underlying assets securitized via techniques similar to those in a collateralized debt obligation (CDO). See also *Collateralized debt obligation (CDO)*.

Audit trails

An audit trail is a clear and indisputable record of an event or transaction that took place, with the information about the actors responsible, and the time. In a trading platform, every action or transformation (like a trade modification, status change, etc.) on a trade needs to have an audit trail because of the sensitive nature of financial transactions.

Back office

In a bank or a financial institution, the back office houses the administrative, record keeping, compliance and settlement functions associated with trading activity. These activities also need to be catered for in a good trading platform design.

Batch job

In computing, a batch job is a computing task that runs largely unsupervised and typically on a regular basis. In a bank, for a trading platform, the batch job may take care of computing the daily marked-to-market values or risk metrics. Usually of high number-crunching and computational intensity, the batch job may run on parallel computers ('Grids') or powerful servers.

Binomial tree

In quantitative finance, the binomial tree option pricing model is a computational technique to estimate the fair value of any option. It divides the maturity time of the option into a number of small time steps and assumes that the underlying price can go only up or down by a constant factor, thereby building a tree with the prices of the underlying at every time node. The tree fans out all the way to maturity. Since we know the option payoff at any node if we know the price of the underlying, we can use the probability of each node to work backwards from maturity to arrive at the option price at inception (backward induction). What may be a bit surprising is that the quantum of upward or downward movement looks arbitrary, and the option price is independent of it. However, the probability of the movement is constrained to be the risk-neutral probability dependent on the quantum. A trinomial tree is an extension of the binomial tree, where the underlying is allowed to stay with no price movement as well.

Black–Scholes price

The Black–Scholes pricing method is the basis of modern quantitative finance. It enables us to compute precisely the price of a call or a put option (of the European kind) analytically. The basic principle behind the formula is that a delta-hedged portfolio containing a derivative (long) and delta times the underlying (short) should yield the risk-free rate of return.

Business process management (BPM)
See *Workflow engine*.

Collateralized debt obligation (CDO)
A collateralized debt obligation (CDO) is a credit derivative (see *Credit derivatives*) that packages multiple debts in such a way as to create the so-called tranches of any desired credit rating synthetically. The synthetic credit rating, and therefore the price of the tranche, depends crucially on the correlation between the underlying debts. The senior tranche is considered the safest and offers the least return. This correlation is hard to measure from the market data and is subject to fluctuation. The way the correlation figures in the pricing is modelled as a Gaussian copula.

Component object model (COM)
In computing, the component object model refers to a software technology that enables binary-level reuse of objects. Commonly used in Windows programming under C++, COM methodology enables run-time resolution of functionalities and interoperability between multiple programming languages.

Credit defaults swap (CDS)
A credit defaults swap (CDS) is a credit derivative (see *Credit derivatives*) that works like an insurance policy against potential losses in dealing with counterparties and assuming positions involving credit risks. For instance, if we own a bond issued by a corporate entity, we have a credit risk exposure. If the entity goes bankrupt or defaults in its payments, we stand to lose the bond value. In order to avoid losses, we can buy a CDS for which we pay a certain amount based on our notional and the entities credit spread. The CDS will guarantee that we will get our money back if there is a change in the price of the bond because of a set of credit events that we agree with the seller of the protection. The problem with a CDS is that we could buy it even if we do not have a credit exposure, at which point CDS becomes a speculative market instrument subject to market forces.

Credit derivatives
A credit derivative is a financial instrument whose payoff depends on the credit event of an entity or an index. The credit event can be a default, or a rating change, or any other predefined event associated with credit. A common credit derivative is a credit default swap (CDS), where a financial institution insures a counterparty against the defaults by a third entity. For instance, if you hold bonds issued by a certain corporation A and you are concerned that it may go bankrupt or otherwise

default on its obligation, you can buy a CDS from an insurer B that will guarantee that you will get your money back in the event of a default. The tricky thing is that you can buy a CDS even if you do not have any credit exposure to A, which may have contributed to the financial meltdown of 2008. Another popular credit derivative is a collateralized debt obligation – CDO (and its variants, as in mortgage-backed security – MBS – or asset-backed security – ABS), where a large number of loans or assets are pooled together and divided into tranches that match various credit ratings.

Credit replicates
To manage credit risk involved in dealing with counterparties, banks compute the maximum potential exposure by simulating a large number of market scenarios for each trade. For complex trades, such simulations may be prohibitively expensive in terms computational resources. Thus, the credit risk managers may try to approximate the payoff profiles of the trades using a set of simpler, easier-to-value trades. These trades are called credit replicates. One requirement in coming up with the credit replicates is that they envelope or find a conservative boundary around the credit exposures involved. In other words, they should not underestimate the credit risk.

Credit risk management
A bank exposes itself to credit risk when it gives loans to its customers. Similar risks exist whenever there is a counterparty that may end up owing the bank a potential future cash flow. Banks try to estimate, price and mitigate their credit risks, and the process (and often the team engaged in the process) is known as credit risk management. The process may use in-house or external credit ratings, quantitative modelling, netting, etc.

Delta equivalent
For market risk management, banks typically have a limit on the aggregate of the notional amount of each trade times its Delta (which refers to the sensitivity of the option price to the spot value of the underlying). This quantity is called the Delta equivalent and is a better measure of the exposure than the aggregate of the notionals. It is closely related to Delta hedging and the Taylor series expansion of the payoff function to first order.

Delta hedging
In quantitative finance, Delta hedging refers to a strategy whereby the issuer tries to minimize the variability in its future obligation (in writing an option, for instance) by holding a fraction of the underlying. This fraction is mathematically equal to the sensitivity of the option price to the spot value of the underlying, known as the Delta. Delta hedging has its roots in the Taylor series expansion of a function to first order.

Derivative

In quantitative finance, a Derivative refers to an instrument whose payoff depends on the price, performance, value or disposition of an underlying asset, variable or index. Note that the underlying does not necessarily have to be a financial instrument.

Dynamic link library (DLL)

In Windows computing a DLL refers to a dynamically linked library. A DLL (in a Windows operating system) holds the compiled functions and subroutines in a separate file that is loaded during run-time. Dynamic linking is to be contrasted with static linking where all the functions needed to run a program are included in the executable image. The Unix equivalent of a DLL is a shared object file (.so).

Encapsulation

In object-oriented programming, encapsulation refers to the modularization of an object, which makes it possible to hold the data structures and functions necessary for its implementation away from the rest of the program. The object talks to the rest of the program through a well-defined interface. This feature of object-oriented programming enables us to change the internal structures and implementation of one object class without affecting the whole program. More generally, an API can be thought of as an interface behind which the module and its functional implementations are encapsulated.

Equity

In finance, equity refers to the asset class of stocks and shares. Equity is considered a medium-risk asset class, and expects returns in terms of stock dividends and capital gain.

Exchange-traded derivatives (ETD)

Exchange-traded derivatives are financial instruments listed and traded in specialized exchanges. They are bought and sold as standard contracts with published bid and ask prices, with the exchange playing the role of the market maker. When you buy or sell an ETD, the exchange is your counterparty, and therefore you have very little credit risk exposure. The exchange demands a margin account from its players to ensure that they will honour their contractual obligations. Exchange-traded derivatives are to be contrasted with over-the-counter (OTC) contracts, which are privately negotiated between two counterparties.

Fair value

In quantitative finance, fair value stands for the price of an instrument either observed in the market or computed using a well-accepted pricing model.

Fixed income
In finance, fixed income is an asset class that deals with bonds that are expected to be low-risk instruments. Bonds and loans can be structured in such a way as to generate guaranteed returns.

Flat file database
A simple database of information can be represented as a single table, with records arranged as rows in the table. A comma-separated file is an example of a flat file database.

Forward
In finance, forward is a contract between two counterparties to buy and sell a commodity at a predefined price at a predefined time in the future.

Futures
In finance, the term futures refers to a standardized contract to buy or sell a commodity at a specified point in time in the future. As opposed to a forward contract (which is between two counterparties in an 'over-the-counter', or OTC, agreement), futures contracts are between a client and a clearing house. There is usually an enforceable payment scheme involved, such as margin accounts.

Gaussian distribution
In mathematics, the Gaussian distribution refers to a continuous probability distribution describing data that cluster around a mean. Plotted in a graph, the Gaussian distribution looks like the familiar bell-shaped distribution that we encounter while studying many naturally occurring populations. Due to a variety of theoretical reasons such as the central limit theorem, the Gaussian distribution tends to be the most common probability distribution in nature. In quantitative finance, the regular returns are typically distributed according to Gaussian statistics. Symbolically, we can write the Gaussian distribution as the probability at any point x:

$$p(x) = \frac{1}{\sigma\sqrt{2\pi}}e^{-(x-\mu)^2/(2\sigma^2)}$$

where μ is the mean and σ is the standard deviation of the distribution.

Greeks/sensitivities
To a quantitative professional, the Greeks are the sensitivities of the option or derivative price with respect to some market parameter. They are so called because of the Greek symbols used to denote them. For instance, Delta is the first derivative of a payoff with respect to the spot of the underlying and Gamma is the second derivative. Rho is the sensitivity with respect to the interest rate and Theta denotes the time sensitivity.

Hedging
In quantitative finance, hedging is the process by which a trader tries to offset the exposure of one position by taking an equal and opposite position in the market. When all the risk exposures are thus hedged out, the trader can expect only the risk-free rate of return. In fact, even if the risks are not actively hedged out, but are hedgeable in the market, the risk premium (the extra return expected because of assuming a risky position) goes away, which is the basis of risk-neutral valuation methodology.

Inception events
In the context of trading, inception events means the workflow events during the saving and booking of a trade. When the trader books a trade and pushes it to the middle office for approval, the inception workflow starts. The MO may approve or reject the trade or the trader may decide to kill the trade before pushing it to the MO. All of these events are considered inception events for the purpose of the discussion in the book.

Inheritance
In object-oriented programming, inheritance is the feature that allows the programmer to derive new classes from other existing classes. Inheritance makes it easy to build a hierarchical class structure, progressively refining the class description. For instance, we can declare a class for a sports car directly or have a hierarchy vehicle ← car ← sportsCar. The advantage of the latter, which uses inheritance, is that we can later add another car class, say familySedan, or different kind of vehicle, say vehicle ← truck ← eighteenWheeler. All the base attributes, behaviour and characteristics common to a vehicle are then described in the base class vehicle, thereby improving modularity and reusability.

Interest rate derivatives
In quantitative finance and trading, an interest rate derivative is an instrument whose payoff depends on the interest rate. Pricing of an interest rate derivative is slightly more complicated than derivatives in other asset classes because of the necessity to take into account the modelled interest rate both in the payoff computation as well as discounting.

Life-cycle events
In the context of trading, life-cycle events refer to the events during the life of a trade that change its characteristics or payoff. They include fixings (such as the rates fixings on the floating leg of an interest rate swap), exercises (as in option exercises), barrier breaches (for knock-in and knock-out type options), cash flows, maturity, etc.

Market risk management
The portfolio of any financial institution is at the mercy of market fluctuations. Market risk is the risk of markets moving in such a way as to diminish the value of the portfolio. Market risk management is tasked with estimating, minimizing and mitigating the risk to the extent possible though risk limits approval and administration, risk measures computation and reporting and general oversight of the trading activity.

Market value accounting
In finance and accounting, market value accounting is the method of reporting the financial well-being of a bank or a company by considering the fair market value of its assets. It is to be contrasted with historical cost accounting where the acquired cost of assets and liabilities is considered constant. While market value accounting (currently practised among all banks since the 1980s) may give a true picture of the firm's financial health as long as the assets and liabilities are fairly simple, it introduces a significant dependence on pricing models for financial institutions that hold complex derivatives and structures. This dependence may prove fatal, as it did in the 2008 financial meltdown.

Mark-to-market
In finance, mark-to-market refers to the process of estimating the present value of the bank's trading book. Marking-to-market is done daily to track the bank's position and its profit and loss. The same phrase is used for the process of estimating the current present value of a trade.

Marshalling, streaming, serialization
In computer science, the terms marshal, serialize, stream, etc., refer to the process of converting objects and their memory layout into ASCII or bit streams that can be stored and retrieved to recreate the original object or memory layout. In the context of quantitative development, we may have to serialize a trade object so that we can store it in a database or pass it between two programs.

Model
In quantitative finance, a model is a mathematical framework to compute the price of a trade or an option. In simple cases where the future cash flows are known (or deterministic), a model merely discounts them and computes the fair value of the trade in question. In nontrivial cases where the future cash flows are probabilistic or stochastic, the model typically models the option as a random process and solves the resulting stochastic differential equation through a variety of methods.

Model validation
In quantitative finance and market risk management, model validation is the process through which the risk controllers try to ensure that the pricing model in use is mathematically sound and appropriate, and that it is implemented properly. Typically, the model validation step involves an independent implementation of the model and a comparison of the model outputs.

Monte Carlo
In quantitative finance, Monte Carlo refers to a pricing model that explicitly simulates a random sample of the future paths an option may take, and estimates its price as an average of the possible future scenarios. Since such simulation is computationally expensive, we use it only as a last resort, or as a quick and temporary implementation.

Mortgage-backed security (MBS)
A mortgage-backed security (MBS) is similar to a CDO (see *Collateralized debt obligation* and *credit derivatives*) where the underlying debt obligations are mortgages.

Normal distribution
In mathematics, the normal distribution is a special case of the Gaussian probability distribution where the mean is zero ($\mu = 0$) and the variance is one ($\sigma = 1$). It can be written as the probability at any point x, defined as

$$p(x) = \frac{1}{\sqrt{2\pi}} e^{-x^2/2}$$

Notional
In trading, the notional amount or value represents the face amount based on which cash flows are estimated. It is called the notional amount because, in general, it does not have to be exchanged.

Object database
An object database is a type of database that uses an object-oriented structure for data representation. As opposed to a relational database, where information is stored in interconnected tables, an object database stores it as persistent images of the memory layout of the objects in the language it supports. Such databases are, therefore, ideal candidates for storing complex data structures in programs such as a trading platform. The downside is that the data schema is so tightly integrated with the associated program that there is very little standardization in terms of querying and retrieval. The persisting data are meaningless in the absence of the associated program.

Over-the-counter (OTC)
In wholesale banking, over-the-counter (OTC) trades are contracts between two counterparties. This is to be contrasted with exchange-traded products. For instance, a forward is an OTC trade, while a futures contract is an exchange-traded product. OTC trades tend to have a higher counterparty credit risk because of the lack of clearing house mechanisms.

Pattern
In object-oriented programming, a pattern is a pre-existing programming theme that may apply to the software problem at hand. Since patterns are well-used and time-tested techniques, they tend to be complete and easy to deploy. On the down side, their usage may entice a developer to complicate the solution unduly in an effort to stretch and make use of a known pattern to the problem.

Persistence
In computer science, persistence refers to the feature of a program to save and retrieve data beyond its execution. In the context of a trading platform, we need to use persistance of the trade data in a database. In fact, many of the crucial design decisions in an in-house trading platform architecture are related to data persistence – where and how to store the data.

Polymorphism
In computer science, polymorphism is a feature, typically of an object-oriented language, whereby different types or classes can interact with a uniform interface. It also refers to the ability of functions to take arguments of different types and return values and objects of different types.

Potential future exposure (PFE)
In credit risk management, potential future exposure (PFE) is one of the techniques used to estimate a counterparty credit risk. The potential future exposure arising from a particular transaction is the largest value of the credit exposure over its lifetime at a given confidence level. Since there are many potential future scenarios, the PFE is estimated using a Monte Carlo simulation. Once the PFE is known, the credit risk managers use its value to approve or reject transactions with the counterparty.

Quant
A quant is short for a quantitative analyst, who is a mathematician working in a financial institution helping it price complex options and derivatives. Quants use probability theories and random processes to model the future evolution of the underlying asset and deduce the current fair value of the transaction,

either as a formula ('closed-form solution') or a computational procedure. Either way, they implement it and deliver it as a computer program or a part of a library.

Quantitative developer

Quantitative developers are typically computer science professionals who pick up where the quants leave off. They deploy the pricing program that quants develop either in an in-house system of their design or in some other system, so that it becomes an integrated part of the trading system where traders can book trades and the rest of the business units can manage the life cycle.

Rate fixing

Fixing or reset is the process by which a reference rate is determined and recorded for the purpose of calculating the amount of a settlement. For instance, in an interest rate swap, the floating leg may have a reference interest rate, to be periodically observed on a particular date at a particular time so that the amount of cash to be paid or received can be computed (as the difference between the floating and fixed rates times the notional of the trade). Given that the rate fixing process results in real cash flows, it is well-specified in the term sheets of the trades and executed exactly in accordance with them.

Reference data

By reference data, we mean auxiliary market information such as an index setup, holiday calendar management, fixing sources, etc.

Relational database

The most popular database model, a relational database organizes data in tables that interrelate to one another. For example, we may have a table of trades, each of which may have a trade type. This table then has a relation to a 'trade type' table where the details of each type are listed. In this way, we do not have to repeat the information for each entry in the trades table, which we would be forced to do if we used a 'flat file' database.

Reserve

In risk management and product control, reserve is a mechanism by which the middle-office professionals create a buffer against potential losses. For instance, if the pricing model computation shows that a particular trade has generated a certain profit at inception, the product controller may have a policy to keep a fraction of it (at times 100 %) as reserve. Once the profit becomes 'realized' at the maturity of the trade, reserves are returned to the book and appropriate incentives are computed.

Settlement risk
In a contractual transaction between two counterparties, settlement risk represents the possibility that one of them may not deliver the security involved after receiving the cash for it from the other, or may not pay the cash after receiving the security. Settlement risks are typically due to legal (bankruptcy, for instance) or regulatory (licence withdrawal) reasons. Since there is a delay of two business days (for most assets) between settlement and delivery, the risk is finite and nonzero, though small. As the transaction volumes grow, settlement risk is something that banks have to manage along with credit risk.

Static Data
By static data, we mean the kind of information we need for validating trade entries, but which is not essential to the quantitative valuation part of the trade. It includes lists of approved products, counterparty details, access rights of staff, account information, portfolio names and hierarchies, profit and cost centre setup, etc.

Structure/structured product
A structure or a structured product is a custom-built or pre-packaged investment strategy, generally made up of multiple assets, that represents a particular market view of the customer. It is usually made up of multiple derivatives and can be priced as an aggregate of them.

Unified modelling language (UML)
In software engineering, unified modelling language is a standardized scheme to consistently describe a program architecture and the various steps in the architecture design, including use cases and object interactions. It finds most use during the software design stages and aids in documentation by defining a natural and common language for software architects and developers to communicate and collaborate. UML diagrams play the role of blueprints in civil engineering. They are used both for design as well as documentation. In this book, we used UML extensively to describe various programming techniques and to illustrate the architecture of the accompanying pricing tool program.

Value at risk (VaR)
In risk management, value at risk is a widely used risk metric. In mathematical terms, VaR assumes Gaussian statistics for the return of individual trades in a portfolio and computes the expected loss at a given confidence level. Thus, a one-day VaR of 100 million at 5 % confidence level indicates that there is a 5 % chance that the portfolio may suffer a loss of 100 million or more the next day.

Workflow engine
A workflow engine is a computer program that models and implements process flows, and helps in process automation. In the process-driven environment of banks and financial institutions, workflow engines can ensure process and policy compliance. They also provide internal control reports for the upper management. For instance, in consumer banking, a loan approval and disbursement process or a deposit account opening process can be well modelled and driven by a workflow engine. In a trading platform, trade approval and life-cycle management can be delegated to a workflow engine. Workflow engines are also known as business process management systems.

Yield curve
The term structure of the interest rate is known as the yield curve. In other words, when we take into account the fact that the interest rate depends on the time to maturity, and therefore consider it a time-dependent quantity, we get the yield curve. The usual shape of the yield curve is that of a function with a positive gradient, but asymptotically flattening out at long maturities. This shape indicates that investors demand higher returns when they invest in the longer term.

Index